A BOOK OF SOCCER

A BOOK OF SOCCER

BRIAN GLANVILLE

New York
OXFORD UNIVERSITY PRESS
1979

Library of Congress Cataloging in Publication Data
Glanville, Brian.
A book of soccer.
1. Soccer. I. Title.
GV943.G56 1979   796.33'42   79-714
ISBN 0-19-502585-7

Printed in the United States of America

CONTENTS

A BOOK OF SOCCER

1
HOW IT BEGAN

To delve into the depths of antiquity, discovering that a form of soccer was played by barbarians with the skulls of their defeated enemies, that it was played at the courts of Chinese emperors, that it was played in Florence while Charles V was besieging the city in the 16th century, seems to me a wholly useless exercise. To propel a round ball with one's foot is so natural a human activity that it is surely no wonder that the practice was known to many different civilizations. It remains irrevocably true that soccer as we know it was invented by the English, developed by the Scots, and that it did not come into its own until Queen Victoria had been on the throne some thirty years.

You might say that soccer was a rough and ruthless street game for many centuries, until it was taken hold of, codified, and made respectable by the English public schools, those very private, fee-paying academies which were such a feature of the expanding, Empire-building Victorian age, of which they were the historical by-product. Parish registers in England had for hundreds of years chronicled the barbarities of the game, of how a medieval father, appalled by the treatment of two of his football-playing sons, had taken out a knife and stabbed two of their opponents, killing them; while the antiquarian Stubbs, no friend to the game—if game it were—had termed it "a friendly kind of fighting rather than recreation." Fitz-Stephen records that London schoolboys, on Shrove Tuesday of 1175, played football after dinner, and that the practice was continued for a long time to come. Shrove Tuesday football was known and played all over England; usually with considerable violence. The kind of football played by the Elizabethan apprentices in Cheapside, London, was described by a shocked contemporary as "a bloody and murdering practice." Various English monarchs tried to put the sport down because they felt that it interfered with the practice of archery, but none of them succeeded.

Rules, it is clear, were more honored in the breach than in the observance, while the goals could consist of the whole end of one village. In Derby, the Shrovetide game became so well established and fiercely disputed that to this very day matches between local rivals are known—even in Italy—as "derby" games.

Football, then, had a hold on the imagination of the country long before 1863, when Cambridge University drew up a set of rules, and the English Football Association was formed at a meeting in the Freemasons' Tavern in London's Great Queen Street.

Why *soccer*, though? The only plausible theory I have ever come across is that the credit, or blame, belonged to Charles Wreford-Brown, a famous center half for Old Carthusians and the Corinthians. Sitting in his rooms in Oxford University, so it is said, he was visited by a friend who asked him whether he were going to play "Rugger," or Rugby football. To this, in a burst of inspiration, Wreford-Brown replied, "No: I'm playing soccer," the word being a corruption of "Association" in the sport's correct name, Association Football.

Though it was never the aim of Dr. Thomas Arnold, Headmaster of Rugby and the chief progenitor of the Victorian public school, these institutions became obsessed by the supposed need to canalize their pupils' erotic drives into more acceptable channels. Muscular Christianity ruled; the boys must be encouraged to exert themselves till there was no energy left for less worthy activities. At the same time, the enormous ingenuity of the Victorian English, who after all invented most modern sport, even track and field, as we know it, ensured that the various leading schools would devise original and enjoyable versions of football.

Thus, at Harrow, goals were known as *bases* and consisted of poles placed 150 yards apart; clearly a much closer approximation to Rugby than to soccer. "If the first day's play result in a tie," said the peculiar rules, "the distance between the poles shall be doubled." To 300 yards, Heaven help us!

Harrow, like Eton—who called it "sneaking"—had an offside rule, known as "behind." It was complicated, but seemed to boil down to the fact that a player needed two opponents between himself and the opposing "base" line to be onside. A rule which had much more to do with Rugby as it would develop than soccer allowed a player who caught the ball when it had been kicked to shout, "Three yards!" and have a free kick.

Harrow it was which initiated the practice of sending a player off for misconduct, enacting that the umpire should "put out of the game any player wilfully breaking any of the football rules." The ball could be handled only when "close to the body," though how close is not stipulated. It was also laid down that "all charging is fair, but no holding, tripping, pushing with the hands, shinning or back-shinning is allowed." The meaning of the term "back-shinning" is deeply obscure.

"Eton," wrote Pickford and Gibson, in their four-volume pioneering work, *Association Football and the Men Who Made It* (1906), "in a dreamy way legislated against the use of the hands, and so marked the incipient divergence between the Association and the Rugby codes." Under Etonian rules, you could stop the ball with the hand; but no more than that. Etonians, however, were permitted to push, hit, or hold their opponents. A player was "sneaking," or offside, when "only three, or less than three, of the opposite side are before him and the ball behind him, and in such case he may not kick the ball."

At Winchester College in Hampshire, bastion of learning and high-mindedness, unending source of intellectuals and leading civil servants, the playing field was 80 yards long but only some 80 feet wide. The touchlines were at first designated by hurdles, but later by canvas stretched on woodwork, to a height of seven feet, with a three-feet-high rope to keep the players at bay. A straight line an inch deep was cut in the turf at either end to represent the goals, and the game was played by those known as "ups" and those known as "behinds." The "ups," or forwards indulged in something known enigmatically as "hots," an attempt to score goals by something which approximated to a Rugby scrum. There was an offside rule called "Behind your side."

Let me say, in passing, that the fact that so many of the great schools in their particular versions of football found an offside rule necessary shows that it is surely central to the game. Any attempt to do away with it entirely would inevitably have negative results, however tantalizing it may be in practice and in application, as it stands.

Cheltenham College in Gloucestershire was actually the first to use the term "offside," and it also initiated the practice of throwing the ball in from touch. Moreover, it seems to have been the first to use the word "crossbar." This though the Cheltenham game was closer to Rugby than soccer, and it was as a Rugby-playing school that Cheltenham would develop.

The problem was that when public school boys got to Oxford or Cambridge, there was no common ground on which to build; and play. In 1862, J. C. Thring, a master at Uppingham, published a code of rules which he called The Simplest Game—these in turn based on much earlier laws, which germinated at Cambridge.

There were ten rules in all. A goal was scored when the ball was forced through the goal and under the bar, save when thrown by the hand, which could be used only to stop the ball. Kicks must be aimed at the ball alone. There must be no tripping or "heel kicking." When the ball was kicked out of touch—an odd rule, this—it must be returned whence it went out by the player who kicked it, "in a straight line towards the middle of the ground."

A ball kicked behind the goal line should be "kicked off from that line by one of the side whose goal it is," a rule with a much more modern flavor. No player should stand within six paces of the player kicking off.

A player was out of play as soon as he got in front of the ball. No charging was allowed when the player was out of play; that is, when the ball was behind him.

A recognizable version of soccer as we know it was plainly evolving though the hands—those "cheats" as the French playright Jean Giraudoux called them in his eulogy of soccer—were still permitted to stop the ball.

1863 was the watershed, the year the Football Association was founded and the partisans of soccer split with the partisans of Rugger; though the strange thing was that the split should take place not over holding but hacking. First, however, Cambridge University produced a new and much clearer set of rules, though the ball was still to be kicked rather than thrown in when it had gone into touch. The size of the field and the goals were, however, established, and the principle of changing ends was laid down. It is notable, given the fact that so many American colleges for many years favored a kick-in rather than a throw-in from touch, that Pickford and Gibson should record in 1906 that there was still quite a body of opinion in England which would favor such a practice. The maximum length of the pitch was set at 200 yards, though oddly enough no width was stipulated. Goalposts were already to be eight yards across, but no provision was made either for tapes or for crossbars. The ball could not be carried, and hacking would be taboo.

This aroused the ire of Mr. F. W. Campbell, secretary of the Blackheath club which may be considered as the true progenitor of Rugby. Hacking, he thundered, was "the true football game." Were it abolished, "all the courage and pluck of the game would be at an end." Long after Rugby and soccer had split, there were those in the Association game who were of his opinion.

Among them was the formidable, red-bearded Honorable A. F. (later Lord) Kinnaird, a Scottish international, and an Old Etonian, who would ultimately become chairman of the Football Association. "So it's to be hacking, is it?" he is said once to have growled when an opponent wiped his studs down his shin. His wife confided to a friend that she was afraid one day her husband would come home with a broken leg. "Don't worry," she was assured, "if he does, it won't be his own."

The newly elected secretary of the Association, a Mr. E. C. Morley, retorted to Campbell that were hacking allowed, schoolboys alone would play the game. On November 24, a second set of rules was put forward, mollifying Harrow and Charterhouse, which schools had their own objections to the first version, but not the Blackheath club, which withdrew to hack and be hacked, without let or hindrance.

The steel city of Sheffield's part in the making of soccer should not be undervalued. As long ago as 1857, Old Etonians resident in Yorkshire had set up the Sheffield club, the oldest of them all. Sheffield rules were to some extent further evolved than the Association's, since they made specific provision for umpires, corner kicks, and a tape or crossbar nine feet above the ground. In 1866, London actually played Sheffield in a representative game, and the fact that soccer was still in embryo is indicated by the fact that the margin of London's victory was given as two goals and four touchdowns to nil. The first goal was scored by none other than Mr. E. C. Morley: a *playing* F. A. secretary. Happy, vigorous, and remote days, when the administrator would quit his office, if he even had one, for the playing field.

1871 was an important year. The Rugby Union was formed, confirming the breach between the two codes. The Football Association Cup, the first of all great tournaments, still wonderfully full of life after more than a century, was founded, and the laws of the game continued to develop.

Now a ground could be 200 yards long at most and 100 yards broad. The ball had to be thrown rather than kicked into play from touch, but in a strange manner; "the first player who touches it shall throw it from the point of the boundary line, and it shall not be in play until it shall have touched the ground, and the player throwing it in shall not play the ball until it has been played by another player." The last part of the rule at least would survive. Throws, however, were still at that juncture one-handed.

The offside law had matured into one which, broadly speaking, would endure until it was changed in 1925, reducing from three to two the number of players needed to keep a man onside. There was still, however, a little way to go towards uniformity, for the Sheffield Association as late in 1870 had a law which required but one opponent between a player and the opposing goal to render him onside.

There were no substitutions; it should be noted that the Eton rules laid it down that no player injured "or otherwise prevented" could be replaced. This inevitably led to many an absurdity, not least in the Final of the F. A. Cup, the very crown and crescendo of the English season. Indeed, for a number of years after World War II, there scarcely seemed to be a Final at Wembley which was not blemished or falsified by injury. Muscular Christianity, an almost sado-masochistic attitude to what passed as sport, no doubt lay at the basis of this dispensation, and the fact it should endure so long. Incredible rationalizations were advanced for it, most of them on the quasi-religious lines that one grows and is purified by suffering.

Not till 1970 did the World Cup allow substitutes for injured players, and English football reluctantly followed suit. There was this at least to be said for its attitude: that it realized and warned that once you allowed substitutes, it would be impossible to ensure that they be used for a genuinely injured player. And indeed, the substitution rule was exploited from the very first in the World Cup itself, substitutes being made for blatantly tactical reasons. The argument now, not least in England itself, seems quite remote. As many substitutes are made for tactical reasons as for those of injury, though in England it remained the practice to allow only one, where World Cups, and certain other countries, allowed two; in the case of Italy, one outfield player and a goalkeeper. That a player as highly specialized and as vulnerable to injury as a goalkeeper could *not* be substituted always seemed an absurdity, especially in important matches. Meanwhile, though at certain American colleges substitution is allowed ad lib, the game elsewhere is still deeply different in this respect from American football.

The advent of the Football Association Cup was a development of huge importance, accelerating the growth of professionalism, a change in the class structure of the sport, and the development of tactics. Had Mr. C. W. Alcock, the Old Harrovian who became the F. A. secretary in 1870, visualized what would happen to the game, one wonders if he would have been so fervent an advocate of a knockout competition based on the Cock House tournament played at his old school, Harrow.

In the early years of the F.A. Cup the competition was dominated by teams made up of former public school players such as the famous Wanderers, who won it three times in a row, the Royal Engineers—all officers, of course—and the Old Etonians. *Noblesse oblige* prevailed. The celebrated Major Marindin, in turn player, referee, and administrator, found himself in an exquisite dilemma in the Cup Final of 1875—played as it was till 1893 at the famous Oval cricket ground in South East London—when he turned out for the Royal Engineers against Old Etonians, his *alma mater*. An Etonian, C. J. Ottaway, one of their best players, was kicked on the ankle and obliged to leave the field. Marindin himself withdrew, to balance matters.

The Etonians played in three consecutive Finals, losing to the Old Carthusians, the ex-Charterhouse boys (it was at Charterhouse that the habit of "run about," whose object was for a boy to retain possession of the ball as long as possible, grew up) then beating the professional Blackburn Rovers, losing to the professional Blackburn Olympic.

These were Lancashire clubs, like the first of the disguised professional teams, Darwen. Players, as it was euphemistically said, *found* money in their boots. Many of these were Scots, attracted over the border to be found jobs in the Lancashire mills, and paid a few pounds besides for playing soccer. For the Scots had revolutionized soccer with their cool skills, their invention of the passing game. Only the fact that the English public school version of soccer was a kind of heroic, death or glory affair in which the individual dribbled and dribbled till he lost the ball can explain how there could be 0-0 draws when forwards out-numbered defenders six to four.

The scientific play of the Scots rendered such chivalrous if self-indulgent methods obsolete. It could be only a matter of time before they dominated the F.A. Cup. Blackburn Olympic, whose existence was short but distinguished, actually initiated the popular expedient of seaside training before an important Cup game as early as 1883, when they took their players to Blackpool before the Final against Old Etonians. Needless to say, they had far too much steam for the Eton men when an extra half-hour had to be played, the more so as the Etonians had been reduced to ten men. Needless to say, there was no Blackburn equivalent of Major Marindin to "do the decent thing" and voluntarily leave the field, a gentle *parfait* knight.

Sophisticated London marveled at the troops of provincial supporters the Northern clubs brought with them for the Final. Already the tradition of "Oop for the Coop," the descent of the North on London for a

12

Cup Final outing, had been established. In 1885, the year in which Forrest, the celebrated Blackburn Rovers halfback, became the first professional to play for England—much to the displeasure of the Scots—and Blackburn reached the Cup Final, the *Pall Mall Gazette* described their supporters as "a northern horde of uncouth garb and strange oaths."

For some years the famous Glaswegian amateur team, Queens Park, competed for the F.A. Cup, twice being beaten in the Final. Subsequently the Scots established their own trophy, and entrance to the F.A. Cup was limited to English teams and the handful of Welsh clubs which were members of the Football League, Cardiff City so far being the only one to take the Cup out of England, when they beat Arsenal in the Final at Wembley with a strange goal scored by . . . a Scotsman.

Professionalism had clearly to come; but would it split soccer apart? Thanks to the English gift for compromise, it did not. Neither for the first nor the last time, the English patricians proved wonderfully accommodating in the face of recalcitrant fact.

In 1884, when Major Sudell, the cotton mill executive who had built Preston North End into the best team in England, and a manifestly professional one, admitted that they paid their players, the gauntlet was thrown down. C. W. Alcock, a flexible, intelligent Secretary, moved at once that "professionalism be legalized." Inevitably there was strong opposition, his motion was blocked, stringent rules against the payment of "expenses" were promulgated, and nineteen rebel Lancashire clubs angrily threatened to form their own British Football Association.

The Football Association itself then appointed a subcommittee which in turn produced a motion demanding that professionalism be made legal "under stringent conditions," one of which was that no pros should compete in the F.A. Cup—which would effectively have left them without a competition.

A further compromise was reached in 1885, whereby pros could participate in the F.A. Cup provided they be qualified for their clubs either by birth or by two years' residence within a six-mile radius of the ground.

Clearly, the F.A. Cup was not sufficient to sustain professionalism, even if the professionals in one way or another were permitted to take part in it. In 1888 Mr. William McGregor, a Scot who had settled in Birmingham about 1870 and was connected with the celebrated Aston Villa club, devised the idea of a Football League. Baseball in the United States had shown the way with its national competitions, but not till McGregor took an interest was a tournament devised in England.

Meanwhile, there had been further development in the rules of soccer. In 1873–74, umpires were officially recognized and free kicks awarded for offenses against the offside rule. The crossbar was introduced in 1875, the referee's whistle in 1878, the two-handed throw in 1883, but it was not till 1891 that the 12-yard penalty kick arrived, the invention of the Irish Association. In May 1889 the "stringent conditions" limiting professionalism were set aside. "A flood of Scottish players filled up the ranks of the League clubs," wrote Pickford and Gibson, "needless to say to the further exasperation of the Scottish Association, whose clubs were depleted of their best."

The night before the 1888 Cup Final, William McGregor presided over a meeting at Anderton's Hotel in London, at which it was decided to set up the Football League. It eventually consisted of a dozen clubs, being won in a canter by Preston North End, with 40 points to Aston Villa's 29. Other great names such as Everton, Wolverhampton Wanderers, Blackburn Rovers, Derby

County, and Stoke, which came bottom, are also to be found. The clubs played each other once at home and once away, gaining two points for a win, one for a draw.

This system has broadly survived until today, which says much for its simple ingenuity, though in its frantic attempt to promote the game in the United States, the North American Soccer League has been moved to give six points for a win and a point bonus for each goal scored up to three; a system which, in my view, contains the seeds of more anomalies than Mr. McGregor's. The chief argument against this system is that it does nothing to differentiate between games won away and games won at home, but against this it may be argued first that such imbalances tend to even themselves out over the season; second, that there would be something a little absurd about a match in which the home team was playing for fewer points than the away team. The draw, anathema to the NASL, was properly rewarded with a point. Drawn games can often be the most exciting of all, while many a goal-less draw—doubly anathema to the NASL—has been dramatic and entertaining; even if the defensive excesses of modern Italian football, especially, have given the result a bad name.

Meanwhile, the split between amateurs and professionals widened, even if, for a surprisingly long time, the amateurs were quite capable of holding their own, a fact which reflected on the training methods of the pros.

Thus, when in 1885 England at last put an end to a long period of Scottish dominance, the Scots having won eight times in the previous nine years, no fewer than nine of the team came from the Corinthians, a wholly amateur club formed specifically for the purpose of giving a backbone to the English national team by the formidable N. Lane "Pa" Jackson. Jackson was a true blue amateur through and through: when it was announced that the F.A. was to send a touring team to Germany in 1899, he protested on the grounds that "professionals had been included," and it might offend the German University men. In fact, the tour was a great success, moving the weekly *Athletic News*, outstanding in its time, to remark acidly, "Strange as it may seem, the pros. somehow managed to behave themselves."

Yet it should be recorded that when the F.A. subcommittee first deliberated on whether to allow professionalism, C. W. Alcock's motion in favor was seconded by . . . Jackson.

The Corinthians, though robust fellows given to the healthy, hearty shoulder charge, and quite capable of "punishing" rough opponents by thundering downfield and deliberately knocking them off balance before they could reach the ball, were the quintessence of sportsmanship. If they gave away a penalty kick, they were expected to atone for the shame by standing aside to give the kicker a shot at an empty goal. Major Marindin had not lived in vain.

Alas, "Pa" Jackson would never allow the Corinthians to compete for the Cup, so we shall never know how they would have fared against the best pros of the day. Such results as their 10-3 victory over Bury, after the Lancashire team had won the F.A. Cup Final 6-0 against Derby County in 1903, are impressive but have the smack of unreality. How hard were the professionals trying?

Still, there is no doubt that the Corinthians could boast some of the finest players of the day, such as the Old Carthusians A. M. and P. M. Walters, two fullbacks inevitably nicknamed "Morning" and "Afternoon," and the peerless center forward G. O. Smith, a legendary sportsman, all of whom played for England with distinction.

Abroad, the game swiftly took hold. The Corinthians, great international tourists, helped to promote it even in South America. How strange and sad to think that while their descendants, the Corinthian-Casuals, labor in the basement of the Second Division of the obscure English Isthmian League, the Corinthians of São Paulo, who named themselves after the English team, are a major force in the coruscating world of Brazilian soccer.

British sailors, gardeners, and businessmen took soccer to the four corners of the globe, and though it did not take root in North America, the rest of the world fell for it heavily.

The Danes were swiftest off the mark; by 1908, when the Olympic soccer tournament was held in London, they were already capable of giving a powerful United Kingdom amateur team a very good run for its money in the Final, as they did again in Stockholm, four years later. The small size of their country and the somewhat over-British, straightforward nature of their play ensured that the Danes would in due course be overtaken by the Central Europeans and the Latins, but as recently as the later 1970s they were producing an abundance of splendid players, most of whom went abroad to play for more highly paying clubs in West Germany and the Low Countries. When all, or most of them, could be reunited, the Danish team was a fine one.

In 1904, FIFA, otherwise the Fédération Internationale de Football Association, was founded, the idea having first been mooted the previous year. Belgium, Denmark, Holland, France, Germany, and Spain got together and sent the Frenchman M. Robert Guerin as their ambassador to London. There, the secretary of the Football Association, the tightly laced Frederick Wall, listened to him dispassionately, head buried in his hands, promising at last to refer the matter to his board.

After several silent months, Guerin was summoned back to London, there to be received by the formidable Lord Kinnaird, once the red-bearded, knee-breeched, stocking-capped terror of the soccer field. "It was like beating the air," Guerin complained, though there is no record that Lord Kinnaird actually hacked him, England did, in the event, help to found FIFA in 1904, but showed little enthusiasm, and seemed almost glad to withdraw twenty-one years later over the payment of broken time expenses to amateur players (i.e. compensation for time lost from their jobs).

"For the last twenty-five years," said a disappointed Guerin, at FIFA's silver jubilee banquet, "Britain's attitude has been incomprehensible to me, and I am afraid that it will remain so as long as I live."

Meanwhile, England for many years retained control of the rule-making, and changing, International Board, which had been formed by the four British Associations in 1885. Eventually FIFA, that is, the whole of the rest of the world, was graciously allowed two members on the Board. At present, the membership stands at equality, four members of FIFA, four from Britain, though there have been great rumblings, not least in South America, that Britain should have only one representative at FIFA. Both on historical and practical grounds, this seems a little absurd, not least when on the basis of FIFA's egalitarian rules, any one country's vote is as good as another's; Zambia's carrying as much weight as Italy's, Malta's as much as Spain's.

By the outbreak of the Great War in 1914, soccer was not only established as immeasurably the most popular spectator sport in Britain—drawing crowds of well over 100,000 to the Cup Final and sustaining a Football

League tournament which since 1892 had had a Second Division, and would before long acquire a Third—but it had spread across the globe.

Such was the force of the expansion, such the growing popularity of the game, that the Olympic tournament would not be sufficient to contain it. A world game it was, and a World Cup it would have.

2
THE GROWTH OF TACTICS

Soccer, it has been said, is a simple game; and so, ideally, it should be. It should never be forgotten, in this era of gnarled terminology and foggy theorizing, that tactics are merely a matter of applied common sense. Soccer is not American football. The heart of its attraction is its very fluidity, and though certain moves can be worked out at the "set pieces"—free kicks and corners—certain basic "plays" can even be decided on when the ball is actually in motion; the reduction of the game to a series of preordained maneuvers is quite impossible. Soccer is in a state of endless flux, and to be committed to a specific move can be at best risky, at worst disastrous.

Nevertheless, tactics do play a crucial part, and in broad terms, it may be said that their development had, until the advent of so-called Total Football in the early 1970s, been towards a greater and greater concentration on defense.

"Without going back to the Ark," wrote Ivan Sharpe, one of the most influential soccer journalists of the interwar years and a leading amateur player in his day—

good enough to turn out in League soccer for Derby County—"one can say that in the beginning football players chased the ball all over the field, leaving only the goalkeepers in a set position."

Dribbling was the name of the game; working the ball deftly with the inside and outside of the feet around as many of the bemused opposition as possible. In 1878 a leading forward of the day bestowed this advice: "A really first class player—I am now addressing myself solely to those who play up—will never lose sight of the ball, at the same time keeping his attention employed in the spying out of any gaps in the enemy's ranks. . . . To see some players guide and steer a ball through a circle of opposing legs, turning and twisting as occasion requires, is a sight not to be forgotten. . . . Skill in dribbling, though, necessitates something more than a go-ahead, fearless, headlong onslaught on the enemy's citadel, it requires an eye quick at discovering a weak point, and *nous* [acumen] to calculate and decide the chances of a successful passage."

The Prince of Dribblers was the sobriquet given to W. N. Cobbold, who played for England between 1883 and 1887, and was one of the most notable products of Charterhouse School's celebrated "run about." Of this the great center forward G. O. Smith wrote, "I don't think I ever dribbled through the whole school at Charterhouse, but I am sure 'run-about' was a great help to learning the art of dribbling."

Of light-heavyweight build, with huge shoulders and solid legs, "Nuts" Cobbold, clearly, was no ethereal figure; one does not have to be slight to be deft on the soccer field. G. O. Smith thought his fellow Old Carthusian the best forward he had ever seen, and N. Lane "Pa" Jackson, founder of the Corinthians in 1882, admired him greatly. Like G. O. Smith, Cobbold had an aversion to heading the ball, and he seems to have prevailed by sheer skill, rather than by ever changing pace; which today has become a *sine qua non*, a coaches' shibboleth. "He was," wrote a critic in 1906, "a powerful dribbler with a pair of shoulders like an ox and a deadly intensity near goal that few defences knew how to cope with." He added, however, the following rider: "How Cobbold would have fared with a modern defence one cannot say with any certainty, but the chances are that against three of our strongest halfbacks he would have had to considerably modify his methods."

Just as the stars of 1906 would have had to modify *their* methods against the exponents of the Third Back Game, while these in turn would have found themselves gasping against the practitioners of Total Football.

In the 1870s, the dribblers dribbled while the rest of the six or eight forwards backed them up, hoping, so to speak, for some crumbs from the rich man's table. There had been eight, yes eight, forwards in the 1860s, seven in the early seventies—two on each wing and three in the center—while the defense was handicapped the more till 1870 when the goalkeeper was finally allowed to use his hands. It should be added, in passing, that only in 1912 was he forbidden to use them outside his own penalty area. There were some jocular keepers who rejoiced in bouncing the ball all the way down the field.

It was the Scots who put an end to the dribbling game with their development of passing, a practice so simple and logical that it seems strange, in retrospect, that it had ever to be thought of at all. "The dribbling style that suited the [public school] old boys best," wrote the historians Pickford and Gibson in 1906, "had been carried to a marvellous perfection, but it was, all things being equal, not the style to last."

Nor alas, was the Scottish style itself; even in Scotland. The great irony was that while it went out to conquer the world, to inspire the Austro-Hungarians, to be adopted then adapted by the South Americans, the Scots themselves, between the wars, steadily forsook it. By 1939, though the Scots could still produce unhurried ball players of the type of Tommy Walker—whose father Bobby had been the great, "technical," inside forward of the early years of the century—the long passing, high crossing, physically committed English type of game was ravaging the old perfectionism.

The always amateur Queens Park club of Glasgow takes most of the credit for evolving the passing game, and changing the face of soccer. Formed in 1867 by members of the Glasgow Y.M.C.A., they made up the bulk of the Scottish international team against England for some years, and competed doughtily in the F.A. Cup.

Six forwards were still the norm in the early 1880s, but by the end of the decade the imbalance had been corrected; one forward had withdrawn to the midfield to become a center half, and the formation, which would remain largely unchanged until the London club Arsenal's revolution of 1925, looked roughly like this:

Clearly, this was no more than an approximation, since the center half could scarcely look after the whole midfield himself, and would need the help of his inside forwards, retreating in the center, and his wing half-backs, who were expected to move up the flanks. What's in a name? The four-in-a-line defense was saluted as a novelty when the Brazilians reinstituted it in the 1958 World Cup, while the overlapping, attacking fullback of today is only the old school wing half writ large; or writ the same.

"Show me your half-back line," said Billy Meredith, the great Welsh international outside right whose career spanned the nineteenth and twentieth centuries, "and I'll tell you what kind of a team you've got." Today, I suppose, one would rephrase his words in terms of the midfield. The center half was the key player, at once attacker and defender. In 1925, first Arsenal then in turn every other club in Britain withdrew him to be a mere defender, devoted guardian of the opposing center forward, but as Charlie Buchan, the inventor of the Third Back Game and one of the greatest inside forwards of his day, has written, "It has many times been said that the change in law brought into operation the 'stopper' centre-half. But there were many such stoppers long before that eventful day. . . . The only difference in the old-time centre-half and the modern is that the 'old-timer' was not just content to clear his lines. He placed the ball on every possible occasion, sometimes moving upfield. He was always there, though, when danger threatened his goal."

That would be a perfect description of Obdulio Varela, the big Uruguayan who captained his team so brilliantly to success in the decisive game of the 1950 World Cup against Brazil, in Rio; a time when Uruguay had yet to abandon the old school methods.

Vittorio Pozzo based his 1934 and 1938 World-Cup-winning Italian teams on such a strategy, having especially in mind the powerful, dominating Manchester United center half Charlie Roberts, whose long, sweeping passes to the wings he especially admired. Roberts also, in Buchan's words, "excelled in defence of his goal." In 1906 a contemporary eulogist wrote of him: "But see him on the field! There you are presented with bottled essence of agility, the personification of unending activity, and a veritable spring-heeled jack. Acrobatics would appear to have been the particular study of this slim youth of twenty-two; and we imagine that should football fail him he might readily acquire fame on the music-hall stage as an expert in legmania" (sic).

Roberts' chief rival for the position of England center half—which he seldom filled, thanks chiefly to his bold opposition to reactionary authority—was Billy Wedlock of Bristol City, a sturdy little center half otherwise known as "Smiler" or "Fatty." Ivan Sharpe, who played with and against both of them, reckoned Charlie Roberts "the best all-round centre-half-back of all time," but praised Wedlock for "his unfailing consistency and non-stop energy; he was football's nearest approach to perpetual motion." Between the two of them, I think they give us some idea of the old school center half at his best, though of course there could be great variations in the interpretation of the role.

Thus Vittorio Pozzo, in the 1920s, controversially dropped the elegant Fulvio Bernardini—who was joint manager of the Italian national team as late as 1977—because he felt he held the ball too long, keeping possession and beating opponents when Pozzo wanted it moved quickly over long distances. "Ball control, tackling and feeding power," wrote Ivan Sharpe, "height for reaching the ball in the air, these are the three prime needs in the player who should be the team's pivot but now is not given the opportunity to be more than a stopper."

That was the direct consequence of the change in the Offside Law in 1925.

For some time the British Associations had been growing increasingly uneasy at the way football was being spoiled, even farcified, by deliberate offside tactics in the English League. These were nothing very new, for they had been practiced before World War I by the two Notts County fullbacks, Morley and Montgomery, one very tall, the other short and thick-set, known to the fans as Weary Willie and Tired Tim, after two characters in a comic strip.

The war over, these tactics were espoused by that crafty and durable Irish international fullback, Bill M'Cracken, who was still scouting for the Millwall club of South East London as an astonishingly vigorous 90-year-old. In partnership with Frank Hudspeth, M'Cracken devised an offside trap, sidling cunningly upfield to put the opposition off limits, which reduced them to gibbering frustration. The story is told that a train carrying a visiting team arrived in the Newcastle railway station, a train guard blew a whistle, and one of the players remarked, with despair, "Blimey, offside already!"

M'Cracken actually left Newcastle in 1923, but the rot had set in. Games were being played in an area confined to ten yards each side of the halfway line, and were stopped time and again for an offside decision. What was to be done?

Whatever it was, the British Associations, who then, it will be remembered, ran the rule-making International Board, did it with indecent haste. "I laugh at their folly and pain," wrote Jimmy Catton, a minuscule fellow who wrote for the *Athletic News* and was the most respected, influential, and far-sighted journalist the sport had produced.

After a perfunctory experiment in London, it was decided simply to reduce the number of players needed to put a man onside from three to two. The alternative was to keep the number at three but restrict the area in which a player could be ruled offside. Inevitably, the balance tipped sharply from defense to attack. Arsenal, which had signed the rangy Charles Buchan, a veteran now, from Sunderland in the summer, went to Newcastle where, irony of ironies, they gave away seven goals and in consequence conceived the third back game or, as it has also been called, the W formation (a third variant, popular in Europe, is the WM).

Charlie Spencer, who played center-half for Newcastle that day, told me in later years that he himself had functioned as a stopper and as we have seen, Buchan himself claimed nothing new for the idea of the center half, once the pivot, as destroyer. There is little doubt, however, that third back theory initiated with him.

Buchan, now thirty-three, had been urging since the start of the season that Jack Butler, Arsenal's center half, be played as an out-and-out defender. He had been made captain of the club which, sixteen years earlier when they were still at Woolwich, South East London, had let him go because it was too parsimonious to pay him £2 a week; though he did not want the job. Herbert Chapman, who had become the Arsenal manager shortly before acquiring Buchan, was against the idea of a "stopper" center half, but the defeat at Newcastle caused him to think again, the more so as, only two days later, they had an evening game to play in East London, away at West Ham United.

So Buchan got his way; up to a point. He had suggested that, to compensate for the gap in midfield, an inside forward, ideally himself, should be withdrawn into midfield, linking attack with defense, receiving the ball from his own defenders with space and time to use it profitably. Chapman liked the idea in principle, but told Buchan, "We want you up in attack scoring goals."

This was understandable enough, for the tall Buchan, seemingly maladroit but in fact a superb ballplayer with a powerful shot, and great creative skills, was a splendid finisher. The son of an Aberdonian soldier, brought up in South East London, he had two brothers who also became professional soccer players, though not as successfully as he. The one blemish on a career interrupted by service in the trenches in World War I was that, in characteristically English fashion, the selectors mistrusted his original brilliance. He played only half a dozen times for England.

The question was, if Buchan didn't do the linking, then who should. "Well, it's your plan, Charlie," Herbert Chapman said—part of his strength as a manager was that he was self-assured enough to listen to other people—"have you any suggestions to make?"

Equally characteristically, Buchan had. He had been impressed in training games by another veteran, a Scot named Andy Neil who played for the reserves and "could kill [bring under control] a ball instantly and pass accurately." Neil, he assured Chapman, "has a football brain and two good feet." Chapman was not easy to persuade, but ultimately Neil played, Arsenal won 4-0, the third back game was born, and the Highbury club—which had moved to North London from Plumstead in the South East of the city only in 1913, one of the very few examples of an American kind of club migration, even if on a somewhat limited geographic scale—went from success to success.

The third back game quickly developed. The fullbacks, who had been playing in the middle of the field since the game originated, now moved to the flanks to look after the opposing wingers. The wing halves, who had regarded practically the whole of the touchline as their beat, would now exercise their craft in the center of the field, marking the opposing inside forwards, both of whom, rather than merely one, would drop back into midfield, playing just in front of the wing halves, with the function of both making and scoring goals. In practice, an inside forward would often tend to exercise one function in preference to the other, but there is no doubt that his position now became physically the most demanding on the field. The formation looked like this:

You will notice at once an evident gap in the center of the defense, where, despite the withdrawal of the center half, there are no longer two defenders, but only one. Pivotal covering was, or was supposed to be, the answer to this. In other words, the stopper third back and the two fullbacks played a pivotal, diagonal system. If the ball was on their right flank the right back moved towards the danger, covered diagonally by the center half, while the left back moved across diagonally to cover the stopper; like this:

So in theory if the right back were beaten the center half would come in to tackle, while if he were beaten, he would be covered by the left back. From this you will also deduce that the system of marking was zonal; you looked after, as a defender, a certain space rather than a specific opponent, though obviously the right back would spend much of his time marking the opposing left winger, the left back the right winger, while the center half would stick close to the center forward.

British players liked the system, mastering the covering aspect of it quite easily, but did not like to play "man to man," that is, to stick close to a single opponent throughout the game and follow him all over the place. The forwards, for that matter, didn't like it either. The illustrious Stanley Matthews, a star for thirty years, once told me how difficult it was to play against a defender, "if you know what he's had for breakfast." But Continental defenders found it less easy to master the zonal covering and, as we shall see, it was Brazil's inability to do so which ended the domination of the third back game and its WM formation—the letters formed if you link up wingers to wing halves to inside forwards—and led to the birth of 4-2-4.

Beyond question the third back game led to a greater concentration on defense, but that was in the air before the offside law was even changed. After all, that law had remained extant and valid for some sixty years, when the equivalent of M'Cracken and Hudspeth could have destroyed it at any time. That no one did so was perhaps the measure not so much of their ingenuousness but of a more generous spirit in the game, a lesser eagerness to exploit the laws in any way one could.

League football and increasing professionalization put an end to that. In G. O. Smith's days, he has recorded, the mighty Corinthians did not train at all; they simply did not find it necessary. But by 1910, according to Charlie Buchan, training was even harder than it would be about 1925. Clearly, to compete, the Corinthians would have to train harder.

This they did in the early 1920s, entering at last, though belatedly, for the F. A. Cup. For they were underdogs now, and though they put up some mighty performances, actually holding Newcastle United to a draw when the North Easterners were a great professional power, their participation was essentially a kind of gallant gesture. Several of them were good enough to win caps for this full England team—among them the Carthusian left back, A. G. Bower, and the inside right, a Cambridge Blue against Oxford, Norman Creek—but the historical process would steadily overtake them.

With the third back game, the romance finally went out of English football. Jimmy Hogan, that fabled coach, who had himself as a player sat at the feet of Scottish "professors," brought his Austrian Wunderteam to play England at Chelsea in 1932, attended a League game there with his players a few days earlier, and was appalled to see the ball constantly banged down the middle to one of two illustrious center forwards, little Hughie Gallacher of Chelsea or big Dixie Dean of Everton. In most cases the "policeman" third back center half simply headed the high ball away. He did not have to be a stylish player, and he seldom was. It was sufficient to be big, strong, and good in the air.

Moreover, as in the case of every tactical revolution there has ever been, the successful use of the new strategy depended on whether you had the players to operate it. Arsenal, under Herbert Chapman, saw to it that they did. Chapman realized that he needed an inside forward of unusual vision, two "raiding" wingers, as they came to be called, of pace and incision who would cut inside and make directly for goal, a robust center forward prepared to give and take knocks in his battle against the third back center half. Charlie Buchan in due course became that inside forward, retiring in May 1928 at the age of thirty-six. Joe Hulme arrived from Blackburn Rovers, a right winger of terrific pace and a fine right foot who admirably filled the bill on the right.

The jigsaw was completed in the summer of 1929 with the signing of . . . two inside lefts. Each had to be, as they say, made over. Thus, the stocky little Scot Alex James arrived from Preston North End with a reputation of being something as a goal scorer, as well as a glorious ballplayer whose foot, fluttering over the ball, could send one defender after another the wrong way. Him Chapman wanted as his lighthouse, his midfield purveyor. Cliff Bastin, a shy 17-year-old, came from Exeter City, a Devonian himself, precociously and astonishingly cool. Him Chapman in due course turned into his perfect outside left, though he would play for England as a splendid inside forward too.

James wasn't very keen on dropping back deeper, giving up all ambitions as a goal scorer, and becoming simply the play-maker; a kind of soccer quarterback, if you wish. It took quite a while for Chapman, the Arch Persuador, to persuade James to play as, where, and how he wanted, but in due course he succeeded; as he did with Bastin, whose debut was made at inside forward. James, lying deep to pick the ball up from his defenders, often from the stopper center half, Herbie Roberts, would send it winging on its way with marvelously accurate passes. The most spectacular was possibly the crossfield ball to Joey Hulme on the right, dropping perfectly into his stride as Hulme went racing on to it. The down-the-middle pass, the so-called through ball, the defense splitter, was for the center forward Jack Lambert (how often Chapman tried to re-place him with a player more refined, and how unsuc-cessfully!) or later, for Ted Drake. Alternatively, the ball was played to Bastin, now at outside left, standing some ten or fifteen yards in from the touchline. In sea-son 1930–31, when Arsenal won the League Champion-ship for the first time, Bastin scored no fewer than 33 goals from the wing.

Purists deplored Arsenal's methods, which brought in their wake a crop of fustian imitators, who had none of the players mentioned above, nor an inside right of the gliding elegance of David Jack, signed from the Bol-ton Wanderers for a huge fee, a player who once scored a goal against Aston Villa in which he beat five de-fenders with his feathery swerves and feints, touching the ball but three times. Without such executors, the third back game became a tiresome, talentless affair in which speed, or what passed for speed in those days, was paramount, while ball skills were at a premium. In training, little emphasis was placed on controlling the ball. British footballers had muscle, stamina and, above all, finishing power—the one quality which for many years the foreigners lacked. So great teams like the Aus-trians of 1932 came to London, gave England a foot-balling lesson, but lost just the same because they sim-ply could not put the ball in the net; a process which sometimes appeared to them—at least to an observer's eye—as the merest vulgarity.

John Goodall, one of the great inside forwards of the 1890s, and a star of the great Preston team, bitterly la-mented what he saw as the sacrifice of skill to speed. In due course, the balance would right itself, though out-side England rather than in it. A player such as Johan Cruyff of Holland would certainly possess as much skill as any of the great players of yore, while at the same time being able to do everything at two or three times the speed; which, with deference to Goodall and other critics of like persuasion, must surely be a gain.

Arsenal dominated the 1930s, winning the English League five times and the Cup twice. Italy, so tactically obsessed in recent times, was incredibly innocent about the new development. Though their national team played England in 1933 and 1934, it was not until England had visited Milan in 1939 that Fulvio Bernardini, by now a journalist, wrote in the Roman daily *Corriere dello Sport* the analysis of the third back game which is generally supposed to have presented it to the Italian public. Vittorio Pozzo, predictably, detested it, and held out against it until the early 1940s, when Italy, too, succumbed to the stopper center half, and in due course produced one of the greatest of them in the Turin club Juventus' Carlo Parola, a splendid compound of power and elegance, famous for his aerial bicycle kick.

It was from Italy that the next major tactical breakthrough would come: *catenaccio*, the development of a Swiss model. But since, in its final and best-known form, it did not really develop till the early 1960s, it would be best now to turn to 4-2-4; and its successor, 4-3-3.

It was the Brazilians who invented it, the direct consequence of a disastrous European tour late in the spring of 1956. At Wembley they lost 4-2 to England and should really have gone down by six clear goals; England missed a couple of penalties and absolutely overran a Brazilian defense which had simply no idea how to cover. The so-called "diagonal" system used in the 1950 World Cup, a kind of compromise between the third back game and the older strategy, had been discredited by the defeat at the hands of Uruguay, World Cup winners in consequence. Now there was a stopper center half, but the backs, known as *volantes*, were, as their name might suggest, flyers down the flanks, wing halfbacks of the classic kind at heart, with little interest in or penchant for the tiresome, pivotal task of covering their center back. I still remember how the wretched Pavao, Brazil's center half, was left alone to try to counter the rampant descents of the powerful Tommy Taylor, then Manchester United's center forward.

By the Swedish World Cup, four years later, the Brazilians had adopted 4-2-4. Whether they were the first team to play it is debatable; it is said that it was brought to Rio by the well-known Paraguayan coach, Fleitas Solich; but it was Brazil who now showed it to the world. In essence, the way around the defensive problem was admirably simple. If your players could not learn how to cover, obviate the need to do so: put four men in a line so that the center half always has a second stopper beside him, while each of the fullbacks has, near at hand, a center back who can come to his aid.

As for the midfield, that was left to two men, a natural wing half and a natural inside forward. The wing half was at first the attacking, free-running Dino Sani, then the slightly less adventurous, defensively more solid, Zito. The inside forward was the coal-black Didì, a splendid, brooding figure, with the face of an African carving, fine ball control, a wonderfully insidious "falling leaf" free kick which swerved the ball through the air and past unsuspecting goalkeepers, above all a marvelous flair for distributing passes.

In the front line, there were four "strikers," as they came to be called, though at this time they were very clearly differentiated. There was a right and a left winger, a forceful center forward, good with his head and quick off the mark, and beside him an attacking inside forward: when he was ultimately fit, the 17-year-

35

old Pelé. Joel was originally the right winger, but when Garrincha came into the team in the third match he gave the forward line an explosive penetration it had not previously had.

The first center forward was "Mazzola," a nickname for José Altafini, given him as a boy with Palmeiras on account of his resemblance to the famous captain of Italy, Valentino Mazzola, who died in the 1949 Torino air disaster. Altafini, a stockily built, fair-haired center forward with good headwork, a quick turn, and speed off the mark, was only nineteen years old then and he did not please the team's coach, Vicente Feola, who felt Altafini's individualism spoiled his tactical schemes and broke up movements. He dropped Altafini after the quarter finals in favor of the Aztec figure of Vavà, a courageous, forcing player who would score two goals from Garrincha's crosses in the Final. But Altafini went on to play at the top level in Italy till 1976; and even then he went on scoring goals in the Swiss league for Chiasso.

The outside left was the extraordinary Mario Lobo Zagalo, destined to win the World Cup twice as a player, once as a coach. With his exceptional stamina, itself the consequence of an unusual lung capacity, Zagalo could run forever, going up and down the left flank like a metronome. In the 1958 Final, he headed out from beneath his own crossbar in the first half, and scored a good goal late in the second, kneeling down to weep with joy. In 1958 he spent the bulk of his time up the field, but in 1962, as we shall see, he became the third man who made the 4-3-3 formation possible.

In these days of 4-3-3 and 4-4-2, it seems extraordinary that there should be only two players in midfield; and it was here that imitators of the Brazilian style tended to fall into a trap. The Brazilians could allow themselves this luxury because they had two players of such immense quality—in Zito and in Didì with his outstanding percipience. If you did not have two midfielders of such quality, however—and who else did?—you were tempting Providence.

Brazil's performance against Sweden in the Final in Stockholm—their enraptured supporters chanting, "Samba, samba!" their gleeful players circling the field, first with the Brazilian then with the Swedish flag, after the game—was the very apotheosis of 4-2-4.

By 1962 and the Chilean World Cup, however, the team was substantially older, while in the second game, against the Czechs at Viña del Mar, Pelé pulled muscles in his thigh and was obliged to drop out.

It was a disastrous blow and forced a reappraisal of tactics by the new manager, Aymore Moreira. Without the transcendent brilliance of Pelé the attack, though still formidable, became merely . . . mortal. It would be prudent and politic to withdraw a forward into midfield, and that forward was at hand, for who could be more ideally suited than Zagalo?

Let it be pointed out, moreover, that Zagalo did not act simply as a midfield player, toiling in the vineyard, serving the forwards rather than making himself still one of them. Time and again Zagalo would dance up the left wing, twist and turn his way past the opposing right back, and put over a center, perfectly measured for the head of the powerful Vavà. Yet he would always have the determination and the energy to drop back into the midfield. If you had a Zagalo, then 4-3-3 was indeed a most practicable possibility; and note that the other two men in midfield were still Zito, a "certified" wing halfback, and Didì, a recognized, creative inside forward. The two formations would look like this:

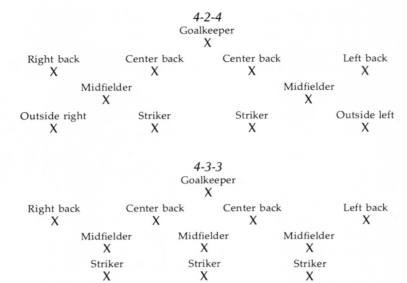

4-2-4

Goalkeeper
X

| Right back | Center back | Center back | Left back |
| X | X | X | X |

Midfielder   Midfielder
X   X

| Outside right | Striker | Striker | Outside left |
| X | X | X | X |

4-3-3

Goalkeeper
X

| Right back | Center back | Center back | Left back |
| X | X | X | X |

Midfielder   Midfielder   Midfielder
X   X   X

Striker   Striker   Striker
X   X   X

Further points should be made. The Brazilian teams of 1958 and 1962 very clearly differentiated between their centerbacks. Bellini in 1958, and Mauro in 1962, was obviously a traditional stopper center half. But Orlando, in 1958, and the little, black Zozimo, in 1962, were what one would call defensive wing halves, more mobile, less dominant in the air than Bellini or Mauro, their function essentially that of covering rather than rigid marking. Today it is often the fashion to play two natural center halves in the middle of a four-man defense, but by and large the best combination has been found to consist of a stopper and a coverer. England's Bobby Moore, one of the finest defenders of the 1966 and 1970 World Cups, was an excellent example of the central defender who was not a center half. Moore was inaccurately known as a "sweeper," in England; inaccurately, because a sweeper, as we shall see, is someone who plays *behind*, not beside, the other defenders. But he was certainly no third back, no stopper, and when he did play there, it was always uneasily. He was never dominant in the air, and preferred to stand off his man, moving in with a tackle at the apposite moment, rather than to mark him tight: a covering player of great gifts rather than a marker.

4-3-3 also demanded an attacking commitment from the fullbacks. This came very naturally to the Brazilian *volantes*, such as the mighty Djalma and Nilton Santos, who had always interpreted their job in this way. The W formation, third back game fullbacks, obliged to play their pivotal, covering game, could seldom permit themselves the self-indulgence of a dash down the wing; for who would cover the center half in case of a breakaway? Fullbacks were essentially destroyers; it was a rarity and a revelation to find even a fullback such as Alf Ramsey, later manager of the England team, who was known in the 1950s for his creative approach to the role, his clever use of the ball. But Ramsey was a heavy, static figure who needed an outside right in front of him, a right half behind him, who would sacrifice themselves to give him the cover and support he needed. He was certainly no overlapper; no practicer of the dash down the wing.

So fullbacks became even physically different. Traditionally strong and heavy, even though some, like Arsenal's Eddie Hapgood in the 1930s, had prevailed by sheer skill, they now had to be lighter, quicker, and fitter, moving into the gaps on the flanks inevitably left by the fact that there were now only three forwards. The W formation, too, had left only three men up, but the inside forwards were supposed to move up, too.

As football became increasingly defensive, 4-3-3 in turn was joined, though never wholly replaced, by 4-4-2, a method of which you could say that Ramsey's 1966 World Cup winning England team was the pioneer. Since 4-4-2 left only two men permanently up, and thus postulated a team without true wingers—since the strikers would have to cover so much ground—it plainly required a huge amount of running. It would be wrong to give blanket definitions of 4-4-2; the 4-4-2 used by Brazil to win the 1970 World Cup often modulated into 4-3-3, and employed the dashing Rivelino, on the left flank, to some extent as Zagalo himself—by now the team's coach—had been used in the past. Not that Rivelino had remotely the stamina of Zagalo, any more than Zagalo had the explosive shot, the clever strategy, of Rivelino; but Rivelino, too, was no mere outside left. He would often drop back into midfield.

England's so-called "wingless wonders" of 1966 were a much more limited team, a triumph, if you wish, of mind over matter. The fullbacks, George Cohen and Ray Wilson, were expected to overlap down the flanks, and did so with varying success. Of the four players in the midfield, one—the right half, tiny Nobby Stiles—was essentially a destroyer, a marker, and a harrier, technically gauche, a very poor passer of the ball, but prized by Ramsey and his own colleagues for his competitive spirit, his potent effect on the morale and concentration of the defense.

Bobby Charlton, the most celebrated and popular member of the team, enormously admired on the continent of Europe, was the chief creative player of the midfield; but very much in his own manner. By nature and endowment he was a front runner, and had begun as a "boy wonder" inside forward of the attacking kind, renowned for his wonderful left-footed shot. To this he added, with commendable diligence, a right foot very nearly as powerful, so that he was a menace to any goalkeeper from any distance up to thirty yards.

From inside forward he was converted into an outside left, and played there for England with much success in the 1962 World Cup in Chile. He was abundantly gifted for the position, having a glorious body swerve, a flowing, elegant run, great acceleration, and, of course, his shot. He was, however, what is called in English football an instinctive player, doing the right thing as though by reflex. He was not a reasoning, thinking, strategic kind of player, changing the course and pattern of the game with his vision and originality. Why should he be?

What he *could* do in midfield was to hold the ball, disrupt the opposing defense by moving forward with it and beating opponents, hit long, crossfield passes to the wings—often more spectacular than effective—and use his wonderful, explosive shot. It brought him three fine goals in the 1966 World Cup.

Martin Peters, another of the midfield players, was in fact the West Ham United right half, with all the attributes of the classical, W formation, wing halfback. That is to say, he could tackle—though this was not his foremost quality—he used the ball skillfully, and he controlled it well. He could also on occasion score goals, but, lacking pace, was at his best when gliding into position from midfield; "ghosting," as it was commonly known.

Ramsey took shrewd advantage of Peters' highly developed positional sense near goal, giving him a freer, more generalized role in midfield than he would have had if he had been playing as an orthodox right half, encouraging him to steal into dangerous places near goal. It was a fine cross from the left wing by Peters which gave Hurst the opportunity to head the only goal of the ill-tempered quarter-final against Argentina; it was Peters who scored England's second against West Germany in the World Cup Final.

Alan Ball, the fourth player in midfield, was "really" an inside forward, a red-haired 21-year-old, himself the son of a professional footballer, whose game was based on sheer energy and determination. It is arguable that he was the decisive player of the World Cup Final with his endless running, first pulling the unhappy German left back Karl-Heinz Schnellinger all across the field, and finally running him silly, down the right wing. Outside right was Ball's nominal position, and he did great damage there, but you could not pretend that he was in any way an outside right as Matthews, Finney, Meredith, Julinho, or Garrincha had been.

Stamina and quickness—these were Ball's assets. He believed in the kind of football known variously as push and run, the wall pass, and the one-two, which simply means a player passing a ball to another, and running on for an immediate return. The second player has, in fact, been used as a wall. Alan, then, was a "short ball player" rather than one who hit the long, searching passes of an Alex James. He had, above all, the character and the resistance to get through the immense amount of running demanded by Ramsey's tactics, which were essentially designed to compensate with endless activity the lack of any great ability.

The Italians, deeply impressed, at once christened this *Calcio Atletico*, athletic football, and kept sending their coaches to England; until England, with what was probably a better team than they had in 1966, lost their World Cup in Mexico. Then everybody wanted again to play like the Brazilians.

To set down the formation of 4-4-2 is, as you will have gathered, only of approximate relevance, given the fact that there are so many ways of applying it, but here it is:

	Goalkeeper		
	X		
Right back	Center back	Center back	Left back
X	X	X	X
Midfielder	Midfielder	Midfielder	Midfielder
X	X	X	X
	Striker	Striker	
	X	X	

Ironically enough, the very undoing of the England team in the 1970 World Cup was probably the fact that they now had two fullbacks eminently capable of overlapping, and delivering splendid crosses. Terry Cooper, the Leeds United left back, was in fact a failed outside left, while Keith Newton, the right back, was a big strong overlapper who delivered the crosses for both England goals against West Germany in the quarterfinal at León.

Unfortunately, the heat and altitude of León were such that both fullbacks were steadily exhausted, and when the game went into extra time both of them wilted, West Germany winning by 3-2.

The Italians, meanwhile, stuck to their *catenaccio,* the origins of which were unquestionably Swiss. There, it was known as the *verrou,* the trough, or the *béton,* and it seems to have been invented in the 1940s by an Austrian coach named Karl Rappan, who for many years had charge of the Swiss international team. Under this system, one forward withdrew to play largely in defense, while the *verrouilleur* lurked at the back of the defense to plug any holes that might appear.

In 1952, when Alfredo Foni, a university graduate who had been Italy's right back when they won the World Cup in Paris in 1938, became manager of Internazionale, Milan, he introduced the system, which now came to be called *catenaccio,* great big chain. It was not quite what it has since become. Foni had a big, heavy right back named Blason who, he thought, needed support. He made him the *battitore libero,* or free defender, usually abbreviated to *libero,* and known in Britain as the sweeper-up, or sweeper. The term is self-explanatory. Any "bits and pieces" which got through the mesh of the defense were, ideally, "swept-up" by the sweeper.

To compensate for Blason's absence from his place on

the right flank, Foni made use of the right winger, the athletic Gino Armano, as a kind of Zagalo, a deep lying outside right, who spent much of his time in defense or midfield, but was certainly capable at times of joining in attacks.

Given the nature of the Italian Championship, the increasingly vast sums of money poured into it, the colossal amounts at stake if a club failed, the commitment by the *nouveaux riches* who had made their pile in more or less dubious ways during the war, it was inevitable that fear and hence caution should prevail. If a club lost a couple of games, the coach would as likely as not be sacked. The Italian footballer is naturally a creative, enterprising, adventurous player, but by sheer overcompensation, he learned to be something else. More and more was the emphasis placed on somber defensive, containing play. Arsenal had been the pioneers of this, the first great exponents of the counterattack, the breakaway. Cliff Bastin, their outside left, once told me that when they had a great deal of the play and pressure, Arsenal would begin to worry. But their methods were almost laughably carefree compared with those developed by Helenio Herrera, again at Internazionale, in the early 1960s.

Herrera, an Argentinian by birth, arrived from Spain, tried to play open, creative football for a time, found it didn't work, and evolved a ruthless *catenaccio*, far more carfully elaborated than Alfredo Foni's had been at Internazionale a decade earlier. His sweeper was a converted fullback from Livorno named Armando Picchi.

In front of Picchi there were four defenders, but the marking was man to man, which meant they followed their opponents about. The left back, the very tall Giacinto Facchetti, a naturally right-footed player, loped eagerly into the attack from whatever position he happened to find himself in, and often scored goals. The left flank was left free for him to go down because the nominal outside left, Mario Corso, a player with an exquisite left foot, played deep on the left-hand side, and kept the attack going with his excellent passes. The chief tactitian, however, was the Spaniard Luis Suarez, a complete inside forward of the old school, strong and deft on the ball, a powerful right-footed shot, adept at binding defense and attack together. There were three rather than a mere two forwards up, however. Jair, a Brazilian international, was a fixed point at outside right, with his great speed and close control. Sandrino Mazzola, son of Valentino, was first used as a "striking" inside forward, flanked by a center forward, then as a center forward himself, abetted by the long-legged Spanish international, Peirò.

The Inter line-up in those early 1960s, when they twice won the European Cup and twice the grandiosely named Intercontinental Cup against South American opposition, was roughly thus:

		Goalkeeper		
		X		
		Sweeper		
		X		
Right back		Stopper		Left back
X		X		X
	Right half			
	X			
	Midfielder		Midfielder	
	X		X	
Outside right		Striker	Striker	
X		X	X	

The right half, sometimes the blond Tagnin, one of the various "discarded" players Helenio Herrera picked up and shrewdly rehabilitated, sometimes Bedin, was expected to lend a hand in the building up of play, as well as simply marking.

By comparison with the game as it would develop in the 1970s, Inter's policy in the 1960s was almost permissive, while Foni's *catenaccio* of the 1950s, so strongly condemned for its negativity at the time, seems wildly romantic. The teams of the 1970s rarely kept more than two forwards up the field, one of which could scarcely afford to be an orthodox winger, though several of the best of them, including the prolific Gigi Riva of Cagliari, the clever Pierino Prati, and Luciano Chiarugi, started on the wing.

The combination of man-to-man marking and the fear of losing led to some ugly football. When a defender knows that a forward is *his* man, and that he "must" be stopped—or else—it is inevitable that he will not always be too nice about his methods.

The greatest weakness of *catenaccio*, however, as the game evolved outside Italy, was seen to be its static sweeper. After Italy had been put out of the 1974 World Cup in West Germany, certain Italian newspapers published lists of the Sèrie A (First Division) teams with their *libero*, or sweeper. In almost every case, he was an ex-defender, usually a fullback or a stopper, though occasionally a defensive halfback. Not, you will notice, an ex-forward. An ability to "read" the game well, weigh up and foresee situations, itself dependent largely on experience, made the sweeper's role a sort of active retirement for many a defender whose legs were rather too old for man-to-man marking.

The Italians rationalized their caution on the curious grounds that they were physically incapable of playing at the rhythm of the English and the Germans and the Dutch. That their players had, indeed, allowed themselves to become thus debilitated was shown in 1975 when a Turin sports daily paper conducted a survey among athletes of various categories and found that the soccer players were easily the least fit. Giampiero Boniperi, who captained Italy and Juventus before ultimately becoming president of the Turin club, and was a celebrated forward of the 1950s, assured me in 1972 that there was no way that the Italians could keep up physically with the English—wryly smiling and shaking his head—that *catenaccio* was a means of husbanding their inadequate energies.

This was physiological nonsense, of course, and by the late 1970s Italian coaches were at last beginning to denounce it as such, demanding more from their players than "postage stamp" marking, as they called it in Italy, and static virtuosity. For a great many years, however, the myth survived, and contributed in its turn to the survival of a pernicious system. Yet Inter's *catenaccio* was to lead, and not altogether indirectly, to Total Football, which would make it, if not obsolete, then at least obsolescent.

In fact the philosophy of Total Football was anticipated and predicted as long before as 1955 by the late Dr. Willy Meisl, a Viennese journalist domiciled in London, younger brother of Hugo Meisl, the father of Austrian football, who had himself kept goal for the national team, as well as excelling in many other sports. In a book entitled, appropriately, *Soccer Revolution*, he spoke of something that he called The Whirl.

"The tactics of the future will be fluid," he wrote, "and fluid flows in all directions." Often, players would desert their normal position and move into "foreign" territory. "This," said Meisl, "is THE WHIRL. However, it is often hampered by the bad conscience, or rather the fears inhibiting the player who anticipated tomorrow's tactics today. He somehow feels that he is ahead of his time and is afraid what will happen to the deserted pitch in his absence. Disaster may come to his team through his action. This fear forces him to hurry and return to his routine position. This hurry usually robs his splendid 'raid' of its chance of success."

Looking at Meisl's exposition today, one is astounded by his prescience, though for those of us who had the fortune to know him well, he was always greatly to be respected for his good, combative Viennese mind, an intellectual in a profession, that of sports journalist, scarcely noted for the breed.

Given the fact that Total Football virtually began in West Germany, it is a little ironic to find him writing that though the Germans—who had won the World Cup the previous year—had had "similar ideas," they had not yet given them sufficient thought, "or, far more probable, they simply have not yet a sufficient layer of first-class players as the true Whirl will need." He felt that the Germans, anxious about leaving holes in their defense, had restructured The Whirl to forward play, calling it The Top, and confining interchangeability to the forwards. They also, he complained, used two stoppers, which "must mean numerical inferiority upfield." Here, as we have seen, he was perhaps wrong, though there is something rather beguiling about his postulation of a team playing The Whirl hitting "into the defence wall with such a devastating impact of five to seven forwards that even two stoppers should prove unable to stop such force." Alas, such a team might well find itself up against eight or even nine defenders!

Meisl went on, however, to talk a great deal more good, almost clairvoyant, sense. "To execute The Whirl," he pursued, "every man-jack must be able to tackle anybody else's job temporarily without any ado." He spoke, hopefully, of "a drive to new old soccer peaks" which could be reached "possibly in a couple of seasons." As we know, it was the better part of twenty years before they were scaled; and it was the Dutch and the West Germans who scaled them.

If Charlie Buchan was the progenitor of the Third Back Game, then Franz Beckenbauer was the true begetter of Total Football. Beckenbauer, in fact, invented a strategy and a role; the latter giving birth to the former. It was Facchetti who inspired him. As a very young footballer with the Bayern Munich club in his native city, he watched Internazionale's triumphs on the television, watched in particular Facchetti's surging forays into attack, and asked himself why, if a left back did it, it should not be done from the right flank; or even from the center. He himself was at the time a right half of great poise and promise, a beautifully fluent mover, eager to go forward and to look for goals. It was as such that he played for West Germany in two World Cups, 1966 and 1970; but with a sense of frustration, for in the meantime he had devised and elaborated with Bayern Munich the innovation of the attacking sweeper.

The idea was in essence simple; though to implement it fully, you had to be a Beckenbauer, a player of his infinite range, immense skill, self-possession, and inspired use of the ball. At his best, moreover, he had a considerable change of pace; it was when he was cutting through the Italian defense at speed, in the semifinal of the 1970 World Cup in Mexico City, that he was callously hacked down, damaging his shoulder so badly that he was a passenger throughout extra time, and the Italians undeservedly squeaked through into the Final.

What Beckenbauer had seen was that a sweeper, or *libero*, was in a sense an invisible man, lurking unobserved at the back, behind the last line of defenders. This meant that he could, if and when the spirit moved him, advance untrammeled from his lair, taking part in the midfield build-up, and even going farther than that, both physically and metaphorically, by joining in the strikes on goal.

Beckenbauer's approach to the game, one based on technique and craft, greatly appealed to Helmut Schoen, who, after years of working under the indestructible Sepp Herberger, German team manager from 1938 to 1962, at last came into his inheritance. The tall and gentle Schoen had been, in his day, a creative inside-forward, clever on the ball, good enough to be capped for Germany. Though he would tell you that with artists such as Netzer, Beckenbauer, and Overath alone, one would not win World Cups, he was still anxious to tip the balance from power to skill, to encourage versatility.

So Beckenbauer, who had for years been playing as attacking sweeper for Bayern, was at last allowed to do the same for his country. The West German team which won the European Nations Cup in 1972 was to my mind a much better one than that which won the World Cup, two years later. Beckenbauer himself was more adventurous and constructive; in 1974 the pressure to win the World Cup was plainly on him; he lurked for the most part at the back, occasionally coming out to hit long, accurate, but unexceptional passes. In 1972, however, when the semi-finals and Final were played in Belgium, he joyfully came out of his own half to join in assaults on goal.

The formation of the team was boldly conceived, for in front of Beckenbauer—or, as it occasionally happened, behind him!—there were only three "markers," each on a man to man basis; the fullbacks, Paul Breitner and Hottges, the center back, Georg Schwarzenbeck. All were encouraged to attack, and this indeed was the stock in trade of the bushy-haired 20-year-old Breitner, with his long, lean legs, socks rolled down to the ankles, his exciting pace, his tremendous shot. A confirmed Maoist, though one who lived high on the hog, drove an expensive sports car, and would join the urcapitalist and paternalist Spanish club Real Madrid after the 1974 World Cup, Breitner's ambition was eventually to make enough money to endow a school for handicapped children. Meanwhile, he and his wife adopted a Vietnamese war orphan.

Schwarzenbeck, the big, blond center back—a Bayern player like Breitner and Müller and Beckenbauer, not to mention the excellent goalkeeper Sepp Maier and the dazzling 20-year-old Uli Hoeness—was technically a modest player, defensively not always reliable, but he, too, rejoiced in going forward and, like Breitner, was capable of scoring some spectacular goals.

In midfield the outstanding figure was Gunter Netzer, an inside forward of enormous gifts, an enormous stride, and . . . enormous feet. To see him, in that European Nations Cup tournament, racing down the field, blond, Viking hair flowing in the wind, ball under immaculate control, to see the long, impeccably accurate passes that he hit across the field, the free kicks that he "bent" with the outside of his right foot, was to see in action one of the greatest players Germany, or Europe, has produced. It was his absence, for all but twenty minutes, from the West German midfield in 1974 which diminished the team, even though the clever, experienced Wolfgang Overath, who regained his place, kept the team on the move with his shrewd, left-footed passing. Netzer's repertoire, however, was vastly greater. Alas, thigh injuries caused by the length of his raking stride were to take the edge off his game, cost him his place and West Germany their finest player, after Beckenbauer.

With him in the midfield was his loyal lieutenant Herbert Wimmer, who had played with him for years at

Borussia Münchengladbach, admiring his great talent, studiously and self-effacingly working beside him, a player who was also capable of moving out to the right and playing as a dangerous winger.

Uli Hoeness, the blond, curly haired forward who had played as a winger when Germany beat England 3-1 at Wembley in the quarter-final, now played a more mobile and versatile game, a "Total" footballer, to the manner born, fast and energetic, ready and eager to probe from anywhere along the line of attack, able to drop back for the ball and make long runs. He had not, then, reached the peak he would reach two years later, but he was already an exciting and incisive footballer.

There were three fully "recognized" attackers and it is interesting to note that two of these were highly specialized. No pretending that Gerd Müller, the prolific, thick-thighed little center forward, an astounding opportunist, was in any sense a Total footballer; he was entirely his own man, a Titan of the six-yard box and, at best, the penalty area. Once, when he was named West German Sportsman of the Year, the girl long jumper Heidi Rosendahl peevishly and publicly enquired why, when all he did was to hang around the goal and score, rather than participate in the outfield play? It was rather as though one were to stigmatize Artur Rubenstein for "only" playing the piano. Müller's flair for scoring goals was what ultimately made the West German team formidable.

Erwin Kremers, the outside left, was precisely that, while Juop Heynckes, he, too, of Borussia Münchengladbach, could operate successfully on the left wing or through the center. Given that the essence of Total Football is fluidity, it is perhaps a little futile to supply a plan, but this diagram will perhaps give some idea of West Germany's 1972 formation.

Remember that all three midfield players were essentially creative rather than defensive players, whereas in 1974, after their defeat by East Germany in Hamburg, West Germany brought into their World Cup team the muscular Rainer Bonhof, whom one would categorize as essentially an attacking *halfback*, strong in the tackle, though always eager to go forward. Remember, too, that the three defensive players in front of Beckenbauer would follow their direct opponents deep or across the field, should they move out of position. It will be quite

clearly seen, however, that the joyful essence of these German tactics was attack. Perhaps it was a little too good to last, but while it did, it was delightful. Franz Beckenbauer himself would later say that the opposition in the European Nations Cup finals—first Belgium, then, in the Final, a leaden Russia—was not exceptional, that teams had become still fitter, more athletic, since then, but the West German team which took Russia to pieces in Belgium that May afternoon was one of the best that I shall ever hope to see.

Meanwhile the Dutch, as personified by Ajax, were just as good.

Ajax had got together a team of phenomenal talent, the most dazzling player of all being the galvanic center forward Johan Cruyff. Dutch football, which had never before been a force, rapidly gained strength when professionalism was made legal, so that the best players no longer went abroad to make money. This, however, cannot wholly account for the astonishing crop of footballers who emerged in the early 1970s.

Under the firm managership of Rinus Michels, Ajax won the European Cup, the virtual club championship of Europe in 1971, against the Greek team Panathinaikos, at Wembley, playing well in the first half but rather disappointingly in the second. By the following year, however, when they beat Internazionale in the Final in Rotterdam, they had developed, like Bayern and West Germany, a new brand of football. The midfield trio of Aarie Haan, Johan Neeskens, and the left-footed Gerry Muhren was immensely dynamic. Mobile, fast, and tireless, these three players could win the ball in the tackle, beat their man, pass splendidly, finish with a powerful shot at goal.

Behind them the fullbacks, Rudi Krol, on the left—and sometimes on the right—and Wim Suurbier had the mobility, pace, and stamina to attack frequently down the flanks, while the powerful center half Barry Hulshoff not only came up to use his head at corners and free kicks, but also liked to bring the ball forward himself, for attempts on goal. The fair-haired sweeper Horst Blankenburg was a West German who, if he had little of the finesse of his more eminent compatriot Franz Beckenbauer, was still an enterprising player, always keen to participate in attacks. Indeed, it was from the left wing that, early in the European Cup Final of 1973 in Belgrade, he delivered the high cross which Johnny Rep headed in for the only goal of the game against the Italian team, Juventus.

Cruyff switched frequently to the left wing, allowing Piet Keizer, the thoughtful and creative outside left, to take up more central positions. The outside right, initially Swart, gave way for the 1973 European Cup Final to Rep, a striker in the more modern sense, able to play as much in the center as on the flank.

There were strong resemblances and a few differences between Ajax and the Dutch team which, with a core of Ajax players, contested the 1974 World Cup. Clearly, they had two wholly dissimilar center forwards: Müller, stationary but deadly; Cruyff, always on the move, giving and taking short balls, sometimes hitting long ones, beating his man with his immense quickness on the ball and off the mark. The Ajax midfield did not have a play-maker of the capacity of Overath or Netzer; the duties tended to be shared around; not merely between the midfielders but also with Cruyff and Piet Keizer.

Who was responsible for the transformation of Ajax into a "Total Football" playing team? Certainly the change coincided with the assumption of the little Rumanian coach, Stefan Kovacs, in place of Michels, and certainly Kovacs has strongly suggested that it was he who implemented it. He has ever since, as team coach to France and to Rumania, sung the praises of Total Football, though without being able to deploy it again. It would probably be fair to say that Total Football emerged from the convictions and predilections of Ajax's senior players—a strong-willed body—encouraged by Kovacs himself. But the heart of both the Ajax and the 1974 Dutch international team was Johan Cruyff, just as the heart of the Bayern and West German teams was Franz Beckenbauer.

When Muhren had to drop out of the 1974 World Cup team as a result of his father's illness, and Haan moved into the back four as a semi-sweeper to replace the injured Hulshoff, Holland called up Wim Van Hanegem; one more example of a player exquisitely unsuited to Total Football, yet gloriously gifted, for all that. With his heavy build, his static style, his superbly strong and accurate left foot, Van Hanegem was quintessentially the midfield general, almost Alex James style. He was none the less impressive and effective for that, even if the Dutch game had to change as the consequence of his presence.

Danny Blanchflower, Northern Ireland's eloquent captain in the 1958 World Cup, their team manager in 1977, has remarked that he believes in specialization, "because I believe that people are different." There is much sense in the observation, and I confess that my opposition to the concept of The Whirl, which lasted many years, was based not only on that but on the awareness that this, after all, is an age of specialization and soccer, always such a mirror of its times, was scarcely likely to be any different.

In fact, I believe that the best modern teams, such as Holland, Bayern, Ajax, West Germany, and—in the 1976 European Nations Cup finals—Czechoslovakia, have proved me partially wrong. Partially; for Total Football itself is, as we have seen, only partial. Within the framework of even the most "modern" team, specialists, quite apart from the goalkeeper, still exist. Recent debate has centered on the validity of the schemer, the new school of thinking which maintains that just as each ordinary soldier should have a field marshal's baton in his knapsack, so each outfield player should essentially be his own schemer. I adhere more closely to the view of Bobby Robson, who made a great success of coaching Ipswich Town in the English League and expressed the view that a midfield which includes two "all action" players is the perfect setting for the talented "schemer."

The implicit demands of Total Football, however, are all commendable ones. It is surely an admirable thing that every player should be superbly fit, capable of covering vast amounts of ground, and running almost throughout the ninety minutes. It is equally good that every player, and not just those in creative or up front positions, should be technically accomplished, able not just to "win" the ball in a tackle but to beat opponents with skill and pass intelligently. The idea of the super specialized defender, which surely reached its nadir with the old-fashioned stopper center half, a player who felt his job was done once he had headed or booted the ball away—though of course there were exceptions such as England's Stanley Cullis, in the 1930s and 1940s—has properly been consigned to oblivion.

Thanks to Total Football, that inexact term for a refreshing attitude, the future of a game which long seemed in danger of being strangled by defensive tactics now seems bright. Dr. Willy Meisl, were he alive today, would I am sure have been pleased: though I am equally sure that he would still have been pungently perfectionist.

3
THE WORLD CUP

The World Cup competition, held every four years for international teams, is the most celebrated, the most distinguished, the most highly esteemed in soccer. Though it was twenty-six years before it matured into a reality, though it began inauspiciously in Uruguay in 1930, though the British, the originators of the game, snubbed it for twenty years, it has long since established itself as soccer's great prize. Its winners set fashions; not only admired but emulated. In a sense, the sport lives from one World Cup to the next, the intervening years colored by what happened in the last tournament.

Nationalism, of course and alas, has something to do with all this; and it was never more displeasingly evident than when Italy won the second World Cup, in 1934. Yet by and large, World Cup final tournaments *have* illustrated what is best in the game at the time; there *has* been a wide appreciation of quality as opposed to mere chauvinism. Everyone admired the way the Uruguayans snatched the World Cup from Brazil in 1950; the way the dazzling Hungarians played in 1954 and the Dutch in 1974, though neither was victorious. Brazil's excellence in 1958, 1962, and 1970 was generally lauded and applauded.

In its half a century or so of life, the World Cup has also been a rich mine of incident and upheaval: America's astonishing victory over England in Belo Horizonte, Brazil, in 1950; North Korea's conquest of Italy at Middlesbrough in 1966. Just as no athlete can really claim to be the best of his time unless and until he has proved it in the Olympic Games, so even the greatest of soccer players—Alfredo Di Stefano, George Best—seems somehow diminished unless he has proved himself in a World Cup. Unfair, of course, for soccer, unlike track and field, is a team sport in which even the greatest individual player can be hobbled by his team, yet true for all that.

The four outstanding countries in the history of the World Cup have been Brazil, three times champions, West Germany, Italy, and Uruguay who have each won it twice, while Italy also lost in the Final. Uruguay's two victories spanned twenty years, Italy's last success was in 1938; Brazil—who might have beaten them then had they not mysteriously and aberrantly pulled their two best forwards off their semi-final team—became a real power only after World War II. That leaves, as the other World Cup winners, England, whose victory in 1966 was a less scintillating one than any of Brazil's, was accomplished entirely at Wembley Stadium, and has seemed somewhat diminished over the years. Nevertheless, England at least won the semi-final and Final with some style, and it was surely appropriate that the country which gave soccer to the world should have its World Cup. Argentina, too, won at home.

Though the idea of such a competition was first mooted in 1904 when, on May 21, in Paris, the first meeting of FIFA, the international football federation, was held. FIFA alone, it was laid down, had the right to organize a world championship. But this was really a dead letter till after World War I, when it became clear that the Olympic Games just could not contain the rapid "professionalizing" of international football. "Today," said Henri Delaunay, at the 1926 FIFA Congress, "international football can no longer be held within the confines of the Olympics; and many countries where professionalism is now recognised and organised, cannot any longer be represented there by their best players." Two years later, when FIFA held their Congress in conjunction with the Amsterdam Olympics, it was decided to go ahead.

Things had become a little farcical. The Uruguayans, elegant and gifted winners of the Olympic tournament in both 1924 and 1928, were manifest professionals; but so by the same token were such European countries as Italy, Austria, Hungary, Spain, and Czechoslovakia; all of which but the first had in fact eschewed the 1928 tournament.

Uruguay, little in size and resources but great in footballing achievement, persuaded FIFA to let them put on the first World Cup. "Other countries have their history," Ondino Viera, the coach of their 1966 World Cup team, remarked to me. "Uruguay has its football." The Uruguayans promised to cover the full expenses for travel and accommodation of every competing team, they promised to put up a new stadium which could take 100,000 spectators, they pointed out that 1930 was the centenary of their independence; and they prevailed. But it turned out to have been a doubtful choice.

Two months before the competition was due to start on July 13, 1930, not one European country had entered! Jet air travel, we must remember, lay far in the future: to reach Uruguay from Europe was a tedious, three-week affair, by boat. Players would be away from hearth and home for two months; and must be paid throughout that time. To the fury of the South Americans, all the major European teams stood aside, while those from Britain were not even eligible; the British had withdrawn from FIFA over arguments about compensatory, "broken time," payments to amateurs.

France was reluctant to make the voyage, and probably would not have done so had it not been for a feeling of *noblesse oblige;* after all, was not Jules Rimet, their own man, president of FIFA, and did not the World Cup itself take its name from him? (It was properly known, till after 1970, not as the World Cup at all, but as the Jules Rimet trophy.)

So the French committed themselves. So did the Belgians. As for the Rumanians, they went because King Carol himself was such a passionate soccer fan. When he came to the throne, his first act was to grant an amnesty to all soccer players suspended from the game for disciplinary offences. Now, eager to have a Rumanian team in the first World Cup, he chose the team himself and interceded with their employers to give them leave to go, after one company had threatened to dismiss any workers who took time off to play. The Yugoslavs, who would become such a power in soccer after World War II, sending team after admirable team to the World Cup finals, went too; though at the time it was not possible to foresee the years of Mitic and Bobek, Sekularac and Milutinovic, Dzajic and Katalinski. To be blunt, Europe's four entrants were of modest quality.

Through the years, World Cups have assumed all sorts of strange shapes. In this, the initial version, it was decided to divide the thirteen teams—ideally there should have been sixteen—into four qualifying pools, run on the basis of miniature leagues: the winners proceeding to the semi-finals which would be played on a knockout, direct-elimination basis.

In 1934 (Italy) and 1938 (France), the World Cup became a straightforward knockout competition, on the classic lines of the English, Football Association, Cup. In 1950, resuming after the war, it became gratuitously complicated. The thirteen teams (again!) that traveled to Brazil were once more divided into four qualifying pools, but the four winners, instead of playing-off on a knockout plan, went into the so-called Final Pool, which was itself decided on a League basis. Thus, though it is customary to speak of that dramatic, memorable, decisive match between Uruguay and Brazil, in Rio, as the Final, it actually was not; even though its winners, by winning the Final Pool, won the World Cup itself.

But the 1950 system was a model of sublime simplicity when compared with the prolixities of 1954 (Switzerland). Now each team in the four groups of four played only two of the others, rather than all three. If, as was only too probable, two teams ended level on points in second and third place, they met in a play-off to decide which should accompany the top team into the quarter-finals; for now it was the last eight teams which were to meet on a knockout basis. This idiotic system allowed the West Germans blithely to throw away a game against Hungary, 8-3, knowing full well that they would easily beat Turkey in the play-off; and then go on to reach the Final in which they defeated . . . the Hungarians. History repeated itself twenty years later when the West Germans were able to permit themselves the luxury of losing in Hamburg to East Germany, but still go on to win the Final, against the Dutch.

What happened on this occasion was that—if you can

still bear with me—again the teams were divided initially into four pools, but this time the first and second teams in each pool would be drafted into two final pools of four teams each. The winners of *these* two groups—Holland and West Germany, as it transpired—would contest the Final.

By now, many a reader's head must be whirling. It should be understood, however, that what the organizers of these World Cups have been trying to do, at least since the end of World War II, has been, in effect, to square the circle. As the late Gertrude Stein might have said, a cup is a cup is a cup; but our well-intentioned FIFA legislators have sought desperately and persistently to give their tournament what one might almost call respectability. Cup tournaments are fascinating but vulgar things; chance plays a horribly salient part. They are not at all like that most worthy and bourgeois of phenomena, a League tournament, which grinds on for months and months until the best, or worthiest, team prevails. Cup competitions are full of strange eventualities. The United States might have played England ten times more in 1950 and lost ten times, but the only time it mattered, they won. Was the United States a "better" team than England? Was North Korea, by the same token, a "better" team than Italy in 1966? Almost certainly not, but theirs were famous victories, which will be remembered and celebrated as long as the World Cup survives.

Curiously enough, the history of the World Cup suggests that, by and large, despite the "Cup" formula, despite the fact that the competition's finals are played off in a few weeks rather than in a matter of protracted months, justice is not only done but *appears* to be done. I don't think it was done in 1950, when Brazil was quite obviously the best team in the tournament, and Uruguay, as we shall see, was given a fatuously easy passage to the Final Pool. I don't think it was done in 1954 when, if Werner Liebrich hadn't kicked Ferenc Puskás in that silly 8-3 game between Hungary and West Germany, the Hungarians would surely have proved their superiority in the Final. But, *grosso modo*, World Cups do tend to be won by the team that deserves to win them.

URUGUAY—1930

Let us, though, return to 1930; and marvel a little at the fact that the United States team was seeded as one of the four group leaders. After all, only two years previously the American team had been thrashed 11-2 in the Olympics by Argentina.

But for some years, as you will read elsewhere, the United States had been importing solid, sometimes remarkable, British players, mostly from Scotland. These weathered pros would, in their turn, bow to the power of Argentina, but they were a great deal better equipped to look after themselves than the hapless amateurs who'd played in the Olympics. Big, muscular fellows they were, for the most part, under the guidance of the Brooklyn Wanderers' coach, Jack Coll, who was sure, he said, that they would spring a surprise. Nor was he wrong.

"We called them The Shot-Putters," said the French center half, the accomplished and fluent Marcel Pinel, looking back many years later on the American World Cup team. "They always amused us when we saw them in training, for they were always clad in tiny shorts which revealed enormous thighs, like tree trunks, and they would go lapping and slogging round and round the track like long distance runners. They were slightly on the crude side."

Crude, perhaps, but remarkably effective. They

played very much in the evolving British manner. Three forwards stayed up the field, while the rest of the team packed the defense and looked for the chance of a fast breakaway. The team was very fit, physically strong, and extremely quick. They won each of their qualifying group matches by the same impressive 3-0 score, first against Belgium, then against Paraguay, showing in the process that they'd been not a bit flattered by their choice as top seeds. Bart McGhee, the left winger, scored two of their goals against Belgium; Patenaude, the center forward, got two against the Paraguayans.

The Argentinians, whom they met in the semi-final, were, however, too much for them. The Americans were but one goal down at half-time; in the second half, however, the more sophisticated Argentinians swept them aside with five more goals, the last three coming in a nine-minute period, before Brown got one, a slender consolation, for the United States.

The most amusing incident of the game, however, concerned not a player but an American official, who was also the team's medical attendant. Displeased when the celebrated referee John Langenus, a Belgian who always refereed attired in leggings and a cap, gave a free kick against one of the Americans, he dashed onto the field to protest, reinforced his diatribe by throwing his box of medicaments on the ground, and was promptly overcome by the fumes of a broken chloroform bottle. Thus overcome, he had to be carried off the field.

Uruguay's promise to finish their new Centenary Stadium in nine months was not fulfilled; just as, twenty years later, the Brazilians were still working on the immense Marcanà Stadium in Rio when the World Cup began. Heavy rains curtailed the building work on the Centenary, and the early games were played on the grounds of the two leading clubs, Nacional and Peñarol.

Themes which have run through the World Cup ever since were early sounded. Refereeing: a French commentator described its level in Montevideo as "a veritable Tower of Babel." Violence: the brawl between Chilean and Argentinian players, provoked when the notorious Argentinian center half, Luis Monti, kicked at a Chilean, presages the Battle of Bordeaux in 1938 and the Battle of Berne in 1954. One referee, Bolivian Ulysses Saucedo, whimsically awarded no fewer than five penalties in Argentina's 6-3 win over Mexico.

The Uruguayans, who might well have won the World Cup had it been held elsewhere, against a fully representative field, prepared with the fervor and dedication one would expect. For almost two months the players were "concentrated" in a hotel in the middle of the Prado park in Montevideo. A curfew was rigorously enforced, and when Mazzali, the splendid goalkeeper, came face to face with the team coach, shoes in hand, while trying to sneak back to his room in the small hours of the morning, there was no appeal. Out of the hotel, the squad, and the World Cup he went, regardless of all his heroics in the Paris Olympics two years before.

Uruguay played, as they would continue to do for the next quarter-century, with an attacking center half rather than a third back stopper. Italy's victorious teams of 1934 and 1938 did the same, though Arsenal had brought the third back game and its "policeman" center half into English soccer in 1925.

Uruguay gloried in their halfback line: the black, ball-juggling José Andrade—whose nephew, Rodriguez Andrade, would be a major star of the 1950 and 1954 tournaments, Lorenzo Fernandez—and the broad-shouldered, handsome Alvaro Gestido, a splendid passer of the ball. Slight, red-haired Hector Scarone was a deadly goal scorer, but the wayward Pedro Petrone, an extraordinarily brilliant center forward of terrific virtuosity, was in his declining years and would give way to Pelegrin Anselmo, a new star from Peñarol. What Uruguay also had, and has always had, was an immense morale, a colossal resilience; never more in evidence than when they withstood the Brazilian assaults before 200,000 frenzied spectators in the Maracanà, in 1950; and won.

Perhaps Argentina, whom they eventually beat in the Final, would have pushed them harder had not Juventus of Turin offered a fortune—and a Fiat—to Raimondo Orsi, their lithe and brilliant outside left, to play in Italy. Four years later, he would score Italy's vital equalizing goal in Rome in the World Cup Final against the Czechs, with a strange, looping shot that flew over the goalkeeper's head, which he couldn't repeat the next day for the photographers, even with no one in goal at all.

What, you may ask, was this Argentinian doing on the Italian eleven of 1934? The answer was that under Italian law Argentinians had double nationality. Monti, captain of Argentina's 1930 team and Guaita, the right winger, were also playing for Italy by now. Grandiosely, the Italian team manager, Vittorio Pozzo, proclaimed, "If they can die for Italy (i.e. do military service) they can play for Italy," a rationalization somewhat undermined two years later when, at the time of the Abyssinian war, Guaita and two other Argentinian players were caught trying to slip across the Italian border . . . to avoid military call-up.

The French did well. Alex Thépot was a fine goalkeeper. A moment's confusion at a free kick, converted by Monti, cost France a game which the watching Uruguayan team thought they deserved to win. France would not play as well in a World Cup till 1958, when they took a merited third place in Sweden. Alex Villa-plane, the 1930 captain and left half, came, alas, to a wretched end when he was shot by the Maquis at the end of the last war for collaborating with the Germans.

While the Argentinians scored six goals in the semi-final against the U.S., Uruguay did the same against Yugoslavia, with Cea scoring three; but few thought the team as good as its Olympic-tournament winning predecessors of 1924 and 1928. Now, as in 1928, when Uruguay had taken a replay before a decision could be reached, they found themselves playing Argentina in an international Final tie.

What passion the match engendered! What excesses of patriotism and local rivalry! The ten packet boats chartered to cross the River Plate from Buenos Aires weren't enough, and crowds thronged the streets shouting for more. When the fleet of ships finally left on the eve of the game, Argentinian fans thronged the quayside with flags emblazoned *"Argentina si, Uruguay, no!"* and "Victory or Death!" Firecrackers exploded in profusion; the chanting was maintained for hours on end.

John Langenus was chosen to referee the Final, but first he demanded the assurance of the Organizing Committee—which was in no true position to give it—that the safety of himself and his linesmen be guaranteed. It was but a few hours before the scheduled kick-off that his fellow referees authorized him to officiate; and as armed soldiers with fixed bayonets encircled the stadium, kick-off was delayed when each side demanded its own kind of ball. In the event Langenus tossed up; and Argentina won. That was the second eventuality to favor Argentina; already the lively young Anselmo, revelation of the tournament, had had to drop out of the Uruguayan team, giving way to Castro, the "One Armed."

Pablo Dorado gave Argentina the lead in twelve minutes, though, and the crowd, limited to 90,000 predominantly Uruguayan, was ecstatic. But Peucelle equalized, then Guillermo Stabile, *El Infiltrador*, the Infiltrator, later to become Argentina's team manager himself, gave Argentina a half-time lead. Against all fears and expectations, the crowd reacted with complete calm; stunned, perhaps, by what had happened.

In the second half, however, Cea equalized after a dazzling dribble, Santos Iriarte, the young Uruguayan left winger, regained the lead for his side, and Castro, in the final seconds, shot high into the net to make it 4-2. Uruguay had won the World Cup in a Final played in a surprisingly sporting manner.

ITALY 1934

Uruguay was not, however, among those present in Italy in 1934. "We are simply doing the same thing to the Europeans as they did to us," was the somewhat petulant explanation. Few believed them. In fact Uruguayan soccer was in the doldrums, after squabbles over professionalism had rent the Federation.

Argentina did make the trip to Italy, but not one of their 1930 team was present; unless you count Monti, who was playing for Italy; while several of the best players had deliberately been left at home, for fear the Italian clubs would poach.

The British teams were still missing, but Hugo Meisl, the cultivated, imperious, and dynamic overlord—what else could you call him?—of the Austrian team gave it as his view that England would not have reached the semi-finals. Since they'd just lost on tour both to the Hungarians and the Czechs by 2-1, he may have been right; though he did say that if his "tired" Austrian team could only borrow Cliff Bastin from the England attack, then Austria could win the World Cup. At inside left or on the left wing, there was no one in Europe quite like Arsenal's Bastin.

Well, Meisl turned out to be right; Austria did not win the tournament, the Italians putting them out by a solitary goal by Guaita in the semi-final in Milan, played on the kind of muddy ground which was anathema to players of the elegant Vienna school, with its emphasis on ball skills and close passing. None symbolized these better than the marvelous, lanky center forward, Mathias Sindelar, known as the Man of Paper; destined to die miserably, a suicide in a gas-filled room, betrayed to the Nazis by a fellow member of the Austrian national team, an ardent Nazi; Sindelar was part Jewish.

The Italians, then, won, but somewhat grimily. John Langenus, there again to referee, put it best: "In the majority of countries, the World Championship was called a sporting fiasco because, beside the desire to win, all other sporting considerations did not exist. Also because over the whole Championship there brooded a certain spirit: Italy wanted to win—it was natural—but they allowed it to be seen too clearly."

Mussolini wanted a victory for Fascist propaganda. Vittorio Pozzo, the stocky, dominating figure who ran the Italian team and had learned his tactics in England, before World War I, was no Fascist, but skillfully used the bombastic, inflated spirit of the times for his own purposes. The spoiled, overpaid, temperamental members of his team had to be welded together by some ethic larger than themselves. Chauvinism would serve; and so it did. But it's doubtful whether that Italian team, by contrast with the one that succeeded in Paris seven years later, would have carried off the Cup anywhere but in Italy.

Pozzo, nicknamed by a French journalist "the poor

captain of a company of millionaires," was later to regret the fact that he chose a large squad of players for training to be gradually whittled down; the process, he felt, was unkind to those rejected. Ceresoli, a superbly acrobatic goalkeeper, broke an arm playing in a training game in Florence, as Pozzo leaned against his very goalpost. "So it's up to me?" said the veteran keeper Giampiero Combi, whose place Ceresoli had taken, as he watched him leave for the hospital. "Yes," said Pozzo, "it's up to you." He also "rehabilitated" the rugged Attilio Ferraris IV, a halfback who at the time was smoking between thirty and forty cigarettes a day. "We'll cut them down gradually," said Pozzo.

Ferraris IV, like Monti, was one of those powerful, aggressive players beloved by Pozzo. He would come to a sad end, collapsing and dying from a heart attack in a veterans' "old glories" game, after World War II.

There was skill in the Italian team, too: Orsi, so fleet and incisive on the left wing; and Peppino Meazza, a beautifully balanced, adroit, elusive forward who was a center by nature, but played at inside right in both the 1934 and 1938 Italian teams. Gioanin Ferrari, a clever inside left, was the only other player to figure in both. Opinions have inevitably differed, but Pozzo always gave me the impression he thought 1938's the better all around team, 1934's superior in individual talent. The team went into "ritiro" in the Tuscan watering-place of Roveta, where the peace was disturbed only by the cries of the peacocks. "Why did they ever save two of them for the Ark?" inquired Schiavio, the Bologna center forward.

The United States was there again, though by a curious arrangement, they were obliged to play Mexico in Rome, just a few days before the competition proper, to decide which of them would take part in it. Watched by, among others, Benito Mussolini, America comfortably and deservedly beat a flaccid Mexican team 4-2, the star of the game being their Italo-American center forward, Donelli. He was far too lively for the Mexicans.

Only three players from America's brave 1930 team survived, however. Moorhouse was still at left back, and had inherited the captaincy from Florie who, together with Gonsalvez, had dropped from inside forward back to wing half.

It was unfortunate that America should now, in the very First Round, be paired with Italy; again in Rome. The Italians in fact had yet to win the belief of their supporters; the players had been jeered on their way down to Rome, at Chiusi, and had had to be restrained from attacking their denigrators. "Now," said Donelli, "it will be enough for me to score a goal against Italy. I would be really proud of that. But will I be able to do it?"

In the event, he was; but Italy scored seven, three of them by the forceful Schiavio. Donelli, who had been born in Naples, now joined the Naples club itself, which led to an ironic welcome: "At last a real Neapolitan in the Naples team!"

In the quarter-finals, Italy played Spain in Florence, and distinguished themselves not at all. The hero of the day was the marvelous Ricardo Zamora, the Spanish goalkeeper. It was fourteen years since, in the 1920 Olympics in Antwerp, he had made his name. Now, with immense bravery and elasticity, he defied the Italian forwards, who used him so roughly—Baert, the Belgian, was a feeble referee—that he could not take part in the replay the next day. The initial game saw Spain take the lead in the first half, Italy equalize in the second, and neither side score during the violent exchanges of extra time. A goal by Meazza gave Italy the game the next day, but it was a shabby victory.

Meanwhile, the clever Austrians were pushed very hard by France in the first round at Turin, prevailing only in extra time. In Bologna they beat their eternal rivals, Hungary, 2-1, in an ill-tempered game. Austria had looked much more impressive than in Turin, but the Italians knocked them out in the semi-final.

The other survivors were the Czechs, who in the semi-finals beat the robust, well-organized Germans, only team in the tournament to play the third back game; Cambal, the Czech center half, was an attacker. In goal, the sturdy Frantisek Planicka was captain and often inspiration; not least in the first game at Trieste against a surprisingly good Rumanian team, when the Czechs were lucky to win 2-1. Puc, their dangerous outside left, and Nejedly, an inside left once described by a French critic as "pure as Bohemian crystal," scored the goals: Nejedly got a couple more against the Germans. Where was the superiority of the third back game, which would in due course sweep the world?

Germany beat Austria for third place in Naples; and so to the Final in Rome, the Czechs' clever short passing against the more robust Italian game. In training camp at Frascati, the Czechs were deluged with gifts: cases of sausages, cuts of ham, silver talismans. The Stadio Torino, its ground smaller than international standards demanded, was no fit place for the Final, while the Romans, by contrast with the Milanese, were strangely indifferent. The Stadium would not even be full to capacity.

With twenty minutes left, Puc, always a danger, took a corner, and drove the resultant loose ball past Combi. That might have been that but for Orsi's freakish right-footed goal, for Sobotka missed an easy chance and Svoboda hit an Italian post. So Schiavio, in the seventh minute of extra time, converted Guaita's pass to win the World Cup for Italy.

The Italians were much more impressive winners in France four years later, even though they made an uneasy beginning in Marseille against Norway. They now had a magnificently endowed center forward in Silvio Piola, a big man, powerful and quick, dangerous in the air—as, indeed, was the smaller Meazza—the star of a tournament rich in fine center forwards. The Norwegians had one of them in Knut Brunyldsen, a large, blond figure tenacious and ubiquitous. Pozzo would describe him as "a cruel thorn in my crown of roses."

The many anti-Fascist Italian refugees in the crowd gave Pozzo's team a fierce reception, jeering them furiously when they gave the Fascist salute before the kick-off. Characteristically, Pozzo made them hold the salute until the jeering stopped; then, with a cry of, "Team, attention! Salute!" he himself saluted again, till at last the tumult abated. Piola quickly made a goal for Ferrari, but thereafter the Norwegians held him well, Brunyldsen overwhelmed the new Italian center half, Andreolo from Uruguay; and Olivieri, the fine new Italian goalkeeper, needed all his agility to keep his goal intact. Finally, in the second half, Arne Brustad, Norway's talented left winger, took a pass from Brunyldsen, cut in, and scored. In extra time, Piola swooped when Johansen could only push out Paserati's shot and Italy, by the skin of its teeth, was through.

Were the Italians in decline? They were not. They proved as much a week later with a fine 3-1 victory in the Second Round, against the home team, France, in Paris. Pozzo brought Amedeo Biavati, of the celebrated double-shuffle trick, in at outside right, and dropped Eraldo Monzeglio, the right back, in favor of Alfredo Foni, who thus renewed the partnership he'd had with Pietro Rava at fullback on the Italian team, so dubiously amateur, which had won at the 1936 Olympics. Monzeglio had been exposed by Norway's Brustad.

Splendidly mobile, enormously quick off the mark, he won the game for Italy with two goals in the second half, the first from a breakaway, the second with a header.

There was no Austria to challenge Italy this time; the *Anschluss* had seen to that. Indeed, several Austrian players were included in the German team surprisingly knocked out by the resilient Swiss, in the First Round. No United States and inevitably no Spain; rent by Civil War. Among the unexpected heroes were two spectacular blond wingers, Gustav Wetterstroem of Sweden, who scored four goals against the Cubans, and Ernest Willimowski of Poland, who would later offend his countrymen by playing for Germany in the war years.

Though the Cubans let in eight goals against the Swedes (a French journalist closed his typewriter after the fifth, announcing, "Up to five goals is journalism, after that, it becomes statistics"), they surpassed themselves by knocking out Rumania.

Supple and unpredictable, the Cubans held the Rumanians to a 3-3 draw after extra time, then dropped their much admired goalkeeper, Benito Carvajales, for the replay. Undeterred, Carvajales called a private press conference. "We shall win the replay," he said, "that's certain. The Rumanian game has no more secrets for us. We shall score twice, they will score only one. *Adios caballeros!*"

And so it transpired; even if Cuba's winning goal seemed to be offside.

The Brazilians, who had gone out 3-1 in the First Round to Spain in 1934, were, however, the revelations; carriers of the flag for South American soccer, in the absence of Uruguay and Argentina—both had refused to come—the Argentinian fans were incensed, and they besieged the Federation's offices in Buenos Aires.

Brazil had another of the tournament's great center forwards in the Black Diamond, little Leonidas, a black player of astonishing acrobatic skill, famous for his overhead bicycle kick, with which he scored goals while in mid-air. He was cleverly supported by the inside forward, Tim, while Domingas Da Guia, the fullback, was described by Pozzo as the best in the World Cup; even though he'd concede a penalty in the semifinal for fouling Piola. In 1974 his son, Ademir, played for Brazil in the Third Place match in Munich.

Brazil hid themselves in the forests of Alsace and told journalists they'd begin training "at 26 o'clock." They began with an extraordinary game against Poland in Strasbourg. Three to one up at half-time, they found themselves pegged to 4-4 at full-time, and ultimately won the game 6-5 in overtime; four goals for Leonidas, four goals for Willimowski. The Poles sent the Brazilians a telegram of good wishes before they played the Czechs in Strasbourg in the Second Round: a violent affair in which the Brazilians seemed the chief sinners. Hardly had it begun when Zeze kicked the gifted Czech Nejedly (who eventually broke his leg) and was ordered off the field. Planicka, the Czech goalkeeper, broke an arm; Brazil's Machados (who had been sent a telegram of good wishes by the ageless French star, Mistinguette) and Riha, the Czech, were sent off the field for fighting.

The result was a 1-1 draw. Two days later, purged, the teams played again; a calm, correct game in Marseille, in which the loss of Nejedly's elegant passing and Planicka's resilient goalkeeping was too much for the Czechs to bear. Did the Brazilians take leave of their senses? Overconfidence had already been suggested when their main party left for the next match, in Marseille, before the replay with the Czechs even took place! Now, before the game with Italy, they blithely left out their two crack forwards, Tim and Leonidas; and booked the only available plane to Paris for the Final!

Vittorio Pozzo visited the Brazilian training camp to point this out to them. "What of it?" said the Brazilians. Pozzo pointed out that should they lose to Italy, they'd be obliged to go to Bordeaux for the Third Place Match, not to Paris for the Final.

"But we shan't lose," said the Brazilians.

They did. Domingas, a fullback of extraordinary delicacy and finesse, for all his bulk, was unsettled by the bustling Piola, chopped him down in the 14th minute, and saw Meazza score coolly from the penalty. Since Colaussi, the fleet left winger, had already gone past Domingas to give Italy the lead, his cup was full. Without Leonidas, Brazil couldn't penetrate Italy's defense, and Romeo's goal, three minutes from the end, was no more than a gesture. So hubris had been punished by Nemesis.

If Brazil were almost certainly the second best team in the tournament, it was Hungary who reached the Final, their attack led by, their team captained by, the polymath Dr. George Sarosi; scholar, fencer, athlete, swimmer, as good an attacking center half as he was a center forward. When Dr. Dietz, Hungary's selector, swore he'd walk back to Hungary if the team didn't beat the Swiss in the Second Round, Sarosi, rejoined, *"Verba volant, scripta manent"* (we shall have that in writing); and did. Luckily for Charles Dietz, Hungary won, and the Long March was unnecessary.

The Hungarians, a force in world football for so many years now, played the "Danubian" style of elegant, short-passing football. When they reached the Final a second time, sixteen years later, as warm favorites, they'd triumphantly conquered their besetting problem of poor finishing. The 1938 Hungarians, however, had no one to match Silvio Piola, or Peppino Meazza, for finishing, even if they defeated the Swedes with surprising ease in the semi-finals at Colombes Stadium in Paris. Nyberg scored for Sweden in 35 seconds; Hungary replied with five goals, three by the splendid young inside forward, Zsengeller.

Would Sarosi show his best form at last in the Final? Would he add to his formidable technique the little touch of devil that he lacked? He and Hungary would need it against the unceremonious Italians. In the event, Sarosi, though he scored, was well mastered; Colaussi was too fast for Polgár, Hungary's right back; while the Italian inside forwards, Ferrari and Meazza, were given too much room. Though they equalized Colaussi's opening goal, the Hungarians were well beaten in Paris, 4-2. Forbidden by officials to sit on the touchline and coach his men, Pozzo got round it by having Luisin Burlando, his chief coach, sprawl at his feet, while he meditated aloud in dialect; meditations which Burlando conveyed quickly to the team.

BRAZIL—1950

By 1950, when the World Cup was resumed after the war years, with Brazil the host, Pozzo was no longer in charge of the Italian team which he had first handled in 1912, at the Stockholm Olympics. A squabbling duo of Ferruccio Novo, Torino's president, and the journalist, Aldo Bardelli, were put in charge of the team; Novo had removed Bardelli even before the team's ship had docked in Rio. Understandably, Bardelli and a number of the players had refused to go by air. In 1949, the year Pozzo left office, his beloved Torino team, seven of them current Italian internationals, had been wiped out on the hillside of Superga, on their way back from a friendly game in Lisbon. Who knows what the Italians might have accomplished with such stars as Valentino Mazzola, the captain and inside left, father of the equally illustrious Sandrino, Maroso at left back, Bacigalupo in goal? All died.

World Cup holders, and thus qualified by right, the Italians compounded those problems they had by picking strange teams, but they could hardly bargain for the fragile form of their best-known player, the majestic center half Carolo Parola, who was turned inside-out by Sweden's center forward, the blond Hans Jeppson, in the opening match at São Paulo. Sweden won 3-2, and since Paraguay was the only other team in the group Italy was almost inevitably eliminated.

England took part; for the first time ever. The British countries had at long last rejoined FIFA, which had indulgently allowed them to use their own British Championship as a qualifying group for *two* teams. But with proud obstinacy, the Scots said they would go only if they won the Championship, England was lucky to beat them in the final match in Glasgow, and although the English players themselves begged the Scots to go, they would not. Far from splendid isolation.

England, on the face of it, had a good team, even though their talented center half, a regular choice for five years, decamped to Bogotá, Colombia, in search of higher pay just before the tournament was due. Neil Franklin, of Stoke City, was sick and tired, like many of his colleagues, of being limited to the iniquitously low English maximum wage; which was not abolished for another eleven years. He fared no better in Colombia, however, and was back within a few months, his career in ruins.

Still England could call on two of the world's greatest wingers in Tom Finney and Stanley Matthews; the latter grudgingly added to the party at the last moment after he had played splendidly for an official team on tour in North America. There was Stanley Mortensen, an attacking inside right of tremendous finishing power, an excellent goalkeeper in Bert Williams, a superb, creative inside forward in the blond Wilf Mannion.

Looking back, one shakes one's head in wonder at the idiotic way the tournament was arranged. First, when teams such as France and Argentina withdrew, no attempt was made to realign the groups. This was compounded by the fact that instead of each set of teams playing off their games in a given center, they were obliged to fly the length and breadth of the vast country. So while England, Sweden, and the rest were hurrying about Brazil, Uruguay had but one match to play and win; against Bolivia, the weakest team in the competition. An 8-0 win and they were in the Final Pool, barely breaking sweat.

So round and round Brazil the caravan trouped, often in killing heat and humidity; from Rio to Recife, from Belo Horizonte to São Paulo. Brazil, under Flavio Costa, had been closeted away and prepared with all the thoroughness the Uruguayans—themselves back in the World Cup after a twenty-year absence—had evinced in 1930. The United States had qualified, but was thoroughly unfancied, thoroughly—as it turned out—undervalued. Their captain, Eddie McIlvenny, was a right half who only eighteen months earlier had been given a free transfer by Wrexham of the English Third Division. Larry Gaetiens, the center forward, was a Haitian. The left wing pair was made up by the two Souzas, John and Ed, from Fall River; no relation to one another. They were under the aegis of a Scottish-born coach named Bill Jeffrey, a selfless, dedicated coach who deserves for all those devoted years at Penn State the reward that is to come his way in Belo Horizonte. More of him elsewhere.

The United States had tightened up since a disastrous trip to the 1948 Olympics in London, where Italy's professionals thrashed them 9-0, and they played with an attacking center half. Now they have a sturdy stopper in Colombo, who likes to play in gloves. Almost everybody is playing the third back game now, even Italy; but not Brazil, which is operating a kind of halfway house system known as the diagonal, in which the center half still attacks; and not the eventual victors, Uruguay, who have a glorious attacking pivot in the massive Obdulio Varela, an international since 1940.

Sweden's victory over the Italians is a kind of vindication; didn't the Italians "steal" Gunnar Nordahl, the big center forward, and the endlessly versatile Nils Liedholm from their 1948 Olympic winning side? Italy's "revenge" will now be more terrible still; they will gobble up practically the complete Swedish team, together with a few reserves; and since the Swedes are still nominally amateurs, it won't be for another eight years, with the advent of permitted professionalism, that some of these players will return to play for them. The team manager is the ebullient Yorkshireman, George Raynor, who has spun together a team out of nothing; not just Hans Jeppson but the marvelous little flaxen-headed Nacka Skoglund, barely twenty, a First Division player for less than a year; Kalle Palmer, his clever, fragile looking partner at inside forward; the burly Knud Nordahl, left behind by brothers Gunnar and Bertil, at center half.

Strange, the part the immense Maracanà Stadium played in this World Cup. Had it been properly finished, without and within, no doubt Rajko Mitic, Yugoslavia's fine inside right, wouldn't have cut his head on a girder just before he was due to take the field for the vital group game against Brazil. By the time he did get out there, bandaged, Brazil was one up, and went on to win 2-0. They really weren't at all convincing in their early games. A 4-0 win in Rio over Mexico was nothing to be proud of, and in their next game, in São Paulo, the Swiss held them to a 2-2 draw and very nearly beat them. In the first two matches of the Final Pool, however, both played in Rio, their marvelous inside forward trio of Zizinho, Ademir, and Jair, stupendous ball players all, splendidly backed up by the attacking right half, Carlos Bauer, tore Sweden and Spain asunder; seven against Sweden, six against Spain. "How To Resist?" asked an Italian paper. The Uruguayans would show how.

And the United States? In their first game, against Spain, at Curitiba, they at once served notice that they were nobody's pushovers. John Souza, no foreign import but the proud product of New England soccer, with its surprisingly long tradition, gave the States the lead after seventeen minutes, and not till the last ten did the desperate Spaniards break through, with two goals in two minutes from the dashing right winger Basora, the powerful center forward Zarra giving them a 3-1 win. Embarrassing though it may be to say it, this American eleven was an infinitely better team than the one knocked out of the 1978 qualifying tournament by Canada.

Then, in Belo Horizonte, it was England, which had already beaten Chile 2-0 in Rio. The city then had a bush league stadium, a mere hovel by comparison with the 100,000 capacity field which stands there now. Disdainfully, the English team stripped in a nearby hotel, having lived luxuriously as the guests of a nearby gold mine, at Morro Velho, owned by Englishmen. It was the nearest they would get to gold in Belo Horizonte.

Several of the American team stayed up till two

o'clock in the morning, dancing and drinking (soft) drinks. What chance had they? A touring English team of far inferior standard to this one had recently beaten them in New York, right after an exhausting fourteen-hour trip from Windsor, Ontario.

England began as if it would walk away with the game; a bombardment during which they hit the post. But McIlvenny marshalled his men, Borghi was an acrobat in goal, Colombo a sturdy bulwark. The American defense fought vigorously, sometimes destructively, to keep the English out; and they succeeded.

Eight minutes from half-time, Bahr, the left half, shot for the English goal. Bert Williams shaped for an easy catch, but Larry Gaetjens intervened with his head—deliberately? who will ever know?—and the ball flew into the English net.

There were no more goals. England played into the hands of the competent American defense by keeping the ball too close; while their wing halves insisted on carrying it forward rather than moving it quickly. John Souza, the clever American inside left, showed them how it should be done, on the rare occasions he was in possession. The field, sparsely covered with grass, bumpy beneath, scarcely favored constructive soccer; to make things worse, only a few inches separated it from the surrounding red cinder track. As an international ground, it was a fiasco; but it scarcely exonerated England.

"Wake up!" the English miners shouted, and Mortensen went tearing characteristically through the middle, to be heavily brought down. Alf Ramsey, later to manage England's 1966 World Cup winning team, took the free kick, Mullen's head met it on the far post, some thought it had crossed the line, after passing Borghi, before it was scrambled away; but the referee gave a corner. America held out, and at the final whistle, hundreds of spectators invaded the field to carry them off shoulder high, while others lit a funeral pyre of newspapers on the terraces.

Sir Stanley Rous, secretary of the English Football Association, remarked, "The Americans were faster, fitter, better fighters."

"This is all we wanted," exulted Bill Jeffrey, "to make the game go in the States." In fact, as we know, it had all the effect of a pebble dropped into a bottomless well.

Years later Walter Winterbottom, England's team manager, an amiable but somewhat remote figure, a little bureaucratic for the job, observed to me, "Everybody who saw the game would say that England didn't take its chances, hundreds of them, and when a team doesn't take its chances, it doesn't deserve to win. Our forwards tried too hard. For the first twenty minutes, they were shooting in (*i.e. as if they were practicing*). Then they began to worry. 'We must have a goal,' they thought. For superiority to show, one must have a good pitch."

If there was little reaction in the United States, there was an outcry in England, where there were absurd complaints that mistaken team selection was responsible for the defeat, that the legendary Stanley Matthews should have been chosen. Second guessing at its silliest. On paper, the English forward line in Belo Horizonte looked thoroughly formidable, a steamroller ready to crack the merest nut.

So the English players flew down to Rio, where they'd lose somewhat unluckily to Spain, 1-0—including Matthews this time—and be eliminated. One reserve said bitterly that he wished he could have a badge to say that he was not playing against the United States. Understandably, perhaps, the Americans' final game, against Chile, in Recife, was an anticlimax. How much they must have given in Belo Horizonte!

Five to two Chile beat the United States, which must have been suffering a considerable physical and nervous reaction. The most amusing moment of the game came near the very end. Chile's center forward, George Robledo, was actually an English League player from Newcastle United, born at Iquique at the foot of the Andes of a Yorkshire mother and a Chilean father. He scored one of Chile's goals, and was subjected throughout to a pungent commentary in English by the American center half. As the final whistle blew, Robledo at last turned to him and addressed him more pungently still, to his astonishment, in broadest Yorkshire.

The Final Pool, then, was made up by Brazil, Uruguay—their eternal bugbear, who'd already beaten them that year in São Paulo—Sweden, and Spain. Among those absent altogether from the tournament were West Germany, still barred from world football since the end of the war; Russia, maintaining grumpy isolation; Austria, who announced that their team was too young to compete, though it would be Europe's best in 1951; and Czechoslovakia and Argentina, each of whom petulantly withdrew.

Having thrashed the Spaniards and Swedes with sublime displays of attacking soccer, compounds of perfect technique, imagination, and stupendous speed, the Brazilians had only to draw with Uruguay in the Maracanà to take the title.

They lost. Their colossal initial bombardment was frustrated by the wonderful goalkeeping of Roque Maspoli, the cool power of the giant Obdulio Varela, the center half, the excellence of the little, black Rodrigues Andrade, left half—though virtually an attacking left back, in "modern" terms—and a worthy nephew to José. How Maspoli reached a terrific drive by Ademir, famous for his shot, will never be wholly explained; but the fact was that for all their pressure,

Brazil by half-time was losing command; Varela was urging his troops forward. It was his own strong shot which Barbosa, the Brazilian keeper, turned for a corner, just before half-time.

Two minutes after the interval, Friaca scored for Brazil; but Uruguay took it in stride. Those two epitomes of the anti-athlete, the pallid, slim Juan Schiaffino, the hunched little outside right, Alcide Ghiggia, won them the game. After sixty-five minutes, Varela sent Ghiggia flying up the wing; Schiaffino, unmarked, converted his pass. Eleven minutes from time, Perez, another fine inside forward, sent Ghiggia flying through to score the winner.

"Our team is a strange one," said Andrade, "it is capable of anything. Against Brazil, we did not keep back one drop of sweat, but what else could we have done?" What, indeed?

SWITZERLAND—1954

If the Brazilians were in some sense the moral victors of 1950—they blamed the defeat on the inadequacies of their "diagonal" system in defense and uneasily embraced the third back game till 1958—Hungary was more unfortunate still, four years later.

Beyond doubt, their team was one of the finest the game has ever seen, marvelously enterprising, technically brilliant, tactically innovative, with its deep-lying center forward in the masterly Nador Hidégkuti, its attacking right half in Jozef Bozsik, its left half, Zakariás, committed to the four-man line of defense. Budai and Zoltan Czibor were natural wingers of exceptional merit, but when Puskás was hurt playing the first game against West Germany, Czibor moved to inside left and performed there as well as he had on the wing. Gyula Grosics, later to be "disgraced" and suspended for a contraband offense (common among that team; his true crime was merely to be found out), was a fine goalkeeper, especially good at dashing beyond his penalty area to kick clear, almost as an extra back.

Ferenc Puskás, inside left and captain, was for all his skill and dynamism an urchin figure, hair slicked smooth and parted down the middle, his grin that of the eternal non-conformist. No surprise that as soon as he could get out of authoritarian Hungary and make some money in Europe, he did. That was at the time of the 1956 Hungarian Revolution when the Honved (army) team into which the Communist authorities had stuffed most of the best players happened to be touring abroad. So Puskás, Kocsis, and Czibor stayed out, though Bozsik, the "good" Communist, member of Parliament (for whatever that was worth), went back.

Puskás' left foot was so incredibly good, such a devastating weapon when shooting for goal, such a delicate instrument when avoiding tackles or making passes, that he scarcely needed his right foot; which he rarely used. Shortish, almost tubby, he was a devastating finisher; and Kocsis and Nador Hidégkuti didn't lag far behind. Hidégkuti, indeed, had scored three times the previous November at Wembley when, in a memorable display, Hungary had shattered England's unbeaten home record against foreign teams. The score that day was 6-3, and when England came to Budapest the following May, Hungary thrashed them 7-1, for good measure.

I have already alluded to Puskás' injury in the 8-3 win over West Germany, in Basle. Switzerland was the scenically attractive but hopelessly ill-organized venue; the four qualifying pools were played in the lee of mountains, by the side of lakes.

The West Germans, now pardoned for the war, were there under the aegis of the formidable little Sepp Herberger, who had been in charge of Germany in the 1938 World Cup, a General Patton-figure who was in the tradition of Pozzo and Meisl. He believed in authority, he believed in strength and combativeness; though in his captain and inside right, Fritz Walter, he had a creative player of enormous skill and subtle strategy.

Hungary's problem over Puskás was compounded by the fact that he was such a strong character. Without him, they still contrived to beat the excellent South Americans, Brazil and Uruguay, in quarter- and semifinal. He wasn't really fit to play in the Final, and it showed, but he talked his way back onto the team and failed to take chances he would have taken when fit; though many thought his late equalizing goal, ruled offside, was in fact a perfectly good one. Moreover, Puskás didn't like Budai; and he had him excluded from the Cup Final team, a manifest error.

This was probably the best World Cup tournament until 1974; the pall of defensive football had yet to settle on the game. Teams expressed themselves and tried to score goals. Australia was there; though the dead hand of the W formation had placed its clammy fingers on their football since the great days of 1951. Yugoslavia was full of elegant football, and played a drawn match against Brazil in Lausanne which was a small classic. England had Stanley Matthews, now thirty-nine years old, yet still a gloriously effective winger, admirable against Belgium and Uruguay.

The Uruguayan wingers, Abbadie and Borges, were newcomers. They ripped Scotland's ponderous defense to pieces in the group game, scoring five between them. Migues, the 1950 center forward, added two more for good luck. England was beaten 4-2 in the quarter-final despite a rash of injuries, with Varela, Schiaffino—dropping back magisterially to left half—and Andrade just as good as ever.

The Battle of Berne disfigured the tournament. Hungary against Brazil; Bozsik and Nilton Santos, two of the world's best players, sent off for fighting, Tozzi, the Brazilian inside left, for kicking, though he went down on his knees to beg Arthur Ellis, the Yorkshire-born referee, to let him stay. Ellis' courageous efficiency allowed the game to be completed. After it, however, the Brazilians invaded the Hungarians' dressing-room, and there was worse fighting still. In retrospect, the Brazilians seem most to blame, reacting violently to minor provocation, though it is still a moot point whether Ferenc Puskás, sitting on the bench, hit Pinheiro, Brazil's center half, with a bottle as he came off the field. Italy's *Corriere della Sera* described the incident in detail and Pinheiro certainly had a bad gash, but FIFA ducked an official inquiry even though Ernst Thommen, Swiss president of the World Cup committee, publicly accused Puskás and said he would be making a report.

Hungary won 4-2, each team scoring some spectacular goals, perhaps the best of the lot being a screaming long shot by the fast, powerful Brazilian right winger, Julinho, whose close control at speed was a marvel.

Then it was Uruguay in the semi-final; an injury to Andrade, doomed to watch from behind the goal as Hungary saved the game, may well have been the turning point. Played in Lausanne under a deluge, the quality of football was phenomenal, and the Uruguayans kept their promise that there would be no violence. Remarkably, it was the first World Cup game Uruguay had ever lost. As holders, of course, they qualified *ex officio;* as did the host nation, Switzerland, who eliminated an ill-tempered Italian team.

The Germans simply got better and better. They hadn't the originality or the brilliance of Hungary, but they were a powerful, compact team with just enough skill and flair dotted about to leaven their impressive muscularity. Helmut Rahn, the huge right winger, called up at the last moment when his club, Rot Weiss Essen, was on tour in South America, had the speed, force, and finish, if not the subtlety, to match Brazil's Julinho. Otmar Walter, Fritz's younger brother, was an incisive center forward, Hans Schaefer a penetrative left winger who, by the 1958 World Cup, would have become a fine inside left.

While Hungary was giving its all in the wearying games against Brazil and Uruguay, the second of which entailed extra time, the Germans had a much easier passage. A careless goal in his own net by the giant Yugoslav center half Horvat, some ruthless German tackling, and three clearances off the goal line by their left back, Kohlmeyer, enabled them to surprise Yugoslavia, a much more technically gifted team, in Geneva. That was hard; but the 6-1 semi-final win against a demoralized Austrian in Basel was a procession. The Austrians were clear favorites; the tall, strong dark Ernst Ocwirk, roving center half turned left half, was one of the best players in the world, the Austrian attack had been scoring many goals. But their selectors blundered, dropping Schmied, none too happy in a 7-5 win against the Swiss, from goal, and restoring the veteran Walter Zeman, though he was known to be off form.

Zeman had an abominable game, inept when it came to handling crosses. Enough to say that of Germany's six goals, two came from high centers, two from corners. The other two were penalty kicks, converted by Fritz Walter.

Yet surely Germany could not maintain their extraordinary momentum at Berne, in the Final? The rain poured down; and within eight minutes, Hungary was two up. Puskás, back again, got the first when Kocsis' shot bounced to him off a defender's back; then Kohlmeyer's erratic back pass squirmed out of Turek's hands and Czibor got an easy second.

The German morale was undented. Within three minutes, it was Bozsik who erred, Morlock who scored. Sixteen minutes gone, Puskás looking heavy, slow, unfit, and Germany had equalized; the third of three successive corners by Fritz Walter, a crafty inswinger which beat the defense, reached Rahn, and was hammered in.

Now it was Turek's turn. At the start of the second half, a catalogue of marvelous saves by the German goalkeeper kept the Hungarians at bay. Kohlmeyer kicked off the line, Kocsis' header skidded off the bar. With seven minutes left, Schaefer's cross from the left ran away from Hungary's Lantos, came to Rahn; and in it went again. The Cup was Germany's.

SWEDEN—1958

Was some kind of stimulant the secret of their endless running? They scornfully denied it, though no one satisfactorily explained the outbreak of jaundice that subsequently laid low half the team. For four years Germany did very little, but by 1958 they were strong again. Rahn, grossly overweight and convicted of drunken driving, was coaxed back to fitness and form by Herberger. Fritz Walter, at thirty-seven, was still a force. There was a dynamic young center forward in the squat Uwe Seeler.

England's chances had virtually perished at Munich, in February, when the Elizabethan aircraft carrying the talented Manchester United team home after a game in Belgrade crashed. Among those killed were three leading England players, Roger Byrne, the captain and left back, Tommy Taylor, the center forward, so dangerous in the air, and the young giant Duncan Edwards, a left half of enormous drive and authority.

The Russians were not only coming; they had, at long last, actually come, lurking in the woods at Hindas, outside Gothenburg, like bears, sneaking through the trees to spy on the noisily extrovert Brazilians, their rivals, who sounded in training like a male choir gone berserk.

Sweden had little George Raynor back to run them, and a clutch of distinguished expatriates back to play for them. The inside forwards, cool, deliberate Gunnar Gren, the Professor, and Nils Liedholm, hadn't played for Sweden since the 1948 Olympics. The two dazzling little wingers, Kurt Hamrin and Nacka Skoglund—the latter an inside left in 1950—returned from Italy, like Liedholm. "We're the slowest team in the competition," said Raynor, cheerfully, after Sweden had beaten Hungary in Stockholm. "If there was a relay race, Sweden would finish last. But we'll still reach the Final."

The Brazilians brought with them 4-2-4, the tactics which would make third back football obsolete; four defenders across the back, a halfback (Dino, Zito), and an inside forward (Didì, marvelous orchestrator) in midfield, four men up the front. The talk was of Pelé, the 17-year-old prodigy from Santos, an extraordinary goal scorer. He was injured at the start, and would play only in the third game; against Russia.

It wasn't a tournament to compare with 1950, even though the Brazilians put on three glorious displays: against Russia, France (hampered by injury to their stopper, Bob Jonquet), and, in the Final, Sweden.

It was, then, an enormously important World Cup in terms of tactical revolution; significant, too, for being the first the Brazilians managed to win. Perhaps their team, for all the genius of Pelé, Garrincha, Didì, wasn't the equal individually of 1950's, but it was better organized on the field.

By whom? By the plump, Buddha-like, intermittently explosive coach, Vincente Feola? Or—as some insisted—by the senior players themselves, the tall, suave left back Nilton Santos and the rest, who certainly went to Feola before the Russian game and begged him to put the wayward but astonishing Garrincha on the right wing. Feola agreed. "Don't let me down," said Nilton to Garrincha, his Rio club mate at Botafogo, before the kick-off. Garrincha turned the Russians inside-out; just as he did the Swedes in the Final.

All four British teams took part; the only time it has happened, or is likely to happen. At that, the Welsh sneaked in through the back door. When all Israel's opponents refused on political grounds to play them, FIFA looked for an opponent for the Israelis. Uruguay, knocked out by the Paraguayans, proudly refused. Wales, eliminated by the Czechs, did not. They played and beat Israel twice, and, as it transpired, acquitted themselves splendidly in Sweden, knocking out tired, diminished Hungary in a play-off, and giving Brazil a terrible fright in the quarter-final at Gothenburg. Had the mighty John Charles, then with Juventus of Turin, been fit to lead their attack that day, who knows what would have happened? As it was, only a lucky, deflected goal by Pelé, who still calls it the most important of his career, let Brazil through. The Welsh defense was magnificent; Jack Kelsey in goal never dropped or missed a high ball. "Chewing gum," he explained to me modestly, afterwards. "Always put some on my hands. Rub it well in."

Bureaucratic England went out to Russia in a play-off, but drew o-o with Brazil. They stayed, inexplicably, in a hotel in the middle of Gothenburg, lost their outstanding winger, Tom Finney, injured, after the opening game with Russia, and inexplicably threw two wholly new forwards, Broadbent and Brabrook, into their final, vital game.

The Northern Irish, who approached the tournament far less pompously, were much better value. They, too, suffered in the Munich air crash, which deprived them of their resilient young center half, Jackie Blanchflower, whose older brother Danny was right half, captain, and joint inspiration of the team with the manager, Peter Doherty, not long since the country's inside left and captain, a player of exceptional verve and quality. The Irish had surprisingly eliminated mighty Italy, and now they knocked out the Czechs in a play-off only to lose, weary and depleted by injury, 4-0 in the quarter-finals to France.

No one, including perhaps themselves, had expected much from the French, but in fact they were astonishingly good. Just Fontaine, a stocky, Morocco-born forward who had come to Sweden expecting to be a reserve, instead found himself chief executioner, the passes for his record thirteen goals mostly supplied by the brilliant little Raymond Kopa, playing—on leave from Real Madrid, where he languished under the shadow of mighty Alfredo Di Stefano—as a deep-lying center forward.

But Brazil, with Pelé now in full, precocious ascendancy, a marvel of gymnastic skill, explosive power, unflurried elegance, scoring three times, beat France 5-2 and went into the Final. At Gothenburg, in the other semi-final, Sweden got the better of West Germany with the help of a blatant hand-ball by Liedholm on the way to one goal, and the sending off of Jusko-wiak, provoked to fury by Kurt Hamrin; who sprang up again to score an electrifying third Swedish goal, dribbling past man after man.

In the Final he, and Skoglund, did nothing, disappearing into the pockets of the massive Santoses, black Djalma, playing his very first game of the tournament, and cool Nilton, in rainy Stockholm. Nils Liedholm picked his way through Brazil's defense to score after only four minutes, but the Brazilians ridiculed George Raynor's forecast that if this happened they would "panic all over the show." Two jaguar bursts down the right wing by Garrincha brought two goals for the forceful Vavà, and in the second half, with their supporters crying, "Samba, samba!" Pelé got two more, Zagalo another. Pelé's goals were phenomenal; one came when he caught a loose ball on his thigh in the crowded penalty box, casually hooked it over his head, and volleyed it in. The second was a majestic header; to be compared with the first goal of the 1970 Final in Mexico City. 4-2-4 had triumphantly arrived.

CHILE—1962

By 1962 it had become, in Chile where Brazil won again, 4-3-3. This was necessitated because Pelé dropped out with pulled muscles after the second game in the little coastal town of Vina del Mar, and made possible because Zagalo of the bottomless lungs could run forever both up and down the left touchline.

Brazil, four years older, deprived of Pelé, hadn't the same panache, though they still deserved their win. For a long time, it seemed they'd make many changes, but when the smoke cleared they were fielding practically the same team, and the 24-year-old inside left Amarildo got in only because Pelé dropped out. Garrincha was the new hero. To his body swerve and amazing acceleration, the sturdy little right winger had added a devastating *left*-footed shot, and the ability to jump amazing heights, head astounding goals. He destroyed England's chances in the quarter-final match at Vina del

Mar with his heading and his shooting; he was the scourge of Chile, the hosts, tumultuously supported, when Brazil beat them 4-2 in Santiago in the semi-final. Eventually he was sent off for a retaliatory foul on a Chilean defender who'd been kicking him all afternoon; his head was cut open by a missile as he came off the field.

Would he play in the Final; or would he be suspended? The very President of Brazil who, it was rumored, had listened to the semi-final radio commentary with earphones, during mass, sent a telegram of appeal. Garrincha was amnestied and, such is the irony of Fate and football, did little or nothing in the Final.

The Czechs were the runners-up; they'd picked their slow but solid way through the tournament, inspired in midfield by the loping, long-legged Kvasniak, by the versatile left half Josef Masopust, who opened the score for them against Brazil. Alas, Schroiff, whose goalkeeping had enabled them to surprise first Hungary then Yugoslavia in the quarter-finals and semi-finals, had a poor day. Brazil capitalized on his mistakes, equalized through Amarildo, went ahead through Zito's header in the second half, and got the third when Schroiff, sunblinded, dropped Djalma Santos' high lob.

ENGLAND—1966

Now Brazil's version of ancestor worship would cost them dear. In Liverpool, four years later, they were beaten 3-1 by a splendid Hungarian team inspired by its ubiquitous center forward, Florian Albert, then again by Portugal, who kicked Pelé out of the game; and didn't need to. The devastating finishing of Eusebio was Portugal's chief weapon though the team played much elegant football, its colored skipper, with Coluña, a tremendous force in midfield, unfailingly composed. Torres, a tall center forward, was dangerous with his head.

The Brazilians brought back Feola as their coach—he'd been absent, ill, in Chile—and Feola went into an orgy of nostalgia, restoring to the team such stoppers as Bellini and Orlando, who hadn't played on it since 1958. A fully fit Pelé might have got him and Brazil off the hook; but Pelé wasn't fully fit, even before the Portuguese kicked him.

England had a new team manager, or coach, in Alf Ramsey, their right back in the 1950 World Cup, a Londoner, impassive, passionate and cryptic, who gave the team a sense of confidence and a morale which the more remote Walter Winterbottom could never provide. Almost unbelievably, till Ramsey took over they'd never even traveled with a team doctor, one result of which was that Peter Swan, a reserve center half, had nearly died in Chile in 1962.

Ramsey looked at his team, saw its limitations, and decided to put his faith in something called "work rate"; if his players couldn't play, then they'd have to run. No wingers; he tried several, right into the World Cup itself, and found them inadequate. Instead, he used Alan Ball and Martin Peters, an inside forward and wing half respectively, as alternates between midfield and attack. Ball ran enough for two men, Peters was adept at gliding into scoring positions. Bobby Moore, at left half, or second stopper, was an Olympian defender, serene and commanding; Gordon Banks an admirable goalkeeper, acrobatic and brave; powerful Geoff Hurst came into the team for the quarter-finals, scored the winner against Argentina, and surpassed any expectations there had been of him.

The blond and balding Bobby Charlton, survivor of the 1958 Manchester United air crash, a forward of immense natural gifts—delightful body swerve, acceleration, two splendid shooting feet—was converted from outside left to the midfield. He was hardly a natural orchestrator, despite the massive crossfield passes which often impressed the crowd, but he beat men beautifully, and his shooting was ferociously good. With a right-footed shot of spectacular power, he scored England's first goal of the competition against Mexico, in the second game, and scored both goals, one in each half, one placed shot, one hooked shot, when England deservedly beat Portugal in an excellent semifinal. At center half was his older brother, the tall, uncompromising Jack, a late developer, a "self-made" star, whereas Bobby had from his schooldays been a golden boy.

And there was Jimmy Greaves, Cockney footballer *par excellence*, a goal scorer of immense renown since his teens, a "striking" inside forward of exceptional opportunism, an almost telepathic gift for being in the right place near goal at the right time, a fine sprinter, a deadly left-footed shot. He had played in Chile—and played poorly—as had that other Cockney, the 1962 team's inside left and captain, Johnny Haynes. But in the pre-World Cup tour of Scandinavia, a volley of goals against Norway in Oslo seemed to demonstrate that he had thrown off the debilitating effects of jaundice and would be a force in the tournament.

He was not. A muffled display in the opening, goalless draw against Uruguay, a moderate one against Mexico (2-0) and France (2-0), an injury that kept him out of the quarter-final against ruthless, cynical, provocative Argentina—whose big captain, Antonio Rattin, was sent off for perpetual protests by the tiny German referee Herr Kreitlein.

Would Greaves play in the Final against West Germany? I myself would have preferred him to the faithful but pedestrian Roger Hunt of Liverpool, a devoted workhorse, a professional footballer's footballer, but a typical "Ramsey" figure in that dedication compensated, or should have done, for lack of flair. In my book, Hunt made two errors in the Final which could have cost England the game: a poorly hit shot when he should have scored late in the first half; and a bad, insufficiently angled pass to Bobby Charlton when England broke away with a three-to-one advantage in men, late in the second.

Ramsey, then, left Greaves out. I think still that he was wrong, but I also think it was utterly predictable. Greaves just wasn't Ramsey's kind of player, nor yet his kind of person. He was touched, as a footballer, by genius. Ramsey liked malleable, straightforward players. His "no wingers" policy may merely have rationalized that preference. In later years it would be said that his success with England set back the English game for years; the emphasis on "work rate" rather than skill, on running rather than technique, led the game into a blind alley.

The 1966 tournament was not one of exceptional quality, and the Hungarians, who did provide it against Brazil, were steamrollered by the Russians, who in turn lost an ill-tempered, rough semi-final to West Germany. North Korea will be remembered as cordially as any team for their astonishing giant-killing; and for the way, alas, that they faded first into splendid isolation, then into sheer mediocrity, when the competition was done.

To qualify, they had to beat only Australia, twice, in Phnom Penh, Cambodia. This they did, 6-1 and 3-1. Jean Vincent, the clever outside left of France's 1958 World Cup team, now coaching in Laos, said they were a better team than France had been; but no one took much notice.

That they had only Australia to play was brought

about by the withdrawal of all other countries from the Afro-Asian group, in protest against the fact that there would be only one qualifier between them, instead of one from Asia, one from Africa. This is not the place to become mired in the politics of the game, but a little explanation is due. The growth of football in Asia and Africa meant a plethora of new international teams, each of whose nations had, under FIFA's rash principle of one country, one vote, as large a say as the great footballing powers.

All would have been well had FIFA acknowledged the invention of the jet plane, de-zoned the qualifying tournament, and thrown the African, Asian, and, yes, the North and Central American, teams into the pot with everybody else. But they stubbornly kept the tournament zoned, which, under Afro-Asian pressure, by 1970 led to the farce of weak African *and* Asian teams getting to the Finals and making fools of themselves, while major powers fell by the wayside, especially in Europe, to other major powers.

The North Koreans, however, were abundantly worth their place. They began, having lived a monastic life in army barracks in Pyongyang, with modest performances at Middlesbrough against Russia (0-3) and Chile, a draw. The Tees-side crowd took the little fellows to their hearts, and actually, remarkably, began talking about them as "us." Italy, beating Chile in a match as quiet as their Battle of Santiago against them, in 1962, had been violent (two Italians sent off and another suffering a broken nose from a Chilean's left hook), was the next opposition.

The Italians, who had left Gigi Riva, one of the country's leading scorers, behind, and were playing their usual cautious *catenaccio*, could havè done with Armando Picchi of Inter as the sweeper-up behind the defense. But Picchi too had mysteriously been left out, and came only as a spectator.

Edmondo Fabbri, the tiny manager, compounded that error by picking a couple of slow defenders and an injured man in Giacomo Bulgarelli, an inside forward, who in fact had to go off the field after fouling a North Korean after half an hour.

There was no way through the determined if tiny North Korean defense for the Italian forwards, and the only goal of the game was scored when Pak Doo Ik, the Korean inside left, tackled the elegant Italian inside forward Gianni Rivera, three minutes from half-time, advanced, and beat Albertosi with a fierce cross shot. It was the most dumbfounding World Cup result since the United States had defeated England.

The North Koreans went on, in the quarter-finals, to shock the Portuguese, at Everton, going three dazzling goals ahead in 20 minutes. It was clear that they had learned at phenomenal speed from their three previous games, and had they not been faced by Eusebio, that soulful, elegant, dynamic figure, a black forward from Mozambique of beautifully fluid movement and a devastating right foot, perhaps they would have won. As it was, Eusebio picked Portugal up from the floor, scored four times, twice from the penalty spot, and Portugal won, 5-3.

In the semi-final, at Wembley, Eusebio was shackled by the tiny, toothless, uncompromising figure of Nobby Stiles, a right half of talismanic rather than technical virtues, a ferocious competitor, who in some sense symbolized the virtues, and deficiencies, of the English team; which had made incredibly heavy weather of beating Argentina's ten men. After that torrid affair, Alf Ramsey had remarked, with much justification, that he hoped his next opponents would concentrate on playing football, "and not act as animals." Unfortunately for him, the worst of the Argentinians' excesses had been committed out of sight, in the dressing-room tunnel, and that word, "animals," had been ringing round the world ever since.

The West German manager, Helmut Schoen, a tall, tolerant, gentle man, had at last emerged from beneath the shadow of Sepp Herberger, whose second in command he'd been for many years. Despite his consistent successes, he was never to gain total acceptance in West Germany, leaving one reluctantly to feel that a *Fuhrer*-figure—such as little Herberger—was still widely wanted there. When West Germany did well, we were told it was despite Schoen rather than because of him. His own assistant coach, the tiny Dettmar Cramer, would criticize him violently in Mexico, four years later, and even when he was winning the World Cup in 1974 he would be widely and cruelly criticized.

From farther away, Schoen, who was in his own day a gifted and fluent inside forward, seems a manager of great substance. His 1966 team was something of a half-way house between what Herberger had created and what he wanted, its salient figure the combative Uwe Seeler, whose first name was a warcry for the German fans.

The England-West Germany Final will turn eternally on England's third goal, scored in the first half of extra time with a rasping shot on the turn by Geoff Hurst at the near, right-hand post, after a run and center by the indefatigable Alan Ball, true architect of victory. The ball hit the underside of the crossbar and may or may not have crossed the line. The Swiss referee, Herr Dienst, was uncertain. The Russian linesman, Bakhramov, a violinist figure with his long gray hair and moustache, urgently convinced him it was a goal. Certainly it was worth a goal, though that is hardly the point at issue. It was a fine move, a fine shot, and the uneasy Tilkowski, in goal, was beaten to the wide.

There has been much less controversy over West Germany's equalizing goal, in the last seconds of normal time, though there is good reason to believe that the free kick which brought it about should have been given to rather than against Jackie Charlton, for a supposed foul on Siggi Held as they jumped for the ball. Lothar Emmerich, the big German left winger, took the kick, which hit the blond Schnellinger in the back, rebounded to Held, was driven across goal again by Held, and put in by the defender, Weber.

England had really done enough to win. They fell behind early when Ray Wilson, usually an impeccable left-back, headed a cross straight to the feet of the skillful Helmut Haller, who promptly put it away. Geoff Hurst equalized with his head from a quickly and shrewdly taken free kick by Bobby Moore, and a third West Ham player, Martin Peters, gave England the lead after half-time when Weber blocked Hurst's shot at a corner. With the new German star, the 21-year-old, elegant Franz Beckenbauer, underemployed in the mere policing of Bobby Charlton, West Germany's attacks seldom flowed, though Banks made two good saves in the first half. In extra time, the tireless running of the little, red-haired Alan Ball on the right overwhelmed Schnellinger and paved the way to the English victory, consolidated in the last minute by Hurst with a fulminating left-footed shot, after Moore had sent him through the scattered West German defense.

MEXICO—1970

By 1970 Brazil was strong again. Pelé was fit again. Beating England 1-0 in a memorable game in Guadalajara, played in appalling mid-day heat, the Brazilians went on to a far easier success in the Final over Italy, in Mexico City. The previous March, the controversial, ebullient, politically radical João Saldanha had locked horns with Pelé and ultimately been forced to resign. His place was taken by the reputedly "lucky" Mario Lobo Zagalo, tireless left winger of the 1958 and 1962 victories.

Zagalo quickly restored harmony in the camp, and solved the problem of having two brilliant, left-footed creative midfield players by playing Gerson—smoking his forty cigarettes a day to no apparent disadvantage— in midfield and the thick-thighed, heavily moustached Rivelino as a deep lying left winger.

Gerson struck long, gloriously precise left-footed passes, and used that same left foot to shoot an important goal in the Final to restore Brazil's lead against Italy. The young Clodoaldo, apart from the silly lapse which gave the Italians their equalizer, had an excellent World Cup, showing precocious enterprise and poise in Zito's old midfield role, while on the right wing, Jairzinho's power, swerve, and pace confirmed him in the distinguished succession of Julinho and Garrincha.

Tostão, the center forward, small, compact, technically adroit, was able to play at the last moment thanks to an operation in Houston for a detached retina—he had been hit by a ball. His skillful linking of the attack, his clever laying-back of passes kicked up to him, were a major factor in Brazil's success; and their absence, when more eye trouble forced him out of the 1974 World Cup, a major cause of their failure in West Germany.

The defense wasn't as good. The center backs were indifferent, Carlos Alberto, the right back and captain, more impressive when surging forward—as he did to score the fourth Brazilian goal against Italy—than when "attacked," and Felix, an astonishingly fallible goalkeeper, especially on high crosses. But the Brazilian tactics, even though it is legitimate to regard their formation as a fluid 4-4-2, with only Jairzinho and Tostão permanently upfield, were solidly based on attack; and the level of sheer technical skill was immensely high.

Moreover, the Brazilians well knew how to woo their volatile Mexican hosts. Where Sir Alf Ramsey, knighted by now, offended them with his indifference—paying a severe penalty—the Brazilians wooed them with bouquets and banners when they got to Guadalajara before the tournament. Just before it was due to begin, they disappeared into a closely guarded training camp into which entry was prohibitively difficult—while the English remained almost overly accessible in midtown at the Guadalajara Hilton. But goodwill had been so solidly established that the Mexicans felt loved and did not care.

By stark contrast, hundreds of them laid noisy siege to the Hilton the night before the England-Brazil game, disturbing the slumbers of the England team until three o'clock in the morning, shouting slogans, hooting horns, while the police made no attempt to disperse them, but merely checked their periodic attempts to invade the hotel. It is always wise to be polite to the Mexicans.

This was not the first extracurricular problem the English had confronted. Bobby Moore, their cool captain, en route to Mexico was arrested in Bogotà, Colombia, accused of having stolen a bracelet in a jewelry shop at the Tequendama Hotel where England had been staying. The frame-up was manifest, the reasons for it less so. Was it one more example of the national Colombian pastime of frame the foreigner? Was it, as a senior United States Senator hinted, jokingly or otherwise, to an English journalist a CIA attempt to promote an ultimate Brazilian victory; knowing how much kudos that would bring the Government in power? Stranger things, after all, have been done by the CIA in their time, and the same Senator even suggested that Gordon Banks' mysterious food poisoning on the eve of the West Germany vs. England quarter-final in León—an illness that cost him his place and England the game—was not fortuitous. Again, who knows? A body that can stalk Castro with an exploding cigar is capable of almost any wild excess.

At all events Brazil, having survived an early goal by the sturdy, blond Petras to beat the Czechs with a glittering fusillade of their own, beat England by 1-0, Jairzinho scoring after groundwork by Tostão—who unquestionably pushed the impeccable Moore off the ball—and Pelé. Banks made an almost miraculous save from Pelé's header, Brazil's goal had several hairsbreadth escapes.

A fine game, as was the West Germany-England match in León, when the Germans recovered from a two-goal deficit, exploiting Peter Bonetti's weakness in goal (lack of match practice compounded by personal mishaps) and the fact that the attacking English fullbacks ran themselves into the ground. These factors were in turn compounded by Ramsey's inept use of substitutes. The opportunism of Uwe Seeler and the heavy-legged, prolific Gerd Müller—skillfully welded together in attack by Helmut Schoen—and the mastery of Grasbowski, the substitute right winger, over the exhausted England left back Terry Cooper, helped Germany to their 3-2 win in extra time.

But extra time saw Italy beat *them* in the semi-final in Mexico City; half an hour in which five goals rattled in; one Italian journalist scornfully and justifiably dismissed it as "basketball." Italy would never have won had they not managed to chop down and "wing" the immaculate Beckenbauer when in full flight for goal, forcing him to play the rest of the game with his arm in a sling.

The Italians, whose post-Pozzo expeditions to the World Cup seemed always to be attended by a touch of *opera buffa,* had to calm turbulent waters over the claims of the rival "generals" of midfield, Internazionale's elegant, incisive Sandro Mazzola and Milan's equally gifted, creative Gianni Rivera. When Rivera heard at second hand that he was going to be left out of the opening match, he strongly criticized the team's officials and was told he'd be sent home if he didn't apologize. Peace was restored and Ferruccio Valcareggi, the team manager, conceived the bizarre compromise of playing Mazzola in the first half, Rivera in the second.

This worked quite well against Mexico in the quarterfinal and West Germany, but Mazzola upset it in the Final by playing with such splendid skill and drive that he just couldn't be taken off. So the desperate much put-upon Valcareggi shoved on Rivera for the last six minutes and took off his most dangerous attacker, Roberto Boninsegna.

Italy also brought Gigi Riva, the striker whom they had left behind in 1966, now grown into a figure of such proportions that one almost thought he would be left to walk across the water to Mexico. He was beyond doubt a fine, fast, strong player, tremendous finisher with foot or head, "Darwinian" product of the battle against superior defensive odds which all Italian strikers had to face, brave man who had twice recovered after breaking a leg, but too much was expected of him. He played well against Mexico, quite well, with a nice goal shot on the turn, against West Germany, and not well at all in the Final.

Not that it was easy to play well, given the conditions of height and climate. The tournament should never have been played in Mexico, any more than the Olympic Games should have been held there two years previously, but the World Cup Committee was no different from most other sports officials in their total indifference to the well being of the players. Things were made worse by the "sell out" of the games to European television, necessitating kick-offs in the noon heat. In the circumstances, the quality of play was amazingly high. Most teams had a period of (attempted) adaptation, while the England team used slow sodium tablets to counteract the heat. For all that, the height and heat of León exhausted them; and as one who drove back afterwards with Geoff Hurst to Guadalajara, I can testify to the exhausted condition of the players.

Peru should be mentioned; they had an exciting team which did everyone a service by eliminating the violent Argentinians in the qualifying competition; the finals themselves were on the whole an agreeable surprise in terms of behavior. Certainly there was nothing to touch or evoke the battles of Bordeaux, Berne, and Santiago. The Peruvians got as far as the quarter-final, and were eliminated by Brazil in Guadalajara, where the Uruguayans—furious, not without some reason, at having to play on a field where the Brazilians were so manifestly at "home"—also went out with honor.

Pelé did many dazzling things. Against Rumania, he attempted to lob the goalkeeper almost from the halfway line, and the ball went over his head to bounce just outside the post. Against Uruguay he sold Mazurkiewicz, that excellent keeper, an astonishing dummy, running around one side of him while the wall went the other. It was kicked off the line. The team which had seemed in Saldanha's last days in a hopeless state of flux and reconstitution was superbly integrated, balanced, original.

So the Final pitted Brazil against Italy, and it was just

no contest, even though Boninsegna, another of the few Italian successes, did equalize Pelé's spectacular headed goal, courtesy of Clodoaldo's aberrant back-heel. In the second half Gerson got his goal, Pelé made two more for Jairzinho and Carlos Alberto, and Brazil had won their third Jules Rimet Trophy; which now very rightly became theirs in perpetuity.

WEST GERMANY 1974

By 1974, and West Germany, Pelé had withdrawn and the Brazilians had gone down the slippery slope again. Tostão had had to retire, as had Gerson, who attended the tournament as a cynical spectator. Clodoaldo dropped out, injured, on the very verge of the competition, Rivelino found the midfield burden too heavy for him. In consequence Brazil became untypically and distressingly defensive. Their big new black center half, Luis Pereira, though he lost his head and got himself sent off in the vital game against Holland in Dortmund, was perhaps the best stopper they'd ever had, Leao was a better goalkeeper than Felix, Ze Maria a right back reminiscent of Djalma Santos.

But the team lacked inspiration and enterprise, and was far too prone to rough, "physical" tactics when things were going wrong. For all that, it failed by a whisker—and thanks chiefly to absurd misses by Paulo Cesar and Jairzinho, now at center forward—to knock out Holland that rainy night in Dortmund.

The West Germans started manifest favorites. Not only were they playing at home, but the team which had won them the European Nations Cup in Brussels two years earlier had been a glorious one. Constructed on the new principles of so-called Total Football—with Franz Beckenbauer interpreting the role of *libero* or sweeper in a totally new, creative way, the other players switching and interchanging with immense fluency and versatility—the West German team had perhaps been the most exciting Europe had seen since the famous Hungarians of the fifties. Gunter Netzer, the inside left with huge feet, a huge stride, and blond mane flowing in the wind had been as exciting as Beckenbauer, the thick-thighed Gerd Muller had despatched goals with foot and head with amazing aplomb, the bushy headed Paul Breitner, an ardent Maoist, said to be at odds with his teammate Beckenbauer whose politics were to the right, attacked explosively from fullback.

The 1974 West German team wasn't as good as that one, though it did represent many of the virtues that Helmut Schoen admired and encouraged; a team built in the image of Beckenbauer rather than Uwe Seeler, now retired. Indeed, its surprising and deserved defeat by East Germany in Hamburg—first time the two teams had ever met—set it by the heels. It needed the insertion of the powerful young Rainer Bonhof, Total Football and perpetual motion personified, to give it new life and direction. Bonhof it was, with a surging run past Aarie Haan on his outside, who made Müller the winning goal in the Final.

No one was quite sure what Holland would do in Germany, though I myself placed them among the favorites, hoping their whole would be as great as the parts. They were, like the West Germans too, a mercenary lot, forever threatening and demanding, but the eleventh-hour arrival of Rinus Michels, former coach of the leading Amsterdam club, Ajax, from Barcelona and Spain gave them the discipline and solidarity they needed. At last the Ajax and Feyenoord (Rotterdam) players bedded down happily together on the field, while Michels was the only man who could command any respect from the remarkable Johan Cruyff; best footballer in the world now that Pelé had decided he would play no more for Brazil, and stayed deaf to every fervent, desperate appeal.

Johan Cruyff had emerged as the best all-round center forward since his idol, Alfredo Di Stefano, the great Argentinian who inspired Real Madrid. Their morphology was very different, Di Stefano being deep chested, broad shouldered, and manifestly strong, whereas Cruyff was tall and slender, an almost boyish figure, with none of the appearance of the professional footballer—until he began to play. Then, his electric speed in the turn, his acceleration, his marvelous close control in full flight, his tremendously quick eye, made him as great a force as Di Stefano had been in his day. With him, the Dutch team was a major power, another of the teams dedicated to Total Football. Without him, even though the Dutch had such other stars as the forceful midfielder Johan Neeskens, who would follow him to Barcelona, the fleet, elusive winger Rob Rensenbrink, the splendid overlapping fullbacks from Ajax, Wim Suurbier and Rudi Krol, Holland was like an immaculate limousine without an engine.

Holland's very qualification had been laborious. They had twice drawn 0-0 with their old rivals, the Belgians, and only the fact that they had scored more goals against the lesser opposition in the group allowed them to get through. Moreover, they lost three of their best players: Van Beveren, the big, blond goalkeeper from PSV Eindhoven, was injured, as was Barry Hulshoff, the powerful Ajax center back, attacker as well as defender, while Gerry Muhren, Ajax's excellent left-sided midfielder, dropped out after the death of his father.

This meant using Aarie Haan, another splendidly gifted midfield man from Ajax, in the back four, which at once cut down his value to the attack, and reduced the solidity of the defense. Good player though he was,

111

it was he, as we have seen, who would be beaten by Rainer Bonhof when the winning World Cup goal was scored.

In goal Holland called up the veteran 36-year-old Jan Jongbloed, who had so little hope of playing that he brought his fishing rods to Hiltrup, the pleasant headquarters of the Dutch, where an extraordinarily relaxed atmosphere reigned. Jongbloed, owner of a cigar shop in Amsterdam, in fact surpassed himself in the tournament, making many excellent saves, and often rushing outside his own area to kick adventurously clear. Moreover, his cheerful, jocular ways were, as Michels had intended, a great help to morale.

England wasn't there; they had been eliminated by the Poles, who beat them clearly in Katowice but were lucky to survive an immense bombardment at Wembley, where Poland's huge goalkeeper, Jan Tomaszewski, made a string of astonishing saves; and had some equally astonishing fortune. In the World Cup finals, he would be consistently splendid.

The extraordinary thing was that though Poland lost its outstanding player, the inside left and striker Wlodek Lubanski, with a knee injury after the first game against England, they should be a better team in Germany than they had ever promised to be. Kasimierz Deyna, no longer overshadowed by Lubanski, emerged as an inside right, or midfielder, of glorious gifts, his clever passing matched by his tremendous right-footed shooting. The wingers: Lato, called up after the withdrawal of Lubanski, and the tough, left-sided striker Robert Gadocha, were a formidably effective pair, switching at will, unselfishly making goals for one another with foot and head, Lato finishing as top scorer of the competition. It was the first time since 1938 either Holland or Poland had competed in the World Cup finals.

Had it not deluged with rain before their game against West Germany in Frankfurt, perhaps the Poles would have beaten them and gone to play Holland in the Final. Many thought that the game should not have been played on the still rain-soaked field, conditions which certainly helped the physically powerful Germans. As it was, only the splendid goalkeeping of Sepp Maier, always at his best in important games, enabled West Germany to hold out, and eventually to win.

For Italy, it was *opera buffa* again. The terror of another "Korea," which had caused them to pack their defense in the early matches in Mexico, was still with them and was resuscitated when Haiti took the lead against them in Munich; the first goal the admirable keeper Dino Zoff had conceded in 1,143 minutes. Italy recovered to win 3-1, but when Giorgio Chinaglia, the big Lazio center forward—a player who'd actually learned his football in Wales—was substituted, he made an insulting gesture at the team manager Valcareggi as he came off the field, then, in the dressing-room, smashed eight bottles of mineral water; full ones, it was reported, empty ones, Chinaglia insisted. He followed this with a public attack on the Italian team managers. It was the Rivera case all over again.

Once more there were threats to send the player home. Once more the officials climbed down. This time, a private plane brought the Lazio coach and president to Germany at the Italian Federation's expense, and, in the Italian headquarters in Ludwigsburg, all was forgiven and forgotten over breadsticks and wine.

There was more, and much worse, to come. Against Argentina, it became very obvious that Italy's dull *catenaccio* tactics, with a *libero* who lurked at the back rather than venturing upfield in the Beckenbauer manner, were obsolete. This was compounded, in the Argentinian game, by a weird error made by the Italian coaches, whose obsession with strategy became counter-productive. Somehow or other, when watching Argentina, they had managed to persuade themselves that little René Houseman, a born, ebullient winger, with superb ball control and abundant pace, was . . . a midfield man. Given as they were to rigid man-to-man marking, they therefore put on him their constructive inside forward, Fabio Capello, who thus found himself transformed into a wholly defensive right back.

Houseman predictably ran rings around him, and had already scored a goal when the penny, or the lira, finally dropped, and Italy marked him with the rugged Romeo Benetti, instead. In the event, Benetti was able to equalize, but it was clear that Italy, with Riva and Rivera now such pallid figures, had little chance against the Poles.

Did they try to bribe them? From my own evidence, culled both in Poland and Italy, I am satisfied that they did; satisfied also that a number of Italian officials were incensed by the attempt, which they saw as thoroughly self-defeating, as well as dishonest. Their reasoning was, and remains, that had both teams been left to their own devices, the Poles, as good (Iron Curtain) professionals, would not have exerted themselves, for they needed no more than a draw to qualify them for the Final Pools. A draw would also have put through Italy.

After the games, various Polish players alleged they had been offered up to $2000 on the field by the Italians to let them at least draw, while the Polish team coach, Kazimierz Gorski, actually made a statement to a Warsaw newspaper that "certain prosperous followers" of the Italian team had attempted such corruption. Rigidly controlled by the Communist Party, all such organs in the Iron Curtain countries can publish nothing unless it has been officially approved, so it was surprising indeed when Gorski then denied what he had said, and forced the journalist who had interviewed him to retract.

The occurrence was far from isolated; only a couple of months before, it had been revealed that an attempt had been made the previous year to bribe the Portuguese referee to favor Juventus, the Italian champions, in a European Cup game against England's Derby County; and it soon became clear that this was no more than the tip of the iceberg. In the event, Italy lost 2-1 to the Poles, whose spectacular goals were scored by the blond young center forward Szarmach, a revelation of the tournament, and Deyna. Italy was out.

Haiti should never have been in. By a curious decision, the complete final tournament of the CONCACAF group, in which the United States is regularly involved, was played in Port-au-Prince, the Haitian capital; where poor Larry Gaetjens, scorer of the famous American goal against England in 1950, had not long since mysteriously disappeared, a presumed victim of the Tons Tons Macoutes.

The Haitians duly qualified, but only after the Salvador referee had disallowed *four* goals scored against them by Trinidad. He was suspended instantly, together with one of his linesmen, but the damage was done.

There were sinister aspects to Haiti's participation in Munich, too. Ernst Jean-Joseph, their red-haired center half, was one of their best men against Italy. After the game, however, his dope test proved positive. Poor Jean-Joseph, suspecting perhaps what would be in store for him, protested that he'd had to take pills for his asthma. The team's French doctor told a press conference this wasn't so, and charitably explained that Jean-Joseph wasn't intelligent enough to know what he was doing.

Jean-Joseph was suspended from the competition,

was to be seen for a day or two sitting tearfully about the lobby of the Penta Hotel, and was finally dragged out of the Grunwald Sports Centre, where his team was staying, beaten by an army officer attached to the party, shoved into a car, and virtually immured in the Sheraton Hotel, whence he was flown back to Haiti next morning. When a sympathetic Polish press hostess, whom the frightened Jean-Joseph telephoned from the Sheraton, and the team's amiable German liaison officer, Herr Renner, who couldn't sleep that night after what occurred, publicized the affair, they were angrily rebuked by the German Organizing Committee. But then, the implicit motto of such bodies is always Don't Make Waves.

Zaire was present, too; legacy of the absurdly structured qualifying competition. The Africans played quite well against Scotland, Britain's only survivors, who neither lost nor won a game, and created a strange sort of record by being eliminated, unbeaten. Against Brazil and the talented but ultimately disappointing Yugoslavs, however, Zaire looked crude. Australia also got through, with an honest, straightforward team which had scarcely a native Australian to its name. The Australians gave both Germanies a surprisingly good, even game, and held the Chileans to a 0-0 draw in Berlin.

West Germany's defeat by East Germany, whose goal was scored with a fine, powerful burst from Sparwasser, perhaps was a blessing in disguise. It meant that they finished second in their group and thus avoided rampant Holland till the Final. The East Germans, so composed and economical against West Germany, didn't win a game in their subsequent group, A.

Brazil, thanks largely to their skilled and potent use of free kicks, somehow kept their heads above water till their third and decisive game in the Final Pools, against

Holland, in Dortmund. They missed, as one has recorded, two concrete chances in the first half, and you cannot afford to do that against a team like Holland, who replied with two marvelous goals in the second. Cruyff made the first for Neeskens, a goal of staggering simplicity, swift and bold execution, with a lightning exchange of passes on the right. Cruyff himself scooped in the second after an almost equally good movement on the left, a cross by Krol.

So the Final pitted Holland against West Germany, and the start, in Munich's Olympic Stadium, could scarcely have been more dramatic. Holland kicked off, almost tauntingly kept possession, till Cruyff sent off on a long, sinuous, electric run, to be brought down at last in the box by a desperate Uli Hoeness. Neeskens scored from the kick.

Was it sheer hatred, a legacy of the war, as some suggested, which made Holland now play cat and mouse with the stunned Germans, rather than drive home their advantage? The Dutch deny it, but the fact remains that they frittered away their advantage till at last Wolfgang Overath, who had won back his 1970 place from a fading Gunter Netzer, sent Hölzenbein away on the left, Hölzenbein cut in for goal, was tripped by little Jansen; and now it was Paul Breitner's turn to score from the spot.

Somehow, Germany allowed Cruyff and Johnny Rep, the blond striker, to break through with only Beckenbauer between them and Sepp Maier. They duly circumvented him, but Cruyff failed to beat the inspired Maier, who would later make a still more spectacular save from Neeskens; and West Germany escaped.

So, when Bonhof beat Haan to cross from the right, Gerd Müller was able to take two bites at the cherry. On his second shot, he dragged the ball past Jongbloed to give West Germany the World Cup; after a twenty-year hiatus. Holland would have been more popular victors, and it is true that both Germany and Beckenbauer had been more impressive in 1972, but there was no doubt of the quality of the team, and none of the superiority that year of European over South American football.

ARGENTINA—1978

The 1978 World Cup was shabby and mediocre by comparison with 1974. Argentina won it, thanks, in the event, to the marvelous opportunism, the individual flair, of Mario Kempes, in the Final against Holland, but they would scarcely have won it anywhere else. The absence of the world's two finest players, Johan Cruyff of Holland, who preferred not to take part, and Franz Beckenbauer of West Germany, splashing in the shallows of the NASL with the Cosmos, reduced the two finest teams of 1974 to mere infantrymen, even though they played briskly and brightly enough when they met one another in Cordoba, drawing 2-2.

The severe inadequacies of the new formula, happily obscured in 1974 but apparent even then, were a further blight on the tournament. The crass notion of perpetuating the League system beyond the first four eliminating groups led to monstrosities such as West Germany's craven performance in a 0-0 draw with Italy, Peru's abject surrender to Argentina 6-0 in Rosario, enabling the host nation to qualify on goal difference at the expense of the Brazilians.

Not that Brazil deserved much out of this World Cup. The third place they eventually gained at the expense of Italy, thanks to two tremendous shots from outside the penalty area by Nelinho and Dirceu, did them a great deal more than justice. They had made the unhappy choice for coach of Claudio Coutinho, an elegant polyglot, an Army captain, a disciple in physical training of the American Cooper. Former trainer of the Brazilian team, Coutinho now tried to instil what he took to be European methods. In the process, he succeeded in crushing the native flair of his best players, ignoring others completely, and instilling a sour, sometimes violent, approach among his defenders.

That Brazil survived their early, qualifying games on the admittedly dreadful field of Mar del Plata, which looked as if it had been ravaged by scores of inept golfers, was a small miracle. Spain would have beaten them there had Julio Cardenosa not perpetrated the miss of the World Cup, delaying his shot into an empty goal from a few yards until Amaral had time to scramble back and block it. Austria would not have lost to them had Bruno Pezzey, the big center back, hitherto so effective, not managed to get himself underneath a long right wing cross by Toninho, allowing Roberto to score at leisure.

Coutinho was humiliated by the egregious Admiral Heleno Nunes, who announced soon after the Spanish game that he was relieving Coutinho of full powers and supervising the team himself, then said, just before Brazil beat Poland in the Second Round, that Coutinho was a man of scarce technical knowledge; Brazil had been saved from the consequences of his failings by its players and by "wise" directors. So wise that they had chosen and kept in office till the World Cup was in full flight a man of "scarce technical knowledge"—second guessing at its worst.

Abominable refereeing was another negative feature of this World Cup. Frequently, as was to be anticipated, it benefited Argentina, whose crowds had seriously intimidated referees in the past. The problem was compounded by the inadequacy of the Referees' Committee, under the chairmanship of the Italian Ar-

119

temio Franchi, who kept insisting, in the teeth of all the gruesome evidence, that all was well. Ludicrously, the Committee made no attempt to standardize practice, above all to see to it that vicious fouls were punished automatically not merely by free kicks but by yellow card cautions.

The Argentinians would scarcely have beaten France, in their second game, were it not for the extraordinary refereeing of the Swiss Jean Dubach, who gave them a penalty so doubtful—for hands against the excellent Marius Tresor—that he consulted a Canadian linesman far less well placed than he, then refused France a perfectly obvious one when Didier Six was felled.

In the Final, the Dutch, though they committed fifty fouls, the first of them in the opening minute, had justification to feel aggrieved with the Italian referee Sergio Gonella. Gonella was chosen only after hours of debate in the Referees' Committee, and on Franchi's deciding vote. He was a disaster, manipulated from the start by the Argentinians, who made a disingenuous fuss about the bandage on René Van De Kerkhof's forearm, and kept Holland waiting on the field five minutes before they emerged.

But the alternative to Gonella was the vacillating Uruguayan Ramon Barreto, who a year earlier, refereeing Argentina versus England in Buenos Aires, had sent off not only Daniel Bertoni of Argentina for hitting Trevor Cherry in the mouth but Cherry himself! Enzo Bearzot, the taut, impassioned manager of Italy, who played so well till they ran out of steam in the Second Round, spoke bitterly about the refereeing of Spain's Angel Martinez when Holland beat his team in Buenos Aires. Martinez certainly made an abominable job of this ill-natured game, in which the Dutch committed many a painful foul, but no manager who regularly fields as rough a player as Romeo Benetti—cautioned in this game when he deserved to be expelled for a savage piece of elbowing—is in much of a moral position.

Italy itself greatly benefited from the bizarre refereeing of Belgium's Francis Rion when they played Austria at River Plate Stadium in the previous game. He should have booked several Italian defenders for persistent fouling, and once, when Claudio Gentile brought down an opponent in the penalty area, gave Austria . . . a corner!

Argentina certainly deserved some reward for their persisting commitment to attack. Their manager, Cesar Menotti, had been greatly and frequently criticized during the four years of his regime, and waiting in the wings was the saturnine Juan Carlos Lorenzo, dark influence of 1962 and 1966, now manager of Buenos Aires' Boca Juniors club.

Many of the best Argentinian players remained in Europe. The only one whom Menotti could and would have had was Oswaldo Piazza, of Saint Etienne, but soon after the big center half returned to Buenos Aires his wife was hurt in a car crash, and he had to return to France. Thus the only "expatriate" in the team was Mario Kempes of Valencia, leading scorer in Spain, 19-year-old center forward in the 1974 World Cup, now matured into a player of immense dynamism and skill. To begin with, Menotti used him most effectively up front beside another big man, the powerful, right-footed Luque. But a dislocated elbow and the death of his brother in a car crash undermined Luque, and after an unhappy attempt to use Kempes as an orthodox center forward between two wide wingers, Menotti eventually settled on playing him as an attacking left midfielder. This, as it transpired, was virtually what won Argentina the Final, since the Dutch, marking man to man on the three strikers up front, gave Kempes the room for three brilliant slaloms, which in turn produced three fine goals.

In midfield, the outstanding Argentinian, till he was injured, was the little, right-footed Osvaldo Ardiles, a strangely anachronistic, tango figure, with his sleeked-down hair, and perhaps a little old fashioned, too, in the marvelous exuberance of his dashes and dribbles. Ubaldo Fillol, the goalkeeper, rescued his team with magnificent saves from Johnny Rep and Rob Rensenbrink in the first half of the Final, while the captain, Daniel Passarella, though he committed some blood-curdling fouls, was a bulwark in defense, a threat when he came up into attack.

Italy beat Argentina 1-0 in the third match of the initial Buenos Aires group, thanks to a goal beautifully worked out between their two most gifted forwards, 22-year-old Paolo Rossi—a revelation of the tournament— and the elegant Roberto Bettega, who faded badly in the later games. But this was a blessing in disguise for the Argentinians, who thus passed into the weaker of the two final groups in Rosario. Even there, they were somewhat fortunate to beat Poland—Kempes punched off the line, from Lato, and Kazimierz Deyna missed the penalty—and not to lose to Brazil. As for the Peruvian game, it was sheer fiasco, Peru collapsing abjectly to lose 6-0, after a bright beginning.

Had Holland been able to call on Johan Cruyff, there is little doubt they would comfortably have won the tournament. Without him, as an Argentine journalist shrewdly recorded after their opening game, they were like a superb machine, deprived of the man who had invented it. They actually lost 3-2 to Scotland, who had played abominably, under the callow management of the inexperienced Ally MacLeod, against Peru and Iran. Worst of all, Scotland had had to send home its left winger, Willie Johnston, after he had been found "guilty" of taking amphetamine drugs before the game against Peru.

Two sizzling right-footed long shots from outside the penalty area, in the second half, enabled the Dutch to beat Italy, after going a goal down. They had, in Johan Neeskens and Aarie Haan, two of the best, toughest, most resilient midfield men in the competition, but the dead hand of their Austrian coach, Ernst Happel (much criticized by his Dutch number two, the Air Force officer Jan Zwartkruis), weighed heavy on the team.

After Kempes had plucked a goal out of the air to give Argentina the lead in the Final—let it not be forgotten, however, that lax marking and his own enterprise gave Passarella no fewer than four chances of a goal—Holland dominated the second half. They equalized late in the game when Haan struck a powerful crossfield ball from left to right, and the never very certain Argentine defense allowed René Van De Kerkhof to center in turn high from the right, Dirk Nanninga, the tall substitute, to head the equalizer. In extra time, however, the Dutch moved their lanky stopper, Erny Brandts, back into defense—after a brief run in attack beside Nanninga—and the virtue seemed to go out of them. By contrast, Argentina found new reserves of energy and morale, to score twice more and threaten at least one other goal.

It was not, however, a World Cup to remember, even if the celebrations in the nocturnal streets of Buenos Aires, ecstatic after every victory, reached hysterical crescendo on the night of the Final.

4
THE AMERICAN EXPERIENCE

It would be very wrong indeed to assume that because professional soccer in the United States began on a major scale only in 1967, the game has no tradition in America. U.S.A. teams distinguished themselves in the World Cup of 1930 and 1950, when the Americans beat England and when John Souza, from Fall River, a wholly "native" product, was described as one of the best inside forwards in the World Cup. St. Louis has produced not only the Anglophile T. S. Eliot, but a host of dedicated soccer players, who developed in the high schools and at St. Louis University. Indeed, the St. Louis Stars team, competing in the North American Soccer League, largely based their teams on locally born and groomed players.

Then there was the determined attempt on the East Coast, during the early 1920s, to get the professional game off the ground; an attempt which led to many fine young Scottish players coming to America. Alec Jackson, later to become perhaps the best Scottish outside right of all time, scorer of three goals against England at Wembley when Scotland's Wembley Wizards thrashed them 5-1 in 1928, very nearly didn't go back at all, he was so happy. And when Glasgow Celtic lost their brilliant young goalkeeper, John Thomson, in a tragic collision with a Rangers forward in 1931, it was to Fall River that they turned for a replacement, bringing the Scots-born keeper James Kennaway back home. Later, in the 1960s, Bill Cox ran an often interesting international club tournament in New York.

Today the professional game in America stands tantalizingly at the crossroads. Much has been done, still more remains to do. Though there is airy talk of attracting the finest players from all over the world to the NASL, though a remarkable coup brought the incomparable Pelé to New York, to be followed by Italy's Giorgio Chinaglia, the true objective must be an American League "staffed" by American players. Soccer is not ice hockey; there are thousands upon thousands of boys, and even girls, playing soccer today, from New England to California, from Washington D.C., to Dallas; in large part the consequence of the young but developing professional game.

If great obstacles stand in the way of developing American stars in quantity, they seem to me essentially artificial ones. Why, when Frenchmen, Italians, Brazilians, Russians, Haitians, Congolese can show such natural aptitude for soccer should Americans, who excel in so many sports, be different or inferior? If they can beat and compete with the world in track and field, swimming, tennis, boxing, then why not soccer?

Clearly, there can be no reason at all, the less so when, as we have seen in Brazil, the blacks are so superbly suited to the game, with their extraordinary reflexes, explosive movement, and natural grace. It is from the black ghettoes that I expect, in due time, America to recruit many of its soccer stars; though, once present obstacles are removed, there should be a steady flow of white talent, too.

What *are* those obstacles? I would classify them as ones of attitude and structure. Structurally, there is no doubt that the college system is an enormous barrier to the development of young American talent. In Europe and Latin America, boys are exposed very early, often too early, to professional clubs. Ajax of Holland, Bayern Munich of West Germany, Fluiminense and Botafogo of Brazil, have many teams; a boy can join one of them as early as eight or nine and, in theory at least, come all the way through to the first team. In Britain, the emphasis on football is placed upon the schools, but a promising boy may be training with a professional club from the age of eleven. At sixteen—it was fifteen until the school-leaving age was raised a few years ago—he can become for three years an apprentice professional, at the end of which period (an insidious system) the club decides whether or not it wants to make him a full pro.

In the United States, the fact that such a vast number of young men go to college obviates anything like this. Nor would it matter were there any equivalence between the position of soccer in colleges and the position of American football. A promising high school football player who goes to college is in fact joining the equivalent of a professional football nursery. He is a football player first and a student second; not a system I have ever found endearing or other, at bottom, than hypocritical, but certainly one well calculated to please the professional clubs. They know that promising young players will be subjected to the most intensive training, the most competitive games, that during their college years they will be progressing. Soccer players mark time or actually go backwards because the standard is low; or, as I would prefer to put it, is not artificially high.

An American college student who plays soccer is a

student first, a soccer player second; however much he might prefer the order to be reversed. The NASL have for some years doggedly gone through the motions of a college draft, on the pattern of American football, but, inevitably, the results have been embarrassing. Even when, in an attempt to encourage a flow of native talent, it was made obligatory for the NASL clubs to sign college, or at least native American, players, of these only a tiny trickle won regular places in the line-ups. The NASL clubs had to survive, to survive they had to win matches and entertain the public, and to accomplish both aims they found themselves relying preponderantly on pro players temporarily imported from Britain.

Some had a distinguished past, some a distinguished future—Gordon Hill played for Chicago in 1975 and in 1976 returned to England as a left winger, making his international debut in New York—a few had a distinguished present. These were supplemented by professionals from many other nations; Yugoslavs, Germans, Italians, Argentinians, Portuguese. It was essentially a holding action; but how long would the NASL be obliged to hold?

Even those college players who *have* come through tend to have been overtaken by anticlimax; as in the case of Kyle Rote, Jr. Kyle Rote, Sr., was, of course, an American football player and commentator of renown. His son seemed all set to follow him, having been offered a football scholarship. But Dundee United had played in Dallas in 1967 as the representative of the Dallas Tornado soccer club in the United Soccer Association. Soccer was in the air, and one day Kyle Rote, Jr., and a few friends were kicking a soccer ball around for fun when a car stopped, out climbed a small, blond man with a Lancashire accent, and he told them all the things that they were doing wrong.

Kyle Rote was a little resentful at first, but then he realized what the Englishman said made sense. He was hooked. The Englishman was a soccer coach, Ron Griffith, who has for many years most enterprisingly been taking his Texan Longhorns and Texan Shorthorns, touring teams of boys, on tour to England—and even Mexico. This, however, must have been the very peak of his proselytizing. In no time at all, Kyle Rote, Jr., had turned down his football scholarship and taken one in soccer to Sewanee University instead.

On emerging, he turned professional with the Dallas Tornado, led their attack, headed some impressive goals, was capped by the United States international team, and won a Super Stars contest of mixed sports on television. Alas, by the summer of 1976 he could no longer hold a regular place on the Tornado team, and his American coach, Al Miller, was saying publicly that he was no better than a modest player.

This was sad indeed, and no fault of Kyle Rote, a natural athlete who would surely have been a very good soccer player indeed had he only begun playing it as early as he began playing American football, had he been attached to a professional club from his early teens.

Soccer gained an early hold on the American colleges but, like cricket, once America's national sport, it could not keep it. On November 6, 1869, Princeton played Rutgers in a football match whose rules were approximately those promulgated by the Football Association at the time of its foundation in London, six years earlier. You could still stop the ball with your hands, but the ball was round, and primarily you kicked it. In 1872 Columbia and Yale followed suit, but Harvard took up Rugby and persuaded Yale to play it too. Within a few years, this in its turn had been modified into the American game.

One day we may know why soccer has for so long been an Un-American Activity. As recently as 1975, Edward Grossman was writing in the New York monthly, *Commentary*, "Despite Pelé's debut, soccer still looks foreign, a game for young UN bureaucrats and for new immigrants resisting Americanization."

There is no doubt that America, in inventing and insisting on its own games, was to some extent insisting on its own separate identity, but there is surely more to it than that. The controlled violence, the massive organization, of football is obviously deeply attractive to an American public. The more fluid, less inevitable, nature of soccer is not. To American fans there seems something imperfect and unjust about a game in which the best laid move cannot only, as Burns would have it, gang agley, but act as the very springboard for a counterattack which itself may produce a goal. Unfair but, to a European or a South American audience, fascinating. The improvisation and fluidity of soccer are far less acceptable to Americans, who also seem to prefer their sports to be broken up into short, fierce flurries of action, followed by a break or pause. Soccer, though the American colleges did for many years chop it into quarters, is a sustained game of two forty-five minute halves, with a minimum of substitutions.

The question of goals is similarly vexed and contentious. The scoring of a goal in soccer is a surprisingly difficult, even a hazardous, business. Good leading up play, like virtue, will frequently go unrewarded because it is so hard to get the ball into that space eight yards wide by eight feet high. There is a goalkeeper, too, who is determined to frustrate you. Perhaps it is not surprising that the NASL have made attempts to have the goal widened, just as they have, in their competition, reduced the area in which players can be offside to 35 yards at each end, and eschewed the very idea of a drawn game by initiating periods of "over-time," penalty kicks-series, and, in 1977, a kind of 35-yard Duel in the Sun between the goalkeeper and a designated opponent. To those who love soccer, the comparative rarity of the goal is one of the game's greatest attractions. Walter Winterbottom, the England team manager from 1946 to 1962, once pointed out to me that were the scoring of a goal to become devalued, facile, then soccer would become like basketball. There is obviously a very thin line between transforming the game for American consumption and destroying its very essence. Moreover, since it *is* an international sport, playing it under your own version of its rules can effectively prevent your ever being able to compete with the world on level terms. Patience should surely be the watchword.

At the turn of this century, a great deal of soccer was being played in New York, New Jersey, and Pennsylvania, though almost wholly by teams made up of immigrants, whether they were British, Irish, or Latin-American. In 1884 the American Football Association was founded, the first such body to be established outside Britain, but seniority alas has been no guarantor of effectiveness. Over the years the history of American soccer administration at the national level has been one of squabbling insularity, and narrowness of vision. This in turn has been caused and conditioned by the fact that, soccer being so minor a sport, those in charge of it have been the "little" people: a Secretary—till recent years—who "moonlighted" as Press Box steward at the Yankee Stadium, a clutch of "ethnics" whose inability to speak English without a strong accent seemed in itself a symbol of soccer's own inability to become a genuinely American game. When, in 1967, a raft of very big businessmen, scenting profits and an international sweep of activity, moved in on the game, it was to find themselves confronted by these same little people, whose very headquarters was then a minuscule suite of offices on Fifth Avenue. For all these years, soccer itself had been similarly obscure; and had done pitifully little to go out into the highways and the byways of the colleges to make converts. Now, these little people blinked in the strong light. Their confrontation with the Big Businessmen was inevitably one of mutual surprise.

There had been squabbling almost from the first in the counsels of American soccer. The New York clubs protested at the League schedule and withdrew to form their own body, the American Amateur Football Association. At the congress held by FIFA, the world governing body, formed eight years earlier, in conjunction with the Stockholm Olympics, both American associations sent representatives. At this the newer body, the AAFA, changed its name to the United States Football Association, co-opted all but the professional clubs, and was joined by them, too, when FIFA accepted their membership in 1913. The first president of the USFA was an English doctor, Ralph Manning, whose aim "to make soccer the national pastime of the winter in this country" proved hopelessly Utopian. Sixty-five years later, the NASL competition was still crammed into the brief, unsuitable weeks of summer, for fear of meeting the Moloch of American football head on.

Despite the attempts by Bethlehem Steel and others to import Scottish pros and build teams in the early 1920s, soccer in America stayed firmly rooted to the ground, noted for its periodic violent excesses rather than for any achievements in the missionary field. Even the partial success in the 1930 World Cup did little or nothing to spread the game; and when America beat England twenty years later in Belo Horizonte, it was much the same story. The periodic reports of violence among "ethnic" teams, Greeks, Poles, Italians, South Americans, Ukrainians, can have done little to enamour the native-born Americans of the game. As late as 1967, I was in the Yankee Stadium when, after a bad-tempered match between Cagliar, representing Chicago, and Cerro Montevideo, representing New York, some forty Italian fans took advantage of a soporific police force to chase the referee across the field. Poor Leo Goldstein, who had already survived a concentration camp, eventually tripped and fell over the infield, kicking out at his pursuers as he did so. Fortunately the stadium police then came belatedly to life and rescued him with no more than a few bruises to show for his ordeal. "Those Italian fans," said the head of the stadium police force, a Mr. D'Alessandro, "behaved like animals." They had done so before and would do so again, on the occasion of a visit by Pelé's Santos club from Brazil, invading the field because it was beating a Milanese team; and finding themselves vigorously opposed by the muscular Brazilians. But then, on other such occasions. Greeks and Poles have behaved just as badly. Perhaps it is not to be wondered at that one of the first preoccupations of NASL's leaders has been to change the "image" of the game, rather than to go out to persuade the underprivileged to play it, professionally. Such organizations as the German-American League, played in and around New York, are all very well in their way, but the connotation, always, is . . . ethnic. Did not the New York Ukrainian club until very recently make all the announcements at its games in Ukrainian? And was there not a match, just a few years ago, in New York in which a Greek player, sent off the field by the referee, went, got a knife from a Greek spectator, returned, and stabbed the referee? On such incidents and their broadcasting has American soccer foundered.

The confusions of 1967 were worse confounded by the fact that the American businessmen concerned knew little or nothing about soccer and the vagaries of the sport. Money would, they were sure, solve everything, but FIFA, though it and its member associations have never discouraged the rich from pouring their wealth into football, has somewhat different ideas. In the first place, FIFA's articles lay it down that clubs are not to be run as profit-making concerns. "If it's a business," as Gianni Agnelli, the head of Fiat in Turin, who have always patronized the Juventus club, once said to me, "it's a losing business." Lamar Hunt, the Texan oil millionaire who has loyally, steadfastly, and crucially stuck by the Dallas Tornado where lesser, and less rich, men have failed, would doubtless agree. Other salient figures in the realm of American sports, such as Judge Roy Hofheinz from Houston, with his inevitable squares of Astroturf to hand around, and Jack Kent Cooke, the Canadian who owns so many franchises in Los Angeles, were in and out of soccer in a trice.

Given the enormous losses sustained by most of the American pro soccer clubs in their early years of existence, the idea that they might ever be profitable may have seemed remote; but the time will surely come when indeed they are, and then some kind of clash with FIFA seems inevitable. Not that I wish for a solitary instant to depict American soccer directors as sharks, the rest of the world's as altruists. Not a bit of it. There are many, many benefits to be derived from running—let us eschew the word "owning"—a soccer club which are not directly financial.

This magic word "prestige" is highly relevant. It was that shrewdest of upstarts Denry Machin, in Arnold Bennett's novel *The Card*. "Why, you silly goose," this Edwardian nouveau riche rebuked his wife, "didn't you know? Football has to do with *everything!*"

Provincial businessmen in England have long been very well aware of that, aware of how much the chairmanship, or even just a directorship, of the local club can transform their position in the community. In 1967 the Pittsburgh club of the National Professional Soccer League managed to lose the bagatelle of $325,000. Things, since then, have got better; but quite slowly.

For the professional game in America, 1967 was a chaotic year. Piqued by the success of the World Cup no fewer than three groups of would-be promoters competed to set up a national soccer league. Two of them eventually banded together, but that still left two competitors. USSFA deliberated on the problem, and when the smoke cleared, it was the group brought together by Lamar Hunt, Jack Kent Cooke, and Roy Hofheinz which had gained favor. In the driver's seat, as chief administrator, was none other than the amiable late Jimmy McGuire, a former Scottish pro, now a manufacturer of shirts, who also happened to be president of USSFA.

The unsuccessful group flew into a fury and decided to go it alone without the benefit of USSFA and, by extension, FIFA. They called themselves, as we have seen, the NPSL. Their authorized opponents ingeniously named themselves the United Soccer Association; or U.S.A. In New York, both the New York Generals, sponsored, albeit briefly, by RKO-General Tires, shared Yankee Stadium with Cerro of Montevideo, alias the New York Skyliners, sponsored by Madison Square Garden. When Jack Kent Cooke telephoned me from Los Angeles to ask me to suggest an English team, I named Wolverhampton Wanderers, just in the process of winning the English Second Division. Wolves accepted, and actually won the League. I had never visualized a first visit to Los Angeles which included the giving of a tactical talk in Spanish to a Uruguayan team about the Wolves, out at El Segundo by a hotel pool; but this was what happened.

Both the Skyliners and the Generals drew minuscule crowds. It was clear enough that before pro soccer ever got off the ground in America, New York would have to be taken; until the Cosmos boldly bought Pelé in 1975, it was difficult to see how. The public seemed divided between native New Yorkers who knew nothing about soccer and cared less, and initiated immigrants, or ethnics, who knew bad soccer when they saw it and wouldn't come.

The Generals had many problems of integration. How could one persuade a solid, down-to-earth English professional from Third Division Scunthorpe to make common cause with a gifted, aging, and overweight Argentinian? An English player informed me with wonder, one day, that at a training session, one of the Argentinians had simply lain down in the goalmouth, complained that he was so tired, and gone to sleep. An English forward complained that he wasn't getting any passes from the Argentinians, "Until I realised I was calling Mas, Plas and Plas, Mas."

After matches, in the dressing room, Freddie Goodwin, the English coach, who would later take over Birmingham City in England and return to do well with the Minnesota Kicks, would labor at the green tactics "blackboard" to try to explain to his Trinidad winger how the game should be played.

The NPSL was an outlawed, an illegal, League, and by definition any player joining it was putting himself beyond the pale of world football. At the end of the season, the NPSL brought an $18 million lawsuit against the USA, FIFA, and USSFA. Inevitably, amalgamation settled the matter; after a fashion. Ken Aston, the English referee who had tried to handle what he called the "uncontrollable" Chile-Italy World Cup match of 1962 and was now a leading FIFA official, remarked that sharks from all over the world scented blood in the waters of American pro soccer; and homed in.

What a jamboree it was for frauds and phonies! Out from under stones crawled obscure ethnics with little but their Central European accents and their wholly putative careers in football, unauthenticated and undocumented, to recommend them. Too often, it was enough. No one bothered to check whether manager X had, as he insisted, once played for Rapid Vienna and coached the first ever Italian Under 23 team, as assistant. As one who was living in Italy when it was formed and attended its first game in Bologna in early 1954, I certainly didn't remember him. But he gained employment, and when an earnest young Canadian journalist crossed the border to expose him to his club directors, it was the journalist and not the coach who was sent away with a flea in his ear.

Dallas Tornado hired a garrulous Hungarian named Bob Kapp who got together a team consisting largely of English unknowns, put them into blazers and big, white Stetsons, and took them right around the world before the season started, playing more than forty games in Europe, Africa, and Asia—it was in Bangkok, I believe, that they were stoned. On arrival, quite exhausted, back "home" in Dallas, they promptly played their first League match against the visiting Houston Stars, and were thrashed 6-0. It said an enormous amount for Lamar Hunt, quiet, undemonstrative, but implacably determined, that he could ride out this sort of thing.

I flew to Chicago and the O'Hare Motor Inn after the Mexican Olympics of October 1968 to attend the crucial meeting which would decide whether the infant North

American Soccer League would carry on or not. The estimable Brigadier Eakins, of the Vancouver club, emerged from meetings grunting that he had identified a new category, "the instant expert." Phil Woosnam, a former Welsh international inside forward of considerable gifts who had been coaching Atlanta, the hope of the Southeast, and would in due time become Commissioner of a far healthier League, sat crew cropped and a little stunned, constantly repeating, "No one's bigger than the game." But was the NASL big enough to survive?

By the skin of its teeth, and woefully reduced, it did so. Only five clubs remained; the instant experts had paid dearly for their hubris. The League headquarters moved for a time to Atlanta, which was most emphatically the power base, if the term be justified, of pro football; for the moment. The Atlanta Chiefs, spawned by the Atlanta Braves, had a series of capable British managers, and did consistently well in competition. It was a blow when Atlanta eventually bowed out; but by then the League was picking up steam again, and if the Generals were in due course cashiered, the New York Cosmos, backed by the potent Warner Communications, arose to take their place, in 1971.

It was they who, in the summer of 1975, signed Pelé, the world's most famous and brilliant soccer player, to a three-year contract for $4.5 million; a coup engineered by the former Fleet Street sports writer Clive Toye, a Devonian who was now general manager of the Cosmos, would become its president, and had boldly leaped into the new soccer League with Baltimore in 1967. In Brazil itself, the departure of Pelé, his emergence from what was said to be definitive retirement, caused mixed feelings, a distinct modicum of bitterness. If he could play for the Cosmos, for all his talk about promoting the game and spreading its Gospel in the States, then why could he not have played for Brazil in the 1974 World Cup?

This, however, was scarcely the Cosmos' problem. They publicized and promoted Pelé all over the country, drew splendid crowds, went back to Yankee Stadium from the wilderness of Randalls Island, and had exemplary co-operation from the star himself, the very personification of Mr. Nice Guy, even though he was carefully kept away from the black ghettoes; from which Toye himself, to give him his due, admitted that the talent would surely and ultimately come.

Pelé was presented to the Cosmos fans in spectacular manner; on May 28, 1975, a helicopter landed on the field in Downing Stadium, Randall's Island, and from the helicopter stepped Pelé. He was followed to the Cosmos in April 1976 by Giorgio Chinaglia, the big Lazio and Italy center forward, still at the height of his powers, whose Italo-American wife wanted to settle in her native New Jersey. Chinaglia, who had property interests there, was released most reluctantly by Lazio. For years he had been their bombardier, their chief hope of goals, a strong, straightforward player with a terrific right-footed shot and the direct methods he had learned as a boy growing up in Wales, where his father had emigrated. In one match against Miami in 1976 he scored five times.

But success in the NASL, which by 1975 had built itself up to no fewer than twenty clubs, an achievement almost inconceivable on that bleak day in the O'Hare motel in 1968, was by no means confined to New York and Pelé. Much more remarkable in its way, and still more encouraging, was the astonishingly rapid progress of the Seattle Sounders, formed in 1974, and the Portland Timbers, established a year later. Neither of these cities had a scrap of soccer tradition. In the case of

Portland, the moving spirit of the club, Don Paul, was a former professional American football player who had seen and been impressed by just one game, in Seattle, before he was inspired to bring the Portland Timbers into being. The club did not find a coach—Vic Crowe, who had played for and coached the Atlanta Chiefs till their demise in 1969, a Welsh international who also managed Aston Villa—till barely a month before the tournament started. Crowe, in turn, got his weary British players to the city five days before the first League match was due; which meant five days after his own arrival in Portland. But then, Don Paul had managed to raise the $30,000 needed to bring the total up to $200,000, to launch the club, only in the last hour on the last day of the scheduled appeal.

Why did Seattle, in 1974, pack its little 15,000 capacity stadium time and again to watch the Sounders? Why was it that Portland, which had snubbed an ill-run, mediocre, arrogant pro football team the year before, should so rapidly take the Timbers to its bosom, a team of aliens playing an alien game?

The fact is that they did, with crowds of 30,000 and 40,000 packing the Civic Stadium; and going mad with joy when the Timbers beat the Sounders in August 1975 to reach the semi-finals of the NASL play-offs. Tampa Bay Rowdies, another new team, under the aegis of the South African Eddie Firmani, once center forward for Charlton Athletic of London, Internazionale of Milan, and Italy would eventually beat them in the Final; but what an extraordinary start they had made!

Their success, so unexpected by themselves, caused embarrassing problems, for Crowe—much against his will—had to keep his British players although their clubs wanted them back for the start of the English season. Neither Portland nor the Football League clubs had ever imagined Portland would do so well, survive so long in the NASL play-offs. The following English season, there would be more trouble when the celebrated George Best, rehabilitated by the Los Angeles Aztecs, wanted with Fulham's blessing to leave the London Second Division club in April 1977 to go back to California. The Football League administration accused Fulham of "arrogance," and of acting as a mere catspaw for an American Club, but it was a little hard on the Aztecs, without whom Best would scarcely have been back in their competition at all.

For Best, when he arrived in Los Angeles in the early summer of 1976, was something of a footballing derelict. The years out of football, the years of drinking, gambling, womanizing, had thickened his girth and taken the edge off his marvelous acceleration. Manchester United, whom he had joined as a shy 15-year-old boy, and whom he had done so much to make the 1968 European Champions, had at last in disgust and despair let him go. He had been playing the odd charity game, making a handful of Fourth Division appearances on a limited basis, in England. But it was the Los Angeles sunshine and, still more, the Los Angeles obscurity which healed him and restored him to soccer. The sheer, soothing anonymity of it all was as important as anything. Whereas in London and Manchester his every step, in his playing days, had been dogged and haunted, absolute strangers insulting him in pubs, in clubs, and in the streets, girls fawning on him, now—as I discovered for myself when interviewing him for television on Hermosa Beach that summer—he could run across the sands, speak in front of a camera, not only untroubled but unrecognized.

"Who's that?" tanned boys on the beach would ask, and, on being told, would answer that they had heard of soccer, but they hadn't heard of Best. Living just above Hermosa Beach, living an easy, undemanding, healthy life, Best regained his appetite for the game. "The standards here," he said, "are good enough to test me. It's not that you can stroll through the games." But it was significant that he had no liking at all for the artificial turf, on which an increasing number of NASL teams play; it was impossible for him to twist and turn as he wished, he said, upon such a surface. Up the coast, at Redondo Beach, the Scottish international forward Charlie Cooke, from Chelsea, expressed his belief that in due course America would get its soccer right, as it got everything else right, in the long run.

The coaching aspect of the game fascinated him; he had just been coaching, with other Aztec players, at a boys' soccer camp, and said the coaching itself was hardly sophisticated, "But by golly, it's very good to see all those sun tanned faces, big smiles and white teeth."

Much groundwork was done in the 1960s and early 1970s by the chief coach of FIFA, Dettmar Cramer, who in fact agreed to become America's chief coach and national team manager, but in 1974 was lured back to West Germany to coach the champions of Europe, Bayern Munich. Understandably, the American soccer association, which has now changed from USSFA to USSF (United States Soccer Federation), was disappointed and embittered. Cramer had, after all, said he would stay for four years. USSF said they would sue him for ten million dollars, Cramer insisted that he had never signed a formal contract, which he hadn't, and the suit was dropped; an unhappy episode. After trying to bring Gordon Jago, the coach of such London clubs as Queens Park Rangers and Millwall, formerly the coach of the defunct Baltimore Bays, the USSF finally appointed as their team coach the Ukrainian-born Walt Chyzowych.

Alas, he could not bring them through to the 1978

World Cup finals. Drawn in an eliminating group against Mexico and Canada, they bravely held the Mexicans to a goalless draw in Los Angeles, thanks in no small measure to the goalkeeping of Arnold Mausser of the Tampa Bay Rowdies, had a 2-0 victory over the Canadians, but were eventually obliged to play off against them in Haiti where, despite Chyzowych's optimism, they lost 3-0; the very score Chyzowych had forecast in favor of America.

Again, the U.S.A. did not disgrace itself—as it had when a motley selection lost 10-0 to Italy in Rome on tour in 1975, and prompted some Italian journalists to write off American soccer and its players with a sneer. In the very first minute of the game in Port-au-Prince, the Americans twice nearly scored. But a long free kick dipped over Mausser's head for Brian Budd to volley Canada's first goal and with twenty minutes left, a stupid foul by the over robust Dallas fullback Steve Pecher had him sent off the field; and expulsion from a soccer field is permanent. The ten Americans played surprisingly well for a while, but eventually conceded two more goals.

For all the difficulty of his foreign name, for all the eagerness of the NASL and its leaders to destroy the ethnic "image," Chyzowych was brought up in the States from early boyhood, and it is no bad thing to have an American coach in charge of the American team. Indeed, one of the interesting features of the NASL itself has been the emergence of American coaches. Terry Fisher was only twenty-five when the Los Angeles Aztecs chose him in 1975. Al Miller was the first of them, and he had the distinction of winning the NASL at his first attempt with the Philadelphia Atoms in 1973. In 1976 he became coach to the Dallas Tornado, succeeding the Englishman Ron Newman, a former Portsmouth outside left, who had done yeoman work coaching the young around Dallas, and who now took over the newly established Los Angeles Skyhawks in the American Soccer League.

This marked a new era of expansion in the ASL, which had in the past been primarily an Eastern seaboard affair. Founded in 1921, but going through any number of incarnations in the ensuing half-century, it could, as Newman himself suggested, perhaps provide the equivalent of a national Second Division for American soccer, though the decision to appoint one of their clubs' coaches to be League president raised eyebrows, and it would obviously take time for the ASL to match the NASL in durability. The expenses of a nation-wide contest in so huge a country as the United States are scarcely small.

One should not leave the subject of American coaches without paying tribute to the admirable work of Bill Jeffrey, the little Scottish-born manager of the American World Cup team which humiliated England at Belo Horizonte, Brazil, in 1950.

Jeffrey came to the States in the early 1920s, worked on the railroad and played soccer for the company team. After a match against a local eleven at State College, Pa., where Penn State is, Jeffrey played so impressively that he was asked to coach the college soccer team on a "temporary" basis. He stayed there for several decades, meanwhile teaching in the machine shop at the college's school of engineering, tirelessly lecturing to civic groups and high school pupils. His success with the Penn State team itself was remarkable. Between 1932 and 1941 it was undefeated in sixty-five consecutive games. Victory against England was the crown of his career, even though his jubilant assertions that this would make the game "take off" in the States were premature.

The club owners of 1967 were criticized in Europe for

trying to impose the game "from the top." I thought at the time and still feel now that this criticism was thoroughly unfair. Since the game had so manifestly failed to take wing "from the bottom," it was surely worth trying to bring it before the public at a reasonably high standard. And so, indeed, it proved. Whether the likes of Woosnam, Toye, and Newman will ever full reap the fruits of their labors I do not know, but there is no doubt that they have made it possible for others in the future to do so, no doubt that the concomitant of all the activity at NASL level has been an astonishing proliferation of the game among the young, the creation of an ever growing base.

There are clearly a number of reasons why soccer at this level has been found to be far from an Un-American Activity. It is, in the first place, physically democratic. Size matters hardly at all, except that a man weighing over 185 pounds, unless he be a goalkeeper or a stopper, tends to be at a disadvantage. Soccer is not mere strength or bulk or even speed—some huge American football players can be remarkably fast. It is a game of stops and starts, twists and turns. You can be as tiny as Billy Bremner—five foot five and captain of Scotland's 1974 World Cup side, eulogized as a halfback and skipper by Pelé—and still excel. In American football and basketball, as we know, it is almost impossible to do so unless you are physically huge; even a freak.

Soccer, moreover, is inexpensive to play. It is still said in Britain, and elsewhere, that ball skills are learned with tennis balls, tin cans, bundles of rags; in the playground rather than on the practice fields. The dazzling products of the sordid *favelhas* of Rio, not to mention its beaches, testify to that fact. By contrast, American football demands heavy expenditure on helmet, padding, and the rest, while many American parents have been appalled and alarmed by the incidence of serious injury. All these things, plus the important consideration that it is truly an international sport from which Americans have been excluded, have brought about a new, more positive attitude and climate. The way to eventual success is still hard and long, but I have little doubt, to quote Charlie Cooke, that America will ultimately "get it right."

Ten years ago, who would ever have believed that soccer would "catch on" in Portland, that more than 50,000 fans would pack the new Seattle Kingdome, in 1976, to watch Pelé and the Cosmos, that the USSF could put on a Bicentennial Tournament with England, Italy, Brazil, and Team America which attracted large, enthusiastic crowds?

It was, alas, a sad and significant thing that Team America was made up almost wholly of foreign "mercenaries." Twenty-six years after the U.S.A.'s victory over England in the World Cup, that mighty country found itself obliged to play them in Philadelphia with a team which included four Englishmen, among them the ex-captain of England, Bobby Moore, an Ulsterman, a Welshman, and a Scot, while only three native-born Americans, Bob Rigby, in goal, Bobby Smith, at fullback, and Chandler, as a substitute, got on the field. Where were the new John Souzas?

On the face of it, it may have seemed that American soccer was going back, rather than forward, though I cannot believe this is so. I would rather see these as important transitional years in which a bridge is built between today's foreign "mercenaries" and the young Americans who will in due course take their place. It may be a long time before the United States again reaches a World Cup semi-final, but when they do, we can be sure that it won't be with a team largely made up of naturalized Britons!

The watershed, the *annus mirabilis*, was unquestionably 1977, whose extraordinary developments could not be even dimly discerned ten years before. Who could have imagined the New York Cosmos playing before a crowd of 77,000 at the Meadowlands Stadium in New Jersey? Who could have imagined the Minnesota Kicks, in Bloomington, heart of the Midwest, drawing an average crowd not far short of 30,000? Who could have foreseen the arrival of Franz Beckenbauer, European Footballer of the Year, in New York?

New York. The quest, the key, the Grail, the enigma. Conquer New York, and American soccer could surely conquer America. So I had thought in that torrid New York summer of 1967; yet how far off such conquest seemed. Manlio Scopigno, Cagliari's coach, may have murmured skeptically, "Ci arriveranno" (They'll get there), but how, and when?

There can be no doubt that the decisive factor was the New York Cosmos' move to New Jersey, to Giants Stadium, whose novelty, comfort, and highly publicized allure drew spectators who would previously not have dreamed of attending soccer matches; not even at Yankee Stadium. As the Cosmos, after a shocking start, rose from their bed of convalescence to challenge for, and ultimately to win, the NASL title, so the attendance crowds at Giants Stadium rose first to an astonishing 50,000 plus, then an inconceivable 77,000. Pelé, of course, had something to do with it, too. Indeed, he played his farewell game at Giants Stadium, to the accompaniment of an orchestrated furor which may have nauseated the true lover of soccer, but appeared to satisfy the crowd. The sight and sound of Pelé intoning hoarsely, "Love! Love! Love!" plumbed depths of vulgarity seldom known in soccer, and the massive scoreboard became an accomplice after the grisly fact, as it flashed up the word in letters of fire. Pelé, by his own confession, had come to New York because he was two

146

and a half million dollars in the hole, thanks to unlucky commercial involvements; love had very little to do with it. Still, the presence of so transcendent and undoubted a star, albeit one who had been taken out of mothballs, was of immense help to the development of the NASL, and American soccer.

Beckenbauer was not taken out of mothballs. Money lured him—a mere couple of million dollars, as opposed to Pelé's four and a half—but he was tempted, too, by the thought that his life would be less hounded. He had just left his wife, and children, in Munich for a blonde young photographer, and he relished, he said, an ambience in which when he went out to eat, he did not read next day in the newspapers just what he had eaten.

There was bitterness in Europe over what the West Germans, and not only they, considered a defection. Beckenbauer, after all, was a major star, one still very nearly at the height of his powers, considered a key player in West Germany's bid to retain the World Cup in Argentina.

Beckenbauer must have known well enough when he went that he was saying goodby to his place in the West German team. "I am thirty-two," he said to me in New York, two months before the World Cup began, "what more can I do for Germany?" A great deal more, clearly, as the West Germans had not remotely begun to replace him in the position of attacking sweeper which he himself had invented. There were late, urgent negotiations between the West Germans and the Cosmos, but in vain. Beckenbauer remained in New York; an alarming portent for future World Cups, which would always and inevitably clash with the season of an NASL that was growing steadily richer and stronger.

In 1978, the Cosmos, above all, reached out to capture other, major players. Dennis Tueart, the Manchester

147

City and England winger, and Vladimir Bogicevic, from Red Star, Yugoslavia, cost some $500,000 each. The Cosmos dressing room, when I visited it out at East Rutherford, was a tolerable facsimile of the Tower of Babel. Eddie Firmani, the South African who had previously coached the Tampa Bay Rowdies, and played football in Italy, sat in his own dressing room, shaking his head in despair.

Along the corridor, one found Giorgio Chinaglia—allegedly the chief mover in the appointment the previous season of Firmani, the defenestration of Clive Toye, president, and Gordon Bradley, coach. One found two winning World Cup captains: Carlos Alberto of Brazil (1970) and Franz Beckenbauer of West Germany (1974). One found Dennis Tueart, and another fine left winger, Steve Hunt, who came to Cosmos from Aston Villa as an unknown, and blossomed splendidly into a star in 1977, joining England's Coventry City in the autumn of the following year. One found a Turkish goalkeeper, a few more Brazilians, a Yugoslav or two, a handful of Americans, several of whom didn't hide their displeasure at the way foreign stars were keeping them off the team.

New clubs, new franchises, had sprung into being. The experiments of 1977 in Los Angeles and Hawaii had predictably failed. Now Detroit, Philadelphia, and Boston were reconstituted, in a League which must now do without Pelé. (The Cosmos, selling over 18,000 season tickets before a ball was kicked, were unworried.) In Boston, Liptons, the tea firm which had launched yachting's Lipton Cup—contested between Uruguay and Argentina early this century—now owned the New England Teamen. Silly names such as Rogues, Roughnecks, and Stompers proliferated, a testimony to infantilism rather than invention. Detroit had a new

148

team, the Express, backed largely by English interests. Pop stars put money into the Philadelphia franchise. The attendance figures of the NASL, which had risen so remarkably in 1977, rose once more.

Yet when the 1978 World Cup was played, there was no America. The USA team had been knocked out in Haiti in a play-off, by untrumpeted Canada. There was clearly still far to go, even if, in March 1978, an American Under 20 team impressively won an international tournament in Bellinzona, Switzerland, beating the likes of England's Wolverhampton Wanderers juniors and the Tunisian Under 20 team. Two of the young Cosmos players, Gary Etherington, a winger, and Rick Davis, a center-forward, were prominently involved. A new trend was in evidence. Good young American players—Davis was a predental student—were now eschewing college, and turning pro straight out of high school, aware that four years of stagnant, mediocre college football, probably ill coached, could sabotage their professional careers.

Trevor Francis, the Birmingham City and England forward, signed that summer for the Detroit Express for some $100,000. Birmingham and its young manager, Jim Smith, were pleased to let it happen, reckoning that this was a way, perhaps the only way, to keep Francis. Others of us wondered how long such players, under such physical and psychological pressure, could go on, so to speak, serving God and Mammon. There was much bitter feeling in England when Charlton Athletic, the South East London Second Division team, allowed two of their best players, Mike Flanagan and Colin Powell, to join the New England Teamen on loan, long before the English season finished. Charlton, in consequence, missed relegation by a touch. "The more we help the Americans," said one embittered English coach to me, "the more they'll kick us in the teeth." Flanagan was a huge success in Boston, once scoring five goals in a single game.

Meanwhile, in the United States itself, there were critics who looked anxiously on the Cosmos and their intention, announced by the knowledgeable Ertegun brothers, proprietors of Atlantic Records, to build the best team in the world. Where would that leave the other NASL teams? The secretary of FIFA, Helmut Käser, publicly upbraided the NASL owners for caring nothing about the game, for having no criterion but money. In many instances, that might be true; but who could be more knowledgeable than the Erteguns, devotees of world football since the 1930s, when they were schoolboys in London? There were manifestly shoals ahead.

The Cosmos retained their NASL title in 1978, but their victory emphasized some of the less satisfactory aspects of the competition. Their exceedingly expensive team duly won its Conference title to reach the play-offs, adding Seninho, the Angolan-born striker from Porto of Portugal, to the attack, and Giuseppe Wilson of Lazio, Rome, to the defense. Yet the team plunged to a humiliating 9-2 defeat before 45,863 spectators in Minnesota, where the former Middlesbrough center forward from England, Alan Willey, scored five of the goals. Eddie Firmani, the Cosmos coach, was incensed by his team's flabby performance. The system was such, however, that goal difference did not count, so that a win by any margin at all for Cosmos in the return game at East Rutherford would put the teams level. This duly happened, Cosmos winning 4-0. Moreover, equality meant that the so-called "mini-game" of half-an-hour which followed should be played at once, on the Cosmos field; a manifest advantage to them. They won this 1-0, on a shoot-out. No wonder FIFA, the world body, was making ominous noises about the NASL's manipulation of the laws of soccer.

The Cosmos now went on to the Conference finals, where Tampa Bay, Fort Lauderdale (who had acquired the errant George Best from Los Angeles), and Portland awaited them. That a League tournament should be concluded on the basis of a Cup, knock-out, competition is itself the most blatant contradiction in terms, the negation of the point and spirit of League football, but here, as in other instances, the NASL has elevated drama and spectacle above tradition and logic.

So the Cosmos found their way into the Final, against Tampa Bay, who were forced at the last moment to play without their best forward, the English veteran Rodney Marsh, whose leg injury had turned septic. Thanks to a couple of goals by the English international Dennis Tueart and one by Giorgio Chinaglia, Cosmos won the game 3-1, in front of over 70,000 fans, on their own field—once again. Yet perhaps the most significant event followed the Final when Steve Hunt, the young Cosmos left winger, left them to play English First Division soccer for Coventry City, though it meant a sharp cut in salary. The challenge of making a name where soccer was real and earnest, rather than a strange, slow summer game, was too tempting to be resisted. Tueart said he quite understood how Hunt felt. "He knows that, whatever acclaim anyone gets here, you have to have done it all first in a league where the competition is really tough."

5
COACHES AND MANAGERS

The tantalizing thing about soccer's coaches and managers is that nobody is ever quite sure what they *do*. Did things happen despite them or because of them? In this connection, I always remember a meeting early in 1955 with Bela Guttmann, a famous Hungarian coach, or manager, as the English would term it, in a restaurant in Rome. Guttmann, who had been an outstanding center half in Austro-Hungary in the 1920s, was in a dejected mood, and with reason. He had just been sacked by the Milan football club, though they held first position in the Italian Championship.

"I shall have a clause in my next contract," he said, "not to be dismissed when the team is top of the League." He then, with a fine irony, told the story of Lucchese and its manager. Some years earlier the Tuscan club, then in the Italian First Division, but one of its weaker teams, had to go to Turin to play the mighty Juventus. On the journey, "their coach, poor fellow, died." Given the talismanic importance placed on coaches—*allenatori*—in Italy, it was clearly unthinkable that Lucchese could go into battle on the Sunday without one. Desperate phone calls were made all over Italy until a new *allenatore* was found. On Sunday he took his place on the bench, Lucchese forced a surprising 1-1 draw; and carried the new coach off the field on their shoulders.

The interaction of footballers with their coaches would provide splendid material for a thesis in group psychology. In the 1930s, Vittorio Pozzo was a stern father figure to the Italian national team, while Herbert Chapman, his friend, as manager of the London club Arsenal, was worshipped by his players. "He told you how to dress," one of them, Eddie Hapgood, an England captain and left back, once told me with fervor, "he told you how to tie your tie." But his partner in so many Arsenal and England teams, George Male, said to me in the 1960s that modern players would not stand for the way Chapman treated his men.

With Barcelona and Internazionale of Milan, the Argentinian Helenio Herrera, brought up in poverty in Morocco, had his players stamping up and down in the dressing room, chanting slogans. They swore by him and, at Inter, became champions of Europe and the world. But by the time he got to Roma, and the capital, in the 1970s, there were those such as the Roma president, a Communist millionaire, Alvaro Marchini, who saw Herrera as an exploiter and a poseur.

Alf Ramsey, Old Stone Face, when he was manager of England's World Cup winning team of 1966 was adored by his players, largely disliked by the press, but he unquestionably created the morale and the tactics whereby England's not truly exceptional team won the tournament. Some five years later, though, he did not even bother personally to inform Geoff Hurst, who had run himself to exhaustion in the English cause, that he was dropping him from the team; while by 1974, his tactical approach seemed ossified.

The problem is that there are so many different ways of being coach, or manager, while there is an immense difference between coaching a club and coaching an international team. Don Revie discovered as much when in 1974 he left Leeds United, the Yorkshire club with which he had had years of steady success, to take over the England team, and suddenly found himself cut off from the invigorating, warm day-to-day contacts of club football, and its myriad games. It was particularly hard for a man with an obsessive, superstitious temperament, a man who wore the same suit to game after game, a man who, once having left his house on the morning of a Saturday match, "could" not return for any reason.

Again, the concept of managers—or coaches—has changed so much over the years. In England, till well into the 1950s, the manager was a curiously remote figure who seldom left his office during the week. The idea of his putting on a tracksuit would have been absurd, though in most cases he was a former professional footballer. As late as 1963, an England player, on a tour of Europe, told me that *his* club manager was so seldom seen at training that when he was the players would say, "They must be mucking out the stable again."

Dismissed by Milan, Guttmann went on in the early 1960s to become coach to the brilliant Benfica team of Lisbon which twice won the European Cup, the major team tournament of Europe. There is no doubt that *he*, in his shrewd, wry, Central European way, was an excellent manager-coach, skilled alike in handling players and tactics. These are two very different functions, while a third, that of wheeling and dealing in the transfer market, is very different again. British managers have traditionally been expected to perform this function, an expectation which has persisted even into the present, when they are also expected to go out and train their players; a job once left to the trainer himself, a menial, unimaginative figure by and large. For the most part, he sent his players toiling around and around the football field to build stamina, seldom allowing them a look at the ball, on the perverse rationalization that the less they saw it during the week, the more they would be pleased to have it on Saturday.

Chapman as a manager, however, was certainly something very special. With Pozzo and the Austrian Hugo Meisl, he formed something of a European triumvirate, united by mutual esteem and affection. Whereas Pozzo and Meisl, however, were highly educated Europeans who had played the game only a little, Chapman, a Yorkshireman, had been a pro footballer, though an undistinguished one, noted chiefly for the curious yellow color of his boots.

While in the reserves of the North London club, Tottenham Hotspur, he suddenly had the chance to become player-manager of little Northampton Town—a club then outside the English League—because the Tottenham center half, Walter Bull, had been offered the job and didn't want it.

He was an immediate success, and from then until his early death in 1934, there was only one stumble. Just after World War I, the Leeds City club, of which he was manager, was accused of making illegal payments to players during the war. The offence was largely a technical one, but Chapman burned the club's books to protect the players, was thrown out of football, took a factory job for a while, was amnestied, and came back to turn another Yorkshire team, Huddersfield Town, till then wholly undistinguished, into the best in England. In 1925 Arsenal persuaded him to come to London. They, too, were undistinguished, but Chapman bought Charlie Buchan, the veteran international inside forward, from Sunderland, in a typically adventurous transfer which guaranteed Sunderland £100 (a lot of money then) for every goal Buchan scored. Buchan elaborated the Third Back Game in a tactical revolution, and Arsenal went on to dominate English football.

Chapman had an astonishing capacity to see the possibilities in people, then to convince them they could fulfill them. Tom Whittaker, who hobbled back to Highbury, where Arsenal played, a cripple after breaking a leg on tour in Australia, Chapman visualized as a trainer; and Whittaker became an extraordinary trainer, a born healer who, in days before treatment was a matter of sound waves and electronics, sent injured players back onto the field in a fraction of the time it would normally take.

When Chapman called George Male into his office to tell him he wanted him to play right back, Male was a moderate left half. By the time he'd left the office, he said afterwards, he was not only convinced that he could play right back; he was sure he would be the best right back in the world. Tactics *did* interest Chapman; unlike so many managers of his era. He held a weekly team conference, and devoted one of them almost entirely to analyzing why Arsenal should not have given away the single goal they did, after they had won a notable victory. On another occasion he broke an umbrella stand in his enthusiasm.

Pozzo came from the mountains of Piedmont. He was a runner till a friend, Goccione, later the first center half for Juventus, told him, "You're very fast, but when you run you look so foolish, just like a motor car: with nothing in front of you." Pozzo was converted to soccer; but slowly. Museums and mountains for some years engaged him still more.

Only when he went to study in England, after attending the International School of Commerce in Zurich, did the sport get its grip on him. He became a passionate follower of Manchester United, who then had the legendary Billy Meredith at outside right, Charlie Roberts as its dominant, attacking center half. Roberts was Pozzo's hero. One day he waited outside the stadium and shyly asked if they could talk. They did; many times. Out of these talks was born Pozzo's concept of football, which he would apply with such success more then twenty-five years later, winning the World Cup twice with Italian teams which scorned the more "modern" third back game.

His parents summoned him back to Piedmont. Pozzo refused. His father cut off his allowance. He made a living by teaching languages all over the Midlands; and went on watching Manchester United. When they did lure him home, it was by a trick, sending him a round trip ticket to attend his sister's wedding, then refusing to allow him to go back to England. Pozzo kept the unused half of the ticket for the rest of his life.

His loss, however, was Italian football's gain. A small, sturdy, bushy-haired, authoritarian figure, with a certain almost child-like egotism, a love for posturing in pictures, Pozzo worked selflessly in Italian football for over forty years. He took an Italian team to the 1912 Olympics at the last moment where it gave Finland a close game, beat the hosts, Sweden, in the consolation tournament, then succumbed 5-1 to Hugo Meisl's Austria.

Relations between Rome and Vienna were thoroughly bad, but Pozzo and Meisl, meeting for the first time in Stockholm, decided to arrange another game in Turin the following Easter between Juventus and the Vienna Amateur Sports Club.

The prefect of Turin sent for Pozzo. "Have you ever been in a lunatic asylum?" he demanded. "So many towns in Italy, and you have to choose Turin!"

Early on the morning of the game, half the garrison of Turin was mobilized, but there was no trouble. Indeed the game was played in a spirit of almost excessive cordiality, players shaking hands if they injured one another. Not all future games between Italy and Austria would be as genial. "When I see Sindelar, I see red!" said Monti, Italy's ruthless center half of the 1934 World Cup, to Pozzo, of Austria's famous center forward. Once, in Vienna, he struck him.

Pozzo became a major in the Alpine Regiment in World War I, and did not resume control of the Italian team, as Commissario Tecnico, till the Parisian Olympics of 1924. Soon afterwards, his wife died, and he resigned the post, taking it up five years later to hold it for over twenty years.

He brooked no nonsense. Even after he'd finally resigned from his position, he snapped at one famous, recalcitrant Italian forward, Benito Lorenzi, "Take that cigarette out of your mouth; and stand to attention while you talk to me!" And while he wasn't a Fascist, there's no doubt that he shrewdly exploited the bloated chauvinism of the time to build his team's morale.

When players had clashed in a League match, his remedy was usually to have them share a room together. They would come to him separately to complain; he would tell them that he knew all about it, "But we have to build a team. You must convince yourself that this man is not an enemy but a friend."

The following morning, his Teddy bear head would appear around the door. "Well, cannibals, have you eaten each other yet?"

Embarrassed grunts. Subsequently each player would usually approach him in turn. "He's not such a bad fellow. It was the crowd who set me against him."

Hugo Meisl, too, tended to be an authoritarian, a

man of formidable intellectual and moral force. He had Chapman's ability to draw the best out of his subordinates; a gift never more clearly shown than in the case of the little Lancastrian Jimmy Hogan who came to him in Vienna as a coach in 1912, simply couldn't put his ideas across initially, but was inspired by Meisl to lay the basis of the postwar *Wunderteam* with its elegant, short passing style, based on the Scottish game.

Meisl came from a wealthy Jewish family, so displeased by his passion for soccer that it "banished" him to Trieste, then still part of the Austrian Empire. Meisl maintained contact while there with a leading Viennese player, Johann Leute, returned to Austria for military service, was subsequently placed in a leading bank, but spent most of his time there, just as he had done when placed in charge of a factory, attending to the correspondence of the Austrian Football Federation. He spoke some eight languages, put large sums of money into the development of the Austrian game, and found his ideal lieutenant in Hogan, who had been imbued by Scottish footballers, while playing inside right for Fulham (the South West London club) with a perfectionist's concept of the game.

Both believed in artistry, ball control, subtlety, the triumph of sheer skill over force. "Don't kick it, stroke it, don't kick it, strike it!" Hogan heard a Viennese exhorting some football playing boys as he walked through the streets one evening. The players he had at his command were largely university students, men of a far higher cultural level than the pros he had known at home, and once he had found the way through to them, they eagerly assimilated his ideas.

Previously, he had coached in Holland, at Dordrecht, in 1910. "Don't leave their center forward!" he instructed his center half, before one game. At half-time he found them in the buffet, enjoying a drink and a cigarette. "You told me not to leave him!" said the center half.

Hogan spent the war years interned in Budapest, where he became an enormously successful coach; so much so that when, in November 1953, Hungary's team came to Wembley to thrash England 6–3, Hogan sat in the Royal Box as their guest. He was never accorded the same respect in England. "Get the ball in the bloody net, that's all I'm interested in!" said the chairman of Aston Villa, a club with an immense tradition of classical football, when Hogan became their manager in 1936. A few months earlier, he had taken to the Final of the Olympics in Berlin an Austrian amateur team most of whose players were half-starved, in those bleak Depression years, when first he took them over.

"People abroad laugh at me when I express the opinion that the British footballer is still the most natural in the world," he said in 1931, after disastrous European tours by both England and Scotland, "but his love and talent for the game have been sadly neglected. . . . We are absolutely out of date as regards our training ideas, and the sooner we realize it, the better." To be fair, the English Football Association did proceed to make him their first Chief Coach shortly before the war, but it would be a long time until the English came around to the idea of coaching, which was something they regarded as being for untutored foreigners, and when in the 1950s coaching did at last gather impetus and strength, it tended to turn into a new orthodoxy. For every naturally gifted teacher there were a dozen oafs mouthing jargon about "peripheral vision," "blind side running," and "environmental awareness."

A few years after World War I, Hogan and Meisl came through one major tactical and ideological crisis when their national team was thrashed 5-0 in Nuremburg on a snow-covered field by Southern Germany. On the fifteen-hour return journey, Meisl and the players ceaselessly argued over whether their Vienna School tactics, so ineffectual in the snow, were truly valid. Should they give up the old, traditional Scottish game, which even the Scots themselves were steadily abandoning, for more direct and physical methods? Meisl thought they shouldn't and he finally won his argument.

England, believe it or not, didn't appoint an international team manager till 1946, though at half-time in the first ever Italy vs. England game in Rome in 1933, Pozzo found his friend Chapman coming out of the English dressing room in shirt-sleeves. Asked what he was doing, for he had no official role, Chapman replied, "The same thing as you're doing for *your* team."

Wales, though, had the extraordinary Ted Robbins, the secretary of their Association, a man who could pull obscure players out of the hat like a conjurer with rabbits, and talk them into being splendid internationals, the man who had established soccer in South Wales despite tremendous opposition from Rugby Football. "Get your legs under the table!" he would tell a shy new player. "I'll be your father!" His job was enormously complicated by the fact that the English League clubs for whom most of his best men played were under no obligation to release players for Wales; and often churlishly didn't. This sometimes left Robbins with half a team a couple of days before a match against the likes of Scotland. On one famous occasion he filled it up with obscure players, some were not even with League clubs, went up to Scotland and forced a draw! The explanation was that thanks to Robbins and what in American sport would be called his "psyching," Welsh players were utterly transformed as soon as they pulled on the red jersey. Thus the Welsh, astoundingly, were quite the equal of England and Scotland in the British Championship, right through the 1930s, giving as good as they got despite their small pool of players.

A superb coach of international teams, Jimmy Hogan had unhappy experiences as an English club master both with Aston Villa and with his former club, Fulham, who sacked him while he was lying ill in a hospital; Hugo Meisl swiftly recalled him to manage the Olympic team. George Raynor, the little Yorkshireman, had much the same experience. He was a moderate Third Division footballer in the 1930s, driving a coal cart in the summer to make ends meet, but he found his true vocation when on army service in Iraq during the war. In Sweden, his ebullience, his honesty, his precise, productive individual coaching, soon won him respect. He was tactically shrewd as well, and after being given a cold reception by the Swedish press, quickly impressed them by devising a plan to beat the Swiss bolt system of defense, explaining it before the game, then seeing his team score six goals. "After that, I was a little king pin," he said. "Before it, I was just a poor fish."

He traveled the country, coaching, lecturing, and explaining, won the 1948 Olympic title with his team, rebuilt it to take third place in the 1950 World Cup in Brazil, and was back in Sweden to get his team to the Final of the 1958 World Cup.

In season 1954–55, I was in Rome when he had a torrid season, in that Byzantine world of intrigue and counter-plot, enabling Lazio to stay out of the Second Division, having taken the team over when it was in dire straits. But when he went back to England and became manager of Coventry City, then a Third Division club, it was another world, demanding other attributes, and his time there was uncongenial. "A good manager for a happy team," they called him in Sweden; but he was shrewd enough to take that team to Budapest in 1953 and gain a 2-2 draw against Hungary with his methods, only weeks before they went to Wembley and trounced England. The best international coaches have often tended to be guerilla generals.

Matt Busby, by contrast, had only brief experience of managing his native Scotland, and then on a part-time basis, but as manager of Manchester United, whom he took over after the war when their old Trafford ground had been devastated by German bombs, he had more success than any manager in English football's history; Chapman included.

An elegant halfback with Liverpool and Manchester City in the 1930s and 1940s, Busby had two great attributes: he was a splendid judge of a player, and he was enormously successful in establishing himself, like Chapman, as a father figure. He was also, in his early managerial days, one of the first British managers to put on a track suit and go out to coach. He was never a great tactician; very suitably for the manager of a Manchester club, he was a believer in *laissez-faire*; get the best players you could, put them on the field, and allow them, by and large, to get on with it. It brought Manchester United the English League, on various occasions, the English Cup in 1948 and 1963, and the European Cup in 1968; the only time, at the moment of writing (1977), that an English team has ever won it. Moreover it was Busby who defied the absurdly chauvinist and insular Football League to enter for that trophy in 1956, when the League was trying to bully and dissuade all English clubs from taking part in it.

He was not a democrat; players who attended his team talks were expected to listen rather than participate. But his readiness to give young players their fling at a time when most clubs preferred a middle-aged caution was at once refreshing and outstandingly successful. His excellent teams of the late 1950s were known as The Busby Babes. Alas, on February 6, 1958, on their way back from a match in Belgrade, Busby's team crashed in an Elizabethan aircraft at Munich Airport, in the snow. Manchester United lost no fewer than eight of their players, while two more never played for them again. Busby himself was severely injured, but with characteristic courage fought his way back to health, took over the team again, and rebuilt it into a side quite as good as any he had had before. It is still painfully tempting, however, to speculate on what his Busby Babes of 1958 might have become had they been spared.

Curiously enough Bill Shankly, Busby's partner at wing halfback in several Scottish international wartime teams—a period in which they were regularly hammered by the English—also became a most successful manager—with Liverpool. Whereas Busby went straight to Manchester United in 1945, his first office a mere corrugated iron hut in a corner of ruined Old Trafford, Bill Shankly served an apprenticeship with several lesser League clubs—Grimsby and Huddersfield (fallen on bleak times) among them—before arriving at Liverpool, where he became something of, as they say, a living legend.

"Some people say football's a matter of life and death," was one of his *mots*, "but it's more important than that."

It's said that in his days as manager of Huddersfield, he once rounded up a group of players in training and told them to come back to the stadium with him. Once arrived, he distributed white shirts to four or five of them—"You're England!"—and blue shirts, the Scottish color, to the rest, himself among them—"We're Scotland!"

They played, on a miniature ground. Twice the then

164

17-year-old left winger Mike O'Leary, who later played for England, "roasted" Shankly and went on to score for "England." On the second occasion, Shankly hissed at him, "Do that again, and I'll break your leg!"

A short, blond, stocky man of pungent opinions and unwavering certitude, "Shanks" took Liverpool out of the Second Division of the English League, into the first, and made them a great power in European football. Moreover, like Manchester United and Revie's Leeds United, they simply went on and on and on. "There are two great teams in Liverpool," Shankly would rumble, carefully ignoring mighty Everton, the city's most distinguished club, "Liverpool and Liverpool reserves."

It became hard to distinguish between those stories about him which were apocryphal, and those which were true. It was alleged that during the freezing winter of 1963 he was once seen with his wife attending a Fourth Division night game. When someone remonstrated with him for bringing the poor woman out on a night like this, he replied, "It's her birthday." Allegedly, again, when someone tried to authenticate the story with him, he answered, "Och, no it wasnae her birthday. It was our anniversary."

Playing first for a Scottish junior team with the delightful name of the Glenbuck Cherrypickers, he made his name with Preston North End in England, and helped them to win the 1938 Cup Final at Wembley with a penalty in the last minute of extra time, given away by the rugged Huddersfield Town center half, Alf Young, and converted by George Mutch.

"I stood next to Alf Young while we were getting our medals," Shankly told me, some thirty years later. "Tears were rolling down his cheeks. I turned to him and I said, 'Ay, and that's no' the first one you've given away.' "

Tactically shrewd rather than original, a hard man on a player who wasn't giving him what he wanted—"He can treat you like dirt at times," one of them, who had been in both favor and disfavor, complained to me—Shankly was so fanatically devoted to football at large and Liverpool in particular that his decision to resign his managership in 1975 came as a thunderclap. It is still a little obscure why he did it; financial panic—the economy was in a troubled state—pressure from his wife; who can say? All one can know with certainty is that—as one might have predicted—he became a ship without a rudder or, to vary the metaphor, a ghost haunting by turn Liverpool's Anfield, and Everton's training ground, nearby his home.

Even the much smoother and more diplomatic Busby found it hard to let go. United's first and second attempts to appoint a manager to serve under Busby's aegis were disastrous. Wilf McGuinness, once a Busby Babe at left half, went white in his brief term of management. Frank O'Farrell arrived from Leicester to find that Busby intended to stay in his large office and keep O'Farrell in a much smaller one at the back. O'Farrell dug his heels in. It was a bad beginning, and things got no better; it is hard to delegate power.

Shankly detested Helenio Herrera, manager of the Internazionale team which so dubiously beat them in the European Cup semifinal in May 1965. Liverpool had won the first leg at Anfield, playing only three days after they'd won the English Cup Final at Wembley, but Inter beat them 3-0 in the return with the help of two deeply dubious goals conceded by the Spanish referee. Shankly especially resented the one scored by Mario Corso, directly from what had been given by the referee as an *indirect* free kick.

There is no doubt that Internazionale was decisively

favored by referees on a number of occasions in European and even Intercontinental competition, no doubt that the club employed the Hungarian refugee Dezso Solti who, a decade later, was belatedly thrown out of European football by the ruling European Union of Football for trying to bribe a referee to favor another Italian club, Juventus. But although controversy unfailingly followed Herrera around, and though he had made many enemies in his troubled career, it is equally undeniable that he has had great success, in Italy and Spain alike.

Brought up in Morocco in the slums of Casablanca, though born in Argentina, Herrera was a moderate professional footballer in France, a coach of consequence in Spain, and it was from Barcelona that the oil millionaire, Angelo Moratti, president of Inter, brought him to Milan.

Herrera believed in hectoring his players, bombarding them with written and verbal slogans: ATTACK: MORE THAN A HUNDRED GOALS! DEFENSE: LESS THAN THIRTY GOALS! He drove his players very hard, trained them to a hair, schooled them in a *catenaccio* (great big chain) system which relied on the counterattack and "mean" defensive play, hauled them into *ritiro* (training camp) for the monastic bulk of every week.

There were some odd episodes in his years with Inter. When only players of Italian descent were allowed to come to Italy and take part in the Championship, Inter signed a Portuguese medical student from Coimbra named Humberto, and produced an Italian who signed a notarized statement to the effect that he was the boy's "real" father. Needless to say, Humberto was not entirely pleased. Herrera believed in pre-match rituals. When Barcelona was competing in the European Cup, he was said to put his players through a ceremony which ended with each of them putting his hand on a football and chanting: "The European Cup! We *must* have it, we *will* have it!"

He never made any secret of his passion for money, and when in 1968 Inter finally dropped the pilot, he went south to take charge of Roma at 100 million lire a season; an enormous salary at the time, though before long Herrera was demanding more. The Roman journalists ate out of his hand, as had the Milanese sporting journalists. The Roman crowd, notorious since the days of the Roman Empire and scarcely less volatile today, was utterly bewitched by him. At the end of one season, Roma lost at home in the Olympic Stadium 2-1 to Bologna, finished the season in eleventh place; and hundreds of their fans swarmed on to the field to carry Herrera off in triumph. Shades of Bela Guttmann's story of Lucchese!

Alvaro Marchini, the Communist president of Roma, wrote most bitterly of this and other events in his dealings with Herrera in his autobiography; above all of the sad case, the pathetic death, of Giuliano Taccola. This was a young, eager center forward who in March 1969 collapsed and died in the dressing-room after a match at Cagliari, Sardinia, in which in fact he had not taken part. But that very morning, Herrera had had Taccola out on the beach with the other players training in a biting cold wind, although he had been informed by a consultant doctor that the player had a heart murmur. Herrera, according to Marchini, had refused to believe anything of the sort, insisting that "the doctors understand nothing! . . . Taccola is an athlete!" It was a wretched and distressing episode.

Herrera himself terminated his career with Roma— who sacked him under Marchini, then took him back again when Marchini left—as the result of a heart attack, but in December 1976 he returned to football as "consultant" to Rimini, in the Second Division. For better or worse, he had made a huge impact on the game, and it is only fair to say that not only many of his best players but also such well-known English coaches as Dave Sexton and Malcolm Allison much admired him.

The case of Helmut Schoen, West Germany's team coach, winner of the World and the European Nations Cup yet perennially criticized and denigrated at home, shows how hard it is to assess a coach or manager and how difficult it can sometimes be, if he has not Herrera's flair and flamboyance, for him to assert himself and win public confidence. The going story during the 1974 World Cup was that the West German captain, Franz Beckenbauer, had Schoen in his pocket and was virtually running the team. Beckenbauer meanwhile was in private eulogizing Schoen and paying tribute to his abilities. The truth of the matter is surely that Schoen had the courage and imagination to change the image of West German football, but could never have done it without Beckenbauer and his genius.

In the 1978 World Cup, there was alas no Beckenbauer to stand by Schoen, whose career ended on a sad, bitter note of anticlimax. Nervously abandoning his previous tactics—two wingers and a center forward—in the dreary opening game against Poland, he thereafter drifted like a rudderless ship, by turns cautious and compromising. For many years, Schoen had labored and languished beneath the shadow of little Sepp Herberger, the dynamic German coach who took control in 1938, won the World Cup in 1954, and bowed out only in 1962. He was a coach cut much more to the pattern of Germanic leaders: forceful, authoritarian, obtrusive. "Look at that!" I heard a German television man say scathingly, as Schoen's face, glum beneath a rain hat, appeared on the screen, during a 1974 World Cup game. "Is this the face of a leader?"

Schoen *was* a leader in his way; a consensus coach, if you like. It was his misfortune that he should lose Beckenbauer at so delicate a moment to New York, and that such other stars as Gerd Müller, Paul Breitner, and Jurgen Grabowski should refuse to play for him.

How much *does* a manager do? In the early 1950s it was fashionable to laud the dazzling Hungarians, yet when their coach, Gyula Mandi, left the country for Israel, he achieved very little. Gusta Sebes, the Deputy Minister of Sports, was said to be the gray eminence of the team, but when Puskás, Kocsis, and Czibo defected in 1956 after the Hungarian Revolution, he was signally unable to rebuild.

Sometimes I am led to think that a soccer coach can do more harm than ever he does good. In the World Cup of 1978, César Luis Menotti, the coach of Argentina, was anything but *dirigiste*. He helped his team by largely leaving them alone, encouraging them to express themselves and attack, as Argentine players prefer, rather than kick opponents and defend, as they'd been doing, by way of over-compensation, in previous World Cups such as 1962 and 1966, under the abrasive leadership of Juan Carlos Lorenzo. Waiting in the wings, as manager of Buenos Aires' Boca Juniors, Lorenzo had his gallery of supporters, who preferred his policies of blood and iron, but Menotti held out, held on, and, in the event, Argentina won.

By contrast, Ernest Happel, the Austrian who coached the Dutch team, was, like Brazil's coach Claudio Coutinho, too rigidly wedded to defensive policies, putting his gifted players in a straitjacket from which they broke out only occasionally. His second in command, the former first choice coach Jim Zwartkruis, an air force officer, publicly criticized him for treating his men as "players rather than human beings."

There is also the question of whether a successful coach at club level will succeed at international level. The jobs are so very different. Men such as Vittorio Pozzo, Hugo Meisl, and Helmut Schoen had no experience of running a club. Enzo Bearzot, Italy's intense and dedicated World Cup coach in 1978, was often sneered at because he had never had charge of a major club team. His performance in getting Italy to Argentina at the expense of England, and almost reaching the Final, proved such critics wrong. As he always said himself, he could not see that one job had the least bearing on the other. The experience of Mike Smith, an Englishman appointed to coach the Welsh international team in 1974, lends strength to Bearzot's argument. Not only had Smith never coached a professional team, he had never even played soccer as a professional, yet he had unusual success with his players, who admired his thoroughness and honesty. He very nearly took them to the 1978 World Cup finals at the expense of Scotland, who beat Wales in Liverpool thanks to a disgracefully unfair penalty decision, the Welsh being punished when a Scots forward actually handled the ball.

By contrast Ally MacLeod, Scotland's team manager, whose life had been spent with professional clubs as player and coach, failed dismally in Argentina, where he was hopelessly out of his depth.

One thing is sure: there is no exact correlation between a coach's playing career and his ability. For every Busby or Shankly there is a Pozzo, Meisl, Raynor, or Jimmy Hogan. Jock Stein, whose Glasgow Celtic teams dominated Scottish football for a decade and won the 1967 European Cup, beating Inter in the Final—to Bill Shankly's joy—was a modest center half who had actually drifted out of League football to play for Llanelly, in

171

Wales, when he was called back to captain Celtic's reserves, and found himself thus launched on a remarkable career as coach.

There are, then, no absolutes, and soccer is so much the better for that. As matters stand, the whole question of coaching—how much the managers and coaches do, why they can succeed in one club and not at another, with a club team but not an international one, remains a tantalizing mystery. Would Pozzo or Chapman succeed today? Was Helmut Schoen a great manager, as his many admirers believe, or a fortunate one, as his detractors would tell you? The image of the Lucchese players, carrying their new manager off the field in Turin, is perhaps the most apposite image.

6
ARE GOALKEEPERS CRAZY?

Goalkeepers, they say in soccer, are crazy. Eccentrics, mavericks, unpredictables, impossible to dragoon, discipline, or domesticate. From "Fatty" Foulke, the 300-pound goalkeeper who picked up offending forwards by their shorts and threw them in the net, through Caxambu, the obscure Brazilian who ate cats to make him supple, to the giant Rumanian Raducanu, who dribbled the ball sulkily around in his area after surrendering too many goals, the lineage is rich and strange and unconventional.

Among soccer players, the goalkeeper is a "loner," the only man allowed to use his hands inside the field of play, the man whose courage and agility can save his team, or the lack of which can condemn it, the one player who knows that almost any error he may make will be irretrievable. In 1927, when Arsenal was playing the Cup Final at Wembley, Dan Lewis, their Welsh international goalkeeper, knelt down to catch a straightforward, easy shot from Ferguson, the Cardiff center forward. Somehow the ball squeezed through his arms, wriggled over the line; and the F.A. Cup went to

Wales. Arsenal decided it might have been his brand new goalkeeper's jersey whose sheen caused the ball to slip; in future whenever they have reached the Cup Final, they have laundered the new jersey before the game. Other goalkeepers, good ones, have been known to prepare to sling the ball out to a colleague; and thrown it inside into their own net.

Playing for England against Scotland at Hampden Park, Glasgow, in May 1976, and still a little dazed from a collision, Ray Clemence of Liverpool let Dalglish's soft shot slip between his open legs: and Scotland won the game. A few weeks later, in New York, it was the legs of Dino Zoff, Italy's goalkeeper and reputedly the best in the world, which were open, as Mike Channon's left-foot shot went through them, to win the game for England. As Disraeli once observed, "The defects of great men are the consolation of dunces."

Bill Foulke was a great man, in every sense. He was originally a coalminer from the mining village of Blackwell, Derbyshire, in the English Midlands. When he played, in the 1890s, in an exhibition match, he punched at a ball, missed, connected instead with the mouth of the illustrious John Goodall, the English international inside right, and knocked out a couple of Goodall's teeth. Derby County wanted him, so did another famous nearby League club in Nottingham Forest, but it was Sheffield United, just across the county border in Yorkshire, which was successful, by the expedient of paying Blackwell, his club, £1 a day—a fair amount of money then—for the remainder of the season. It was a bargain. Foulke went on to help them win the Cup, and to play for England.

He was a violent, an emotional, and a caustic man. When a brash young reserve at Sheffield once demanded, "Why am I always in the second team?"

Foulke mordantly replied, "Because we have no third team, my boy." If, in his opinion, his defenders let him down so that a goal was scored, he would make no attempt to save next time there was a shot at goal. It was said that his Gargantuan stomach was a temptation Steve Bloomer, the most famous goal scorer of the day, could not resist; that twice his fierce right foot drove shots into Foulke's belly, but that the third time it happened, the ball sailed into an empty goal; whence Foulke had fled!

That may or may not be apocryphal. What certainly rings true is the story of Foulke and Harry Hampton, the Aston Villa center forward, well known for his penchant for charging into goalkeepers who had none of the protection from rules and referees they enjoy today. Hampton was not very big, weighing 150 pounds or so, but he was nothing if not aggressive. Once in a game at Villa Park he managed, who knows how, to charge into Foulke and miss him, do a somersault, and end hanging upside down in the goal netting, for all the world like the victim of a *retiarius*. To his anguished appeals for help, extrication, Foulke merely replied over an enormous shoulder, "Tha got oop there, tha can get thysen doon."

A celebrated referee, J. T. Howcroft, told two stories of Foulke's fearful temper. In 1901, after the F.A. Cup Final was held at Crystal Palace, South East London, Foulke was in a rage because he thought—wrongly, as it happens—that a goal scored by Southampton against him had been offside. Stark naked, he padded down the dressing-room corridor, looking for Tom Kirkham, the referee. Frederick Wall, the F.A. secretary, begged him in vain to go back to the dressing room. Howcroft shouted to Kirkham to lock his cubicle door, and this he did in time. "But what a sight!" Howcroft recalled.

"The thing I can never forget is Foulke, six feet tall and tremendous in size, striding along the corridor without a stitch of clothing."

When Chelsea, the South West London club, was formed in 1905, Foulke moved south to become its first goalkeeper; and captain. "Come and see Chelsea's 23 stone (322 pound) goalkeeper!" said sandwich boards carried by a group of derisory fans, when Chelsea arrived to play an away game. "Twenty-three stun!" rumbled Foulke. "I'll give 'em twenty-three stun!" He shuffled his feet, and the men ran away.

"A football wonder is Willie," wrote historians Pickford and Gibson the season he joined Chelsea. "Perhaps the most talked of player in the world. A leviathan with the agility of a bantam. Abnormal yet normal. The cheeriest of companions; brims over with good-humour; and at repartee is as difficult to 'score' against as when between the posts. His ponderous girth brings no inconvenience, and the manner in which he gets down to low shots explodes any idea that a superfluity of flesh is a handicap."

But Foulke, we know, had his darker side, and J. T. Howcroft saw it when he refereed a match at Burslem, between Chelsea and Port Vale. Foulke was in his blackest mood, and when a Burslem forward advanced on goal, he grabbed him round the waist and hurled him into the net. Naturally Howcroft gave a penalty kick. "Then the fun started," he wrote. "It took quite a time to persuade Foulke to get into his proper position, and it seemed to me he was after my scalp. Eventually, J. T. Robertson, captain of the side (*actually its player-manager*), took the bull by the horns and told Foulke either to go into goal or clear out. He did not try to save the shot but stood glaring at me. His face was a picture. I kept a respectable distance until the close of the game, and then made my way quicker than usual to the dressing room. If Foulke had put one of those large hands on me, I might have been short of some part of my anatomy."

Alas, Foulke died a pathetic death. On retirement, the poor fellow could find no better way of earning a living than stopping penalty kicks from holiday-makers at the seaside. There one day he caught a chill, grew worse, and subsequently died.

"There is a proverb which says, 'Before you go to war say a prayer,'" wrote Leigh Richmond Roose, a Welsh doctor, an amateur, another of the great goalkeepers of that period, "'before going to sea say two prayers; before marrying say three prayers.' One might add: Before deciding to become a goalkeeper say four prayers. He's the Aunt Sally."

Dick Roose was known as a practical joker, yet even he could scarcely have perpetrated the joke, if joke it was, played by Bill Foulke on the rest of the Sheffield United team, when they were in special training for a Cup tie.

One morning, the trainers and players, but not Foulke, set off on a run before breakfast. They never did have breakfast. Foulke slipped into the dining room soon after a waiter had put fifteen large English breakfasts, each covered by a silver salver on the table. Foulke ate one. He ate another. He ate all fifteen. When the other players got back, it was to find Foulke sleeping quietly on a sofa, and decided they would eat his breakfast. They sent for the waiter, who told them they were making fun of him; he'd cleared away five minutes ago. It was then that they hurled themselves on Foulke.

The goalkeeper, with his license for acrobatics, his daring, his diving and his leaping, at once became a popular figure on the Continent. When Southampton, before World War I, traveled to Vienna to play they took with them their famous international keeper, Jack Robinson, and the Viennese demanded that he give an exhibition before the game. The Southampton players, tongue in cheek, deliberately placed all their shots within his reach, but the Viennese were mightily impressed, and for years to come they called any spectacular goalkeeping save a Robinsonade.

Goalkeepers of this era were a robust and eccentric lot. There was, for example, Albert Iremonger, who played for the oldest League club of all, Notts County. He stood six feet, four inches, not too tall for a basketball player but very tall indeed for a goalkeeper, played for Notts County for twenty years, was exceedingly thin, wore woolen gloves and a very long, loose jersey. His reach was such that Steve Bloomer, who had, even he, a hard time trying to get the ball past him, remarked that his head reached the crossbar and his arms reached up to Heaven.

All sorts of stories were told about him, some unquestionably embellished in the telling. He was one of those goalkeepers who liked to take penalty kicks. It still happens; as recently as January 1977 in Rome, Christian Piot scored from a penalty kick for Belgium against Italy. One day, so it was said, Albert Iremonger took a penalty kick, hit the crossbar, then had to run like mad to get back to the other end. What happened when he got there is largely a matter of choice. The most exotic version of the story has it that he lashed out desperately and kicked the ball into his own goal.

Iremonger was an excitable fellow. "What we need today," Steve Bloomer remarked before a match, at Meadow Lane, Nottingham, "is a couple of boys with orange-peel behind Albert Iremonger's goal." There were times when Iremonger would leave his goal, trot over to the touchline, and take a throw-in.

Much more sober and scientific in approach was

Harry Rennie, Scotland's fine goalkeeper in the early years of this century. When he was playing for the Glaswegian club, Greenock Morton, it was supposed that the little grandstand was haunted. Gasps and thuds had been heard from the dressing rooms beneath it, at dead of night.

One night, a football fan looked through the window. It was not a ghost, it was Harry Rennie, stripped for football, periodically shouting, "Shoot!" and hurling himself to the wooden boards. He would do this all alone, after training, every day. Another of his penchants in training was to run backwards, an admirable discipline for a goalkeeper who may be caught off his line by a lob. Rennie, least crazy of goalkeepers, had most carefully worked out his positional play—which, with the ability to come out and catch high crosses, is surely the most important aspect of a goalkeeper's art.

He believed in being some twelve yards off the goal line, so he could move diagonally to block shots from the wing, move out to catch a cross, double backwards to deal with a lob. "Open the gate!" the crowd behind the goal would shout as he took up his position, but Rennie knew full well what he was doing.

He also had a theory about what he termed the Shooting Gesture; the drawing back of a player's foot before he shot for goal. Once that "gesture" had been made, Rennie, observing closely, knew whether shot or center was intended.

Sam Hardy, of Liverpool and Aston Villa, who became England's goalkeeper a little later, was a similar, unspectacular, perfectionist, as was Harry Hibbs, England's fine keeper of the 1930s. Both men were only about five feet, nine inches tall, but each was so tremendously skilled in calculating angles that it didn't matter. Hibbs never did have a good name for England, in what was then the premier game, against Scotland, but he was a wonderfully consistent keeper, his positioning so good that often the opposition's fans accused their forwards of shooting straight at him. In truth, it was difficult to avoid him.

Early in 1955, in Rome, the late Giuseppe Moro, a wily fellow who was then the Roma goalkeeper and played numerous times for Italy, told me that he felt a goalkeeper could decide any game with the saves he made, "Not just by encouraging his own side, but by demoralizing the opposition."

Continental goalkeepers were, from the first, protected. Games could die a small death while they picked the ball up, mused on it a little, bounced it about, and finally deigned to kick it up the field. Guarded by referees from the violent onslaughts British keepers were for long exposed to, the European and the Latin American keeper became a kind of licensed acrobat. John Macadam, a well-known Scottish journalist, a great celebrator of Harry Rennie, once described with barely concealed disgust the antics of Aldo Olivieri, Italy's 1938 World Cup winning keeper. Where a British goalkeeper would stoop solicitously to pick up an easy ground shot, Macadam said, one knee up, one knee down, gathering the ball in, a goalkeeper like Olivieri would wait till the last moment, fling himself into the air, then pounce on the ball.

It was partly true, but a little unfair. Olivieri, after all, was the goalkeeper who, in the estimation of Italy's team manager, Vittorio Pozzo, made the most important save of the 1938 World Cup tournament. Italy against Norway at Marseille, Norway and the huge center forward Brunyldsen rampant, the score 1-1, Brunyldsen in front of goal with only Olivieri to beat, a tremendous high shot to Olivieri's right, a stunning reaction, a stupendous save, and Italy in a position to win a game they might have lost. There would scarcely have been any time left to equalize, but thanks to Olivieri the game went into an extra half-hour.

Besides, though Italian goalkeepers, a distinguished breed, have often been spectacular, they have not all been as extrovert as Olivieri, who appalled Macadam by his exhibitionism in a game at Amsterdam, in 1938. Playing a warm-up, for the Rest of Europe, en route to play England, against a weak Dutch team, he had virtually nothing to do, so he called on the two trainers and made them shoot in at him throughout the half-time interval, while he went through his antics.

Carlo Ceresoli, who should have kept goal for Italy in the 1934 World Cup but broke an arm in training, wasn't of that breed, though he could be just as dramatic to watch. Nor was the keeper who did play, and win a medal, in 1934, the accomplished Giampiero Combi. A few months after the World Cup, Ceresoli kept to the Arsenal Stadium at Highbury and played a staggering game against England. The poet Alfonso Gatto wrote of him:

> Ceresoli seemed occupied and preoccupied by his job, in every match. He was expressionless on the field, grey of spirit and of jersey, and with a heavy mien. Then one came to realise that this unawareness of his body, this indifference towards muscle and nerves, were his means of being able to transcend himself in the game, depersonalised and powerful. The whole force of his being seemed concentrated in his eyes, with none left over for his legs and arms which he held rigidly and carefully positioned in the lee of a glance that, seemingly languid and pale, was yet magnetic. From this ambush, he would sally out infallibly; he turned one white with his lightning interceptions and with his furious clearances which he used to watch anxiously before going back to lie in wait again. He was a wild beast in the goal, all

alone, his own shadow: he was everywhere at once, rolling over and over, crawling, diving recklessly into the mêlée, his prey between his hands.

Italy, however, can scarcely have had a better goalkeeper than the sober, dedicated, infinitely honest Dino Zoff, who, on the eve of the 1974 World Cup, had gone over 1100 minutes in international football without conceding a goal. Zoff's saves could be as astonishing, as picturesque, as any Italian goalkeeper's, but the foundation of his game was courage and logic. A northeasterner from Udine, he eventually went as far south as Naples, where the enormous crowds at Fuorigrotta mourned him when he went north again, to Piedmont and Juventus. A professional to the fingertips of his goalkeeping gloves, and always an admirer of England's Gordon Banks, whose one-handed tip over the bar of Pelé's header in Guadalajara, in the 1970 World Cup, remains among the finest saves I shall ever see.

If Europe, in the pioneering stages of the game, admired British goalkeepers, then Britain has admired Europeans. In the early 1930s, Herbert Chapman, manager of Arsenal, tried hard to buy the Viennese baker, Rudi Hiden, to play in North London, but labor regulations frustrated him. Hiden, with Zamora of Spain, was the most highly estimated of all European goalkeepers between the wars, a consummate acrobat who eventually took out French nationality, played for the French international team, then wandered the world, keeping goal even in Russia, until a sad retirement, during which he lost a leg.

Ricardo Zamora's experience in England says much about the fate, what the Italians would call *il dramma*, of the goalkeeper.

Ever since the 1920 Olympics when, young, proud and daring, he conquered the European football public, Zamora had been a hero among goalkeepers. His agility, his authority, his courage, his consistency made him remarkable. He was in goal for Spain when, on a hot Madrid afternoon in 1929, they became the first foreign country ever to beat the full English international eleven, by four goals to three.

Two and a half years later, Spain came to Highbury for the replay, and the crowd forced the locked gates at the Arsenal Stadium. There, within a few minutes, both Spain and Zamora's reputation toppled. Overcome by the tension, struggling pitifully in the mud, Zamora had given away a couple of ridiculous goals, one of them between his legs, before the game had really begun. England went on to score seven. Spain scored one. "If Zamora," wrote one English critic, "earns £50 a week [*a huge sum then*], then Hibbs [*England's goalkeeper*] is worth a benefit once a fortnight."

That evening, at the banquet, a Spanish interpreter, standing by the crestfallen Zamora, told Dixie Dean, England's prolific center forward, who had scored some of the goals, "He says he is nothing in Madrid tonight." "Tell him he's not much here, either," said Dean, heartlessly.

Arsenal did not get Hiden, but Manchester City was fortunate enough to sign Bert Trautmann. When Frank Swift, their renowned and immensely popular England goalkeeper, retired in 1949, after more than fifteen years with the club, it seemed unlikely that City would ever find a comparable successor. They turned to a huge, blond German, playing non-League football for a little Cheshire club; Berg—or, as he was known in England, Bert—Trautmann. Trautmann's story was a strange one. A paratrooper, he had fought in Russia, been captured eventually by the British, put in a prisoner of war camp in the northwest of England, and kept there long after most of the other prisoners had been released, because he would not renounce his Nazi allegiance. Ironically, when he was released, he stayed; to marry an English girl, to play football in England, to develop a strong Lancashire accent.

When City signed him, there was trouble, particularly among their Jewish supporters, who resented the acquisition of an ex-Nazi, but City held firm; and Trautmann in time became as warmly admired as Frank Swift. For so huge a man, he was astonishingly agile, and his power was equaled by his bravery. Plunging at the feet of Peter Murphy, the Birmingham City inside right, during the 1956 Cup Final at Wembley, he saved a goal, kept the ball; and broke his neck. This he discovered only after he had played out the rest of the game, when he was X-rayed at the hospital.

Frank Swift, too, had had his troubles in the Cup Final, of 1934. A Lancashire fisherman, whose brother kept goal for Bolton Wanderers, "Swifty," six feet, two inches tall, inveterately good humored, and a humorist to boot, was only nineteen when he played for City against Portsmouth in the Cup Final. Inexperience cost him and his team the first goal, against Portsmouth. Uncertain whether to put on his goalkeeping gloves or not, Swift looked down the other end, after a light shower of rain, and saw that the Portsmouth keeper, Gilfillan, had not troubled to do so. Nor did Swift.

Thus when, after half an hour, the Portsmouth outside right cut in for goal and shot, the ball slipped through Swift's hands and into the net. City, however, scored twice in the second half, and were holding their one goal lead when, in the closing minutes, the photographers behind their goal began telling Swift, "Three minutes to go . . . only two minutes . . . one minute . . . only fifty seconds, you're nearly there, lad . . . forty . . . thirty . . . There's the whistle, it's all over." Swift bent into his goal net to retrieve cap and gloves; and fainted.

Despite his bulk, Swift's goalkeeping was immensely acrobatic. Playing against Switzerland at Chelsea, in 1946, he changed direction in mid-air, stretched out his endless left arm, and just got his huge left hand on a ball which had skidded off a defender. Bert Williams, the blond, compactly made Wolves goalkeeper who succeeded him, performed the same feat three years later at Tottenham, to save a "certain" Italian goal, the crown of a staggering performance which had the Italian forwards beating the ground in their despair, and rob them of a victory they well deserved.

At the other end, by contrast, "Beppe" Moro let a soft lob from Billy Wright, the England halfback, sail over his head for England's second goal, late in the game, when mist and darkness—there were no floodlights then—had made visibility negligible.

Swift was happy enough to tell stories against himself. One concerned a famous referee, Ernie Pinkston, almost as large as Swift himself, who early in Swift's career with City came running up to him in an away match after he had hung on to the crossbar, to "see over the top" a shot from afar.

"Where do you come from, son?" asked Pinkston.

"Manchester, sir," said Swift. They were much more respectful to referees in those days.

"Manchester, eh?" said Pinkston. "Haven't they got a big amusement place there?"

"Yes, sir, Belle Vue."

"What have they got in there?"

"Speedway track," said Swift, somewhat baffled, "fun, fair, zoo . . ."

"Ah, that's where I've seen you before," said Pinkston, "in the monkey house. Don't hang on to the bar again!"

In Swift's day, British footballers earned little money. Now, they drive about in expensive automobiles. Then, they went by streetcar or bus; as Swift and his wife Doris did after he had played a home match at Maine Road for City. The bus they took, full of City fans, was so crowded that he had to sit beside one of them—a little fellow—and his wife elsewhere. Swift's neighbor turned to him abruptly and said, "Goal which beat City should have been saved," at which the man sitting in front of him disagreed. The small man turned to Swift and asked, "Were you at the match?" A classic Manchester dialogue was developing.

"I was," said Swift, "and I had a very good view of the game."

"If tha had such a good view of the game," the little man said, "then tell me this, should the big dope have saved the goal?" Swift said no, and argument raged, though the little man withdrew from it, sitting and eyeing Swift.

When he got up to climb down the stairs of the bus, he took a few steps, came back, and said to Swift, "Tha knows, I've seen thee before. What's tha name, son?"

"Frank Swift," said Swift, "and I still don't think I could have saved the goal."

Goalkeepers have a hard time of it. Elisha Scott, a splendid Irishman who played fifty-one times for his country and many years for Liverpool, was so used to plunging and leaping to the headers of Dixie Dean, center forward for the other Liverpudlian club, Everton, that it's said that when they met at Lime Street railway station and Dean nodded a greeting, Scott instantly and automatically dived onto the platform.

That may or may not be true; it has certainly entered the lore of the game. What does appear to be true is the story of Elisha Scott keeping goal at Burnden Park, Bolton, on an exceptionally muddy day against the formidable Albert Shepherd, Bolton's center forward, a man with colossal thighs and a pulverizing shot. One such was coming straight at Scott, in the Liverpool goal, and Scott went down assiduously to gather the ball in, did so, then found the sheer force of it taking him irresistibly back, sliding in the mud across his own goal line, ball in his arms.

The Zoffs and Clemences of the game, like Rennie before them, place a high premium on training, but Scott never did. Ted Crawford, who signed for Liverpool in the early 1930s, told me that on a training morning, Scott would beckon him over, take him to a secluded corner, stretch his arms once or twice in a perfunctory exercise, then light a cigarette. It seemed, in practice, as good a recipe for longevity as one has met.

Britain, which has always known and appreciated a good goalkeeper when it sees one, greatly appreciated the squat and cropped-haired "Tiger" Khomich of the Moscow Dynamo, when the Russians toured in 1945. Khomich was enormously lithe, strong, and capable.

When he got back to Russia, he, or perhaps some ghost, wrote a modest and agreeable account of his tour, familiarizing us with the term "Spot 9." He had mentally divided each section of the goal into a spot, or square, giving it a number. Spot 9, the fateful spot, was that area just inside the angle of post and bar which he considered the hardest for a goalkeeper to cover.

Khomich's mighty successor in the Russian goal was Lev Yachine, whose emergence coincided with the emergence of the Russians themselves; out of splendid, or, if you prefer it, sullen isolation, into the world game. Thus Yachine was able to take part in three World Cups and to give at Wembley, in the first half of a game between England and the Rest of the World, in 1963, a fabulous display of goalkeeping.

With his long, strong, lean, black jerseyed body, his reckless boldness, his immense reach, his anticipation, elasticity, and, yes, his chivalry, Yachine was surely the outstanding keeper of his day. More than any of his innumerable fine saves, I remember the moment in the World Cup semi-final of 1966 at Everton between Russia and West Germany when he rose from a mêlée, ball in his firm grasp, and wagged a reproaching finger at a German forward who had come in at him late and dangerously. There was a nobility about Yachine's approach to goalkeeping.

Curiously, it was not Khomich who inspired him but a blond Bulgarian goalkeeper named Ivanov whom he saw on tour in Russia, and who impressed him particularly by his dash out of goal, out of his own penalty area, to kick the ball clear. Yachine was wont to complain, during his long career, that things had been made much harder for a goalkeeper by the era of the massed defenses, first because he was no longer the unchallenged master of his own domain, second because, thanks to the number of legs and bodies round the goal area, often he would see the ball very late, and perhaps have a shot deflected at the last moment.

A good example of what he meant was given by Franz Beckenbauer's goal against him in that same semi-final, at Everton; the ball curled round the outside of the "wall" of defenders, and sneaked just inside Yachine's right-hand post. After the game the Russian coach publicly blamed Yachine for defeat, which I thought at once ungallant and inaccurate. The goal was scarcely his fault, and he had made a number of superb saves in the game.

It would have been more justifiable to blame him for Russia's surprising defeat in the quarter-final of the previous World Cup, up in the north of Chile at Arica, where for once Yachine had a strangely distracted day, allowing two Chilean long shots to sail past him, so that Chile went on to the semi-final.

Yachine started goalkeeping in actual games at a surprisingly late age, sixteen. But then, so did one of the finest goalkeepers of the 1970s, Northern Ireland and Tottenham's Pat Jennings.

Where Yachine, however, was a Muscovite, Jennings came from the little town of Newry in the Irish countryside. Professional soccer, he has said, "was only something I read about." He did not play soccer at all; instead he played Gaelic Football, which has in fact produced so many gifted soccer players, and involves both handling and kicking.

Leaving school at fifteen, he worked in a timber gang, felling trees on a mountainside, and probably would have stayed in the job for good, hard though it was, for he found it most enjoyable. One day, however, now seventeen years old, he watched a team in Newry, thought he could do just as well as their goalkeeper, played for them, and in no time at all was picked for the Northern Ireland youth international team which played in the annual European Youth tournament finals, held that year, 1963, in England. Within eighteen months, he had become a professional footballer with Third Division Watford, and been transferred to Tottenham Hotspur, in the First Division; since when he has easily beaten Elisha Scott's record of Irish international caps.

"I've never had any coaching in my life," he has said. "If I'd come up the normal way, I'd have had professional coaching from the age of eleven and been full time on the ground staff at fifteen. When people get on to me, trying to make me do something a certain way, I might as well pack up. I can't do it. I was naturally good at it from the minute I tried it; so I'm just as likely to say bollocks if someone tries to tell me what to do."

It is difficult to think what they could tell him, what there is in his game that could possibly be improved, though like every goalkeeper, he has his little lapses. Just under six feet tall, very powerfully built, Jennings is one of those keepers who makes so many "impossible" saves that they tend in time to be taken almost for granted. He is completely versatile; can fly through the air to tip the ball over the crossbar, plunge to the ground to get one of his vast hands to a ball which seems bound for the corner of the net. He can come rushing out and block with his legs in the manner initiated by European goalkeepers, and espoused by English keepers in the 1960s; a method which gives the keeper just that vital fraction of a second of time.

Jennings has, moveover, a stupendous kick, either from hand, as punt or drop-kick—on a windy day, he once scored a goal against Manchester United—or from goal kicks, which it has always been customary for English goalkeepers to take. He is of placid, even temperament, holds the high crosses with all the fearlessness and security he shows in every other facet of his goalkeeping, and since Gordon Banks retired, victim of a car accident, has been the best of British keepers.

Yet he says he probably enjoyed his football more when he was playing for Newry. A goalkeeper's life is tense and very hard.

7
DEFENDERS

The defender as artist has, after long travail, come back into his own. There could scarcely have been a more versatile, elegant, constructive defender than Franz Beckenbauer, West German inventor of the attacking sweeper, with his absolute poise, his almost impertinent calm. How many other players, at a tense moment in the European Nations Cup Final of 1976 in Belgrade, would volley a high cross from the wing neatly, firmly, and deliberately into his own goalkeeper's arms?

In the days of the all around, attacking, center half, which ended in Britain in the late 1920s, but persisted in South America and Europe for many more years to come, adventurous defenders were still often to be found; not merely among center halves, or "pivots," but among the wing halfbacks, lying wide on the flanks, who conceived attack as part of their job. Note, by the bye, how misleading the nomenclature of football became after the birth of the third back strategy. The so-called center half withdrew to become a mere center back, the so called wing halves came into the middle of the field and had nothing to do with the wings at all.

Two of the first exponents of scientific defense were the burly brothers Walters, fullbacks in the 1880s for the Old Carthusians—old boys of Charterhouse School—the Corinthians and for England. Between 1885 and 1890 they were the regular choice as England's fullbacks in the premier game against Scotland; only in 1888 was the partnership briefly broken, owing to an injury to the right back, A.M. "It is doubtful," wrote chroniclers Pickford and Gibson, in 1906, "if the game has ever produced a better pair of defenders than the two old Charterhouse boys with the 'meridian' initials. Individually each was a great back; collectively they were superior to any club pair that ever took the field."

C. B. Fry, himself a fine amateur fullback in the early years of the century, a member of the otherwise professional Southampton team, described the Walters as tall, exceptionally fine-looking fellows of the Nordic type.

Weighing about 185 pounds apiece, a large build for a soccer player, they indulged freely and forcefully in the shoulder charge so beloved of the amateurs of their day, kicked powerfully, moved quickly and enterprisingly up the field in support of their halfbacks, and had a famous understanding with the excellent Old Westminsters goalkeeper, W. R. Moon, who played behind them both for the Corinthians and England. A.M. won his blue for Cambridge, and P.M. played for Oxford, so that they were on opposite teams in the varsity match of 1884.

G. O. Smith, a Carthusian and a Corinthian of a slightly later era, told with glee the story of how the brothers reacted to the tarnished morals of the game, when they returned after long absence.

> A.M. and P.M. Walters gave up the game for some years, but were persuaded to play for the Old Carthusians against Sheffield Wednesday at Crystal Palace (which succeeded The Oval as the Mecca of the game).

They had been accustomed to the hardest knocks but were unaware of the tricks that had been acquired by some of the professionals during their absence.

One of the Wednesday forwards had the temerity to give P.M. a nasty hack on the calf. There was a roar of fury, and P.M. rushed at the man, who took to his heels and fled. The game was supposed to be going on all the time, but no one paid any attention to it. All eyes were focused on the race. The Wednesday forward ran far beyond the pitch, pursued by his foe, who eventually caught him up about twenty yards beyond the touchline and, with a fair but hardish charge, hurled him to the ground. After this, the two calmly returned and the game was resumed, though we were all too convulsed with laughter to do much about it.

It is said that the Walters gave up the game reluctantly, at the behest of their parents, because an unfortunate younger brother, Hugh, died after an accidental blow in the stomach from an opponent's knee. Later, P.M. became a Chancery barrister, A.M., a London solicitor. They would have a successor in A.G. ("Baiche") Bower, another Old Carthusian, good enough, as late as 1925, to play as an amateur for Chelsea and to captain the full England international eleven.

I treasure a reminiscence of the late Charlie Spencer, center half for England at Cardiff against Wales, when Billy Ashurst, the Notts County fullback, was cursing and swearing. "Now then, my man!" snapped Bower. "We want none of that!" But Ashurst was clearly unaware of his place in the feudal hierarchy. "Thee!" he retorted, "Thee, fook off!"

After the Walters, there came Crompton and Pennington, the great English fullback partnership of the years preceding World War I. Crompton, a mighty shoulder charger, was heavy and robust. There was a memorable duel in 1912 between him and the equally muscular and physical "Sunny" Jim Quinn, the

Glasgow Celtic center forward, who was placed that day on the left wing with the evident intent of bringing the two dreadnoughts into conflict. Charlie Buchan, who was reserve that day to the England team which met Scotland before a record 127,307 spectators in huge, wind-swept Hampden Park, related, "They went at it hammer and tongs throughout the ninety minutes. It was an example of robust charging the like of which will never be seen again. It would not be allowed today."

Crompton was a Blackburn man, who spent his whole career in the Lancashire town with Blackburn Rovers, winning a record number of thirty-four international caps for England. Why, you may ask, are they known as "caps"? The answer is that in Britain, it has been customary to give international players after each appearance a small, peaked cap, usually velvet, often with a tassel, the front suitably inscribed with the date and details of the game.

Where Crompton was bluff and vigorous, Jesse Pennington, left back for West Bromwich Albion, the Birmingham club (to be absolutely precise, it stands fractionally outside the city limits), was slighter and more circumspect, yet a player of great judgment and exactitude. Like Eddie Hapgood, the Arsenal man who would follow him in the 1930s, he was a supreme sportsman. "If Pennington had been rougher and tougher," wrote Ivan Sharpe, "he would have been a better player. I played against him half-a-dozen times, and his very gentlemanliness gave me confidence. One knew that one could try out tricks, that Pennington would always play the game. Like Crompton, the Albion idol failed to obtain an F.A. Cup-winner's medal. There are better 'medals.' I can testify that, in the crisis and although it looked his last chance, Pennington preferred loss of the medal to a trip when Tufnell of Barnsley swerved past him to score the winning goal in the Final tie of 1912."

Nice guys, as Mr. Leo Durocher has assured us, finish last.

Crompton was solid rather than brilliant, consistent rather than inspired. One might perhaps make comparisons with the likes of Alf Ramsey, another solid, heavy, competent right back in his England days of the 1950s—though of course Ramsey played out on the flank, while Crompton played in the middle. There would certainly be no comparison with the brilliant "overlappers" of today; with such as the Dutchmen Suurbier and Krol, the West Germans Vogts and Breitner, the Scotsmen Gemmill and McGrain. Crompton was never very fast. The story was told of a match between the representatives of the English League and Scottish League at Newcastle, when he was marking the tremendously fast Glasgow Rangers forward Alec Smith. They ran fifty yards together, in pursuit of the ball, and Crompton astonished everyone by finishing dead level. Afterwards, he confessed that he had hold of Smith throughout by the seat of his shorts.

Prudent and methodical both off the field and on it, Crompton had his own successful business while he was still playing. "The result is," wrote Pickford and Gibson, "that besides possessing the affection of the football public, he has been able to accumulate a snug little competence, and is now accustomed to drive down to his training at Ewood Park in his own motorcar."

Rara avis indeed, in 1906.

Eddie Hapgood came from Bristol, a southwestern city which has been remarkably prolific in turning out fine soccer players; the attacking center half Billy Wedlock being one of the first, and best. Hapgood was so thin and fragile when he came to Arsenal, in 1927, as a

19-year-old that he used to be knocked out when he headed the heavy, mud-caked ball—the lighter, plastic balls of today lay far in the future. Arsenal put him on a diet of beefsteak, and built him up sufficiently to make him resilient, but he was never physically powerful, and his game depended essentially on science and skill. Indeed, though he, too, was certainly no overlapper, no dasher down the touchline in the modern manner, the fact is that the thick-thighed, vaguely Neanderthal full-backs of bygone days were becoming obsolete.

Hapgood, an enormously dedicated player who worshipped Arsenal's manager, Herbert Chapman, never really got over his sense of abandonment when the club first dropped him from its team during the war, and then wouldn't offer him a job, when he had lost his own, in soccer management. He died, bewildered and disappointed, in the 1970s. Forty-three times capped for England, thirty-four times England's captain, winner with Arsenal of seven Cup and League medals, he could indeed have expected something better than to be sent an *ex gratia* payment of £50 when he was down on his luck.

He preferred to intercept rather than to tackle, though he could tackle crisply and well, to "jockey" the winger out of the game, rather than to "dive in" for the ball, as the professionals say, committing himself to a tackle which, if missed, would put him out of the game and expose his defense. He suffered a broken nose in the Battle of Highbury, the notorious England-Italy game of November 1934, when an Italian player deliberately smashed an elbow into his face; then laughed at Hapgood when he saw him with his nose bandaged after the game. Hapgood restrained himself from "going over the table at him."

His partner both for Arsenal and for England was the

less exuberant but physically heavier George Male, a quiet Londoner who would stay on with Arsenal till retirement as a coach to the junior teams, making few demands on life and soccer, while Hapgood, with his boyish naïveté, was floundering in a career as a coach doomed by his very, unsophisticated, virtues.

In 1937 Hapgood was joined on the England team by a defender who *would* succeed in management, Stanley Cullis, a third back center half who was one of the first with the enterprise and skill to move up into attack, beat men, give cogent passes, rather than merely bang the ball out of danger. Cullis in his smooth style presaged such polymaths of today as Josip Katalinski—the big Yugoslavian center half, never so happy as when he is heading, shooting, or thundering down on goal—Barry Hulshoff of Holland, Anton Ondrus, the Czech giant.

Cullis became the youngest England captain of all time when Hapgood stood down from the game against Rumania in Bucharest in May 1939; he was then twenty-two, and he would retire when only thirty-one to become manager of his own club, Wolverhampton Wanderers.

For some years he was enormously successful with his long passing tactics, his fast, "raiding" wingers, Hancocks and Mullen; but when the style was overtaken, he could learn no new tricks, and soccer left him by the wayside as casually and coldly as it has so many less successful coaches. "Here it comes!" Cullis would complain, in his strong Black Country (Midlands) accent, when his team started to pass the ball short, rather than boot it long, "tip-tap, tip-tap; the classical stuff!" What scorn there was in his use of the word classical; yet he himself was, in the best sense, a classical center half, and the wartime halfback line of Brit-

197

ton, Cullis, and Mercer, representing both the Army and England, was surely one of the best there has ever been.

Cliff Britton, another Bristol man, and Joe Mercer both played for Everton of Liverpool, and both were complete halfbacks in the fashion of the W formation; fine tacklers, neat on the ball, good distributors. It is fair, I think, to regard such halfbacks primarily as defenders. Tommy Docherty—one of the best of Scotland's halfbacks in the 1950s, a player who marked the tall, pale, defense-splitting Juan Schiaffino of Uruguay, a still finer inside-foward than Ferenc Puskás of Hungary—used to say in his playing career that he felt his job was "70 percent defense."

Yugoslavia produced a distinguished line of such halfbacks: Zlatko Cjaicowski, Boskov, Radakovic. Brazil, in 1950's World Cup, provided the strong and accomplished Carlos Bauer. England had the young prodigy Duncan Edwards, with his exceptional physique and phenomenal left foot—sadly killed by the Munich air crash of 1958, when still only twenty-one. Scotland, which has always turned out these players in abundance, has seldom had a better one than Jim Baxter of Glasgow Rangers in the 1960s; a left half who, till he broke a leg, was the epitome of finesse and virtuosity.

In its way, Baxter's left foot was as distinguished as that of Edwards or Puskás. Less powerful than Edwards, he was a better ball player, with an attitude to the game of casual superiority. He it was, in the Scotland dressing room in 1967, at Wembley, before the game against the World champions, England, remarked casually at the end of a long team talk that the English could "play nane"; that is, couldn't play at all. He it was who, during that impassioned game, calmly strolled on to a ball left for him by his fullback, McCreadie—who simply walked away from it—and played what the Glaswegians call, "Keepy-up"; juggling it from foot to foot. A broken leg, alas, wrecked his career, while his way of living was a little too near that of a George Best, a Joe Namath, to be consonant with the demands made on a professional footballer.

The 1950s produced no better, more magisterial, defender than Ernst Ocwirk of Austria, one of the last, great exponents of the so-called Vienna School with its emphasis on sheer technique, unhurried virtuosity. Curiously, Ocwirk was one of those who, in the middle 1950s, called for the end of the Austrian style, with its roving center half, of which, powerfully made, dark, with an exquisite left foot, he was the last great example. At the 1954 World Cup, where Austria took third place, he appeared as an orthodox—if that word can ever properly be applied to him—W formation style left half.

The combination of strength and manipulative skill, together with his wide vision of play, made Ocwirk a remarkable player. There was no taking the ball away from him when he wanted to keep it. He could indulge in the close control, the close passing dear to the Viennese as adroitly as any of them: but he could also hit the kind of magnificent long, sweeping pass from left to right that he did at Wembley in 1951, when Ernst Melchior ran on to the ball to volley a spectacular goal. Later, he would play for Sampdoria of Genoa in the Italian League.

The Italians themselves produced many formidable, unceremonious, fullbacks in the 1930s: Rosetta, Monzeglio, Caligaris, Allemandi. None, however, made quite the impact, nor won as many international honors, as the towering Giacinto Facchetti, who won the first of more than eighty Italian caps in 1963. Playing under the Argentinian-born coach Helenio Herrera for the Internazionale club of Milan, Facchetti became the attacking fullback *par excellence,* not merely "overlapping" down the left in the space afforded by the absence of an orthodox left winger, but attacking and shooting for goal with his strong right foot, from wherever he might happen to be. Man to man marking meant following one's direct opponent around, so that Facchetti would not necessarily be striking for goal from the left.

Possessed of an excellent temperament—it came as a great surprise when, infuriated by a disallowed goal, he started hurling punches at the English fullbacks at Yankee Stadium in May 1976—Facchetti played for Italy in three World Cups, then became their sweeper, in the latter 1970s, by now thirty-four years old.

The sweeper of the Inter team of the 1960s, however, was the late Armando Picchi who died, sadly early, of cancer, a dark, stalwart little man whose competitive instinct transcended mere considerations of prestige, significance. During the World Cup tournament of 1966 in England, when for some arcane reason Italy left him out, I found myself playing with Picchi in a casual Sunday morning game in Battersea Park, beneath the chimneys of the power station. There was nothing at stake; no referee. One team consisted of Italian tourists, three League players, including Picchi, and myself. The other was made up by young Englishmen. Picchi, who played in his undershorts, could scarcely have taken it more seriously had it been the World Cup Final. He challenged energetically for every ball, ended by scoring the decisive goal, and did not spare a plump little middle-aged friend who was playing, without much conviction, on the left wing: *"Ah, Pasta'asciutta! Non è come dalla tribuna!"* (It isn't like watching from the stand!)

Picchi was the original, defensive sweeper, or *libero, par excellence,* covering, anticipating, filling spaces.

Beckenbauer, however, would draw his inspiration not from him but from Giacinto Facchetti.

Of modern English defenders, none did better than Bobby Moore, captain of England and voted the outstanding player of the 1966 World Cup, better still in the World Cup of 1970, although, as we've seen, he was "framed" and kept under arrest for alleged theft of a bracelet in Bogotá, on his way to Mexico.

Moore was, by his own confession, a self-made player, and none the worse for that, yet those who played with him in youth football will tell you that even then, he was colossally calm. A Cockney, an East Londoner, tall, fair-haired, and strongly built, a magnificent "reader" of the game, forever seeing a move or two ahead, a powerful tackler and a fine coverer, his ideal position was that of the defensive wing half—the secondary stopper if you wish, in a back line of four. His debut, however, was made for England in the 1962 World Cup in Chile as a more or less orthodox wing half, expected to go forward as well as to defend. This was not Moore's strength or penchant. He *could* score the occasional goal, he could often make excellent use of the long, sweeping pass, but he did not like to move forward with the ball, as opposed to moving it; any more than he liked to mark his man tight and close. He played 108 games for England, most of the impressive ones, though he had a strange, half reckless, tendency to make abysmal mistakes in important matches. Sometimes he escaped the consequences, sometimes—as in the quarter-final of the European Nations Cup against West Germany in 1972, at Wembley, or, in Poland, a year later, when he carelessly let Lubanski rob him to score in a World Cup eliminator—he, and his team, paid heavily. Ron Greenwood, his mentor and manager at the West Ham United club, a man to whom Moore reacted with some ambivalence, even a sporadic petulance, spoke of him as "an occasions player," which was a polite way of saying that he could and would raise his game magisterially when it was necessary, but could look surprisingly fustian when he felt that it was not.

Brazil, as one would expect, has steadily turned out defenders who add imagination and skill to their solidity; Djalma and Nilton Santos in their first World Cup winning teams, the exciting blond left back, Francisco Marinho, in the World Cup of 1974; when the center-half was the mightily dominating black Luis Pereira, nicknamed early in his career "Chevrolet" for his impulsive dashes down the field. It was an impulsive foul which had him sent *off* the field during the semi-final at Dortmund against Holland, blemishing what had previously been so distinguished a tournament for him. Katalinski played in that World Cup, too, as did Elias Figueroa, the splendid Chilean, known as the best center half in Brazil—where he was playing in Porto Alegre—until the emergence of Pereira. Figueroa, too, had enormous presence, strength in the air as on the ground, the ability to command while making command look easy.

"Total Football" has given us a new and better breed of defenders, no longer content to be mere destroyers, but eager to join in the build-up of attacks; and even to consummate them. Nils Liedholm, who himself became a wing-half after his years as an inside forward with Sweden, Norkopping, and Milan, told me late in 1977, now the coach of Roma, that he even felt that future *creative* play would come from the back. Defenders alone, he felt, now had the room and time. It is an interesting concept, and it shows how far the game has come since Crompton caught hold of Smith's football shorts.

8
SOME SCHEMERS

That some forwards make chances, other forwards take them, was long a commonplace in soccer. Only in very recent years has it been disturbed, a new orthodoxy propounding that the schemer, the general, the midfield director, or *regista*, as the Italians call him, is a mere luxury. My own view is that until his particular gifts of vision, anticipation, and execution become generally diffused, the schemer will remain necessary; though he will have to do more than lurk about and just distribute.

Often, to give him his due, he has. The stocky little Gerson, of Brazil, began the 1970 World Cup in Guadalajara with an amazing, pin-pointed, fifty-yard left-foot pass, straight to Pelé's chest, in the middle of the Czech penalty area. Pelé, being Pelé, brought the ball down and scored. In the last match, the Final against Italy in Mexico City, it was Gerson, with a sudden dash, a rasping left-footed cross shot, it was Gerson who regained the lead Brazil had thrown away just before half-time.

Even Alex James could score goals when he chose,

though his role in the great Arsenal teams which dominated English football in the 1930s was essentially that
of purveyor, striker of long cross and through-balls
from the deep midfield. Once, allegedly because his son
told him that he "couldn't score goals," he got three in
a game against Sheffield Wednesday, while in the 1930
F.A. Cup Final at Wembley, his was the first. Arsenal
was awarded a free kick, James raised his eyebrows at
the referee, Tom Crew, and received an assenting nod,
while the Huddersfield Town players were waiting for
the whistle to be blown. James pushed the free kick to
the 18-year-old Bastin, out on the left, moved on to take
the return pass, and put the ball into the net. Later, it
was his through pass which sent the burly center forward Jack Lambert galloping down the middle to get
the second.

Schemers, directors, can be imperious and temperamental. When James was going through such a phase,
Herbert Chapman, the Arsenal manager, a formidable
paternalist, told him he'd be sent on an ocean voyage.
James, accompanied by the club trainer, Tom Whittaker, went down to the docks, expecting to be put on a
"luxury" liner, and found the boat to be a mere cargo
vessel. "The Boss's orders," said Whittaker, when
James objected; and James went.

The Scots have long been adept at producing such
players, little inside forwards with immaculate close
control and a sublime gift for reading the play. One of
the first and best of them, in the early 1900s, was Bobby
Walker of the Edinburgh club, Heart of Midlothian,
who looked slow, even in those remote times, but had
such admirable ball control, such a clear sense of what
he wanted to do, that he bent football games to his will.
Later, in the 1930s and 1940s, his son, Tommy Walker,
was an inside right little less talented.

The only equivalent I can think of, a father and son

who both excelled as inside forwards, was provided by Italy. Valentino Mazzola was a blond, powerfully built, omnicompetent inside left, born in Milan, who captained the Torino team of Turin to five successive Italian championships, till he was killed in the Superga air crash of May 1949, just outside the city. Sandro, slighter and slimmer, joined Internazionale of Milan as a boy, played first as a striking, scoring inside forward, then as a center forward, exploiting splendid gifts of ball control and speed—he once juggled the ball all the way through Switzerland's penalty area before scoring— eventually to drop back into midfield.

A sensitive, intelligent, combative man, a reader, a theorist, and a fluent talker, it was not surprising that Mazzola should want to run things on the field, rather than merely be part of them. He was quite different in style from Gianni Rivera, who had played, from the age of seventeen, for the other great Milanese club, A. C. Milan, was equally gifted as a ball player, could himself score spectacular goals at times, but preferred to lie quite deep, compose the play with broad, sweeping strokes, finely conceived long passes. His detractors accused him viciously of being "afraid" to enter the penalty area, yet it was rather a question of style. Mazzola was a dasher and a dribbler more than a great passer of the ball. He played glorious games against Brazil, in the 1970 World Cup Final, and Argentina, in the 1975 tournament; each time raising an Italian team from the ground. Rivera, with whom he served turn and turn about, one replacing the other, in the 1970 tournament, was either a general or he was nothing: whatever the worth of his occasional goals.

Of Alex James, the most masterly of "generals," his partner, Cliff Bastin, told me that he was one of the fastest footballers over ten yards whom he had ever seen; though he doubted whether he could have lasted a hundred; that the accuracy of his cross-field passes was such that he once met a goal kick on the volley and dropped the ball right at the flying feet of Joe Hulme, on the opposite wing; that he was forever calling for the ball.

James, moreover, was extremely strong; he could hit passes of a length beyond what many schemers would attempt. These, capable of giving only the shorter passes on their own side of the field, were known in English football parlance as One Wing Players.

James did not have the all around dynamism of another little Scottish inside forward, the fair-haired Billy Steel, who would end his playing career in Los Angeles—where he still lives—in the 1950s. A young soldier in World War II, Steel returned to play for the Glaswegian club Greenock Morton, and to become an instant star with an ebullient performance for Scotland against England at Wembley Stadium in April 1947.

England was expected to win easily, but Steel, with miraculous energy, amazing ubiquitousness, superb control, virtually took over the game. The classic criticism of the Scottish inside forward—that he is too slow, that he needs time to adjust to the rhythm of English football when transferred to a club across the border—was ridiculed. If anyone was made to seem slow, it was the English players who tried to contain Steel.

The following month, he was preferred at inside left in the Great Britain team, the first that had ever been fielded, against the Rest of Europe, at Hampden Park, to the illustrious Raich Carter of England and Peter Doherty of Ireland. What's more, the Continentals could no more control him than the English. In partnership with an equally brilliant English inside forward, the blond Wilf Mannion of Middlesbrough, he tore the European defense to pieces. Each man showed he could score as well as scheme, Steel with a rasping shot from twenty-five yards which sailed into the top corner of the European goal; Mannion, a splendid dribbler as well as playmaker, getting two of the six British goals. Such players could scarcely be described as "luxuries"; but then neither could Carter and Doherty, who had briefly come together in refulgent partnership for Derby County, helping them to win the 1946 F.A. Cup Final against Charlton at Wembley, in 1946.

A lean, wiry redhead with a glorious left foot, Doherty was the stormy petrel of his day, an inside left of tireless energy, vast versatility, forever kicking against those in the soccer world whose dice were heavily loaded against the player. As a boy, he had been given a trial game by his local club, Coleraine, when one of the first choice players was late arriving. Nobody spoke to him, nobody passed him the ball, and when the player turned up at half-time, he was ordered to give up his shirt. A tearful Doherty vowed he would never play again for Coleraine, and it was from Distillery that he eventually went into English football at Blackpool, going on to Manchester City, Derby County, Huddersfield Town, and Doncaster, a player as capable of playing his part in defense as in attack, of dribbling at speed for long distances as of heading brave goals among swinging boots. Both he and Carter, prematurely silver-haired, a fine strategist and a tremendous shot, became player-managers, Doherty with Doncaster, Carter with another Yorkshire club, Hull City.

Perhaps Doherty's finest achievement was not as a player, gifted though he so abundantly was, but as team coach of the Northern Ireland team which reached the finals of the 1958 World Cup at the expense of Italy. He had always retained bitter memories of the way Irish teams had been thrown to the lions when he was playing, gathered together at the last moment, everything perfunctory and off the cuff, leading players as likely as not kept back by their English clubs. Doherty, with admirable lieutenants in Danny Blanchflower, his captain, and Jimmy McIlroy, his cool, creative inside right, both of whom had admired him as boys, welded together a fine team, which beat England at Wembley for the first time ever, in 1957, then went on to knock proud Italy out of the World Cup eliminating tournament.

Doherty, Carter, Mannion, Steel, then, would all live up to the picturesque description of another fine inside forward of the 1930s, Ray Westwood, of whom the *Topical Times* sporting handbook for 1935 said, "he is no mere schemer without powder or shell." Denis Law of Scotland was in the same category; did he not once score six goals in an (abandoned!) F.A. Cup tie, for Manchester United, at Luton?

When Law arrived, a 15-year-old from the Scottish city of Aberdeen, in the Yorkshire town of Huddersfield, he was a skinny blond waif wearing spectacles, the antithesis of what he was and what he became: an inside forward of exceptional stamina, bold, strong, and commanding. With Huddersfield Town, he became a star, who was sold to Manchester City. From City, in 1961, he went briefly to Torino, where the fans thought him a better inside forward even than Valentino Mazzola, and from Torino he went back to Manchester, but to play, now, for United. He would end his career with City, returning, too, to the Scotland team, and at last playing for them in a World Cup—1974—ironically, many years after he could have expressed the full, fine range of his talent.

There was always something of the scamp about Law; the gamin grin matched his personality on the field; abrasive and impertinent, forever trying, and often bringing off, unorthodox things. He was one of the first British players to master the overhead bicycle kick. He was enormously effective in the air, another relatively small man who could climb vast heights. Sometimes he was used at center foward, but he was, so to speak, an "all court player," as effective in midfield as up the front, a Scot whose style, in its vitality, was essentially English; but then, so was Billy Steel's and Steel, unlike Law, did not come to England, and Derby County, till he was already a mature player.

Law, for all his years in England, was Scottish to the backbone. It is very hard for one who is not a Scot to know just how truly and fiercely their fans and players feel the rivalry with England. When England played the World Cup Final of 1966, Law went out that afternoon to play golf. He could not bear to sit by a television set and watch an English win.

South America has produced any number of distinguished generals, and it is significant that where in Britain they bleat generically of "midfield men," the Brazilians, who invented the category, still distinguish between wing halves and inside forwards.

There can seldom have been a more consummate schemer than the black Didì, who played in the 1954, '58, and '62 World Cups, then coached Peru to the finals of 1970. After him came Gerson, and after Gerson, the shrewd if irascible Rivelino.

The Argentinians showed us, in the 1970 World Cup, the blond, curly headed Carlos Babington, a player of English descent, who would once have joined Stoke City had his father not allowed his English passport to lapse. Babington, originally left behind in Argentina by the World Cup squad, had all the traditional schemer's immaculate control and ability to strike the killing pass, one of which made a spectacular goal in Stuttgart for little René Houseman, against Italy.

In Chile's 1962 World Cup, Didì was matched as a creative inside forward by Yugoslavia's Dragonslav Sekularac, a dark, sturdy little player of gypsy origin, utterly adroit in his control of the ball, subtle and penetrating in his use of it, a joker and a maverick quite capable of hiring an airplane to fly out of Belgrade for a date with a girl, a wanderer who finished his playing career in Colombia, possessor of a searing temper which twice had him suspended for eighteen months by the Yugoslav Federation, on one of these occasions being bundled into the army.

Later still, there has been the massive Wim Van Hanegem of Holland, whose build belies his exquisite use of the ball, his subtle evaluation of the game, while such Swedes as the "Professor," Gunnar Gren, the impeccable Nils Liedholm, the effervescent Nacka Skoglund, who died a sad and early death in Stockholm, must be recorded. These, too, could score goals when they wished; I remember in particular how Gren, a veteran by then, winged his shot high into the top corner of the West German goal in the World Cup semi-final of 1958, in his native Gothenburg; how Liedholm picked his way through the penalty box to score against Brazil, in the Final. No mere schemers without powder and shell. And certainly no "luxury" players.

9
SOME STRIKERS

In the beginning, there was Bloomer. Well, not quite in the beginning, but Bloomer, in the 1890s and the early 1900s, was the first of the legendary striking inside forwards, whose line of descent leads directly to Pelé.

Not that the word "striker" would become common till the latter 1960s, when it would come to connote one of the two, three, or very occasionally four forwards who lay well up the field, their task that of scoring goals. The players of whom we are talking were initially attacking inside forwards, players to be, as they often still are, easily distinguished from the classical center forward, on whose shoulder, one might say, they tend to "lean," snappers up of unconsidered trifles. They tend as a rule not to be as big as the usual center forward. Bloomer—or his ghost—wrote in 1906: "It is true that a centre-forward may be able to play an effective inside game, or an inside forward take the centre with a fair amount of success: but you will find, as a rule, that it is the player who has filled one position, and brought out all his energies and intelligence to the end of playing the game as it is generally understood it should be played by one filling that particular place, who will do best."

For all his 352 goals in League football, his 28 in 23 games for England, his five for England against Wales in March 1896, his fearsome right-footed shot, Bloomer looked no athlete: indeed, he was a slender fellow, whose nickname was Paleface. "In the dressing-room," wrote a contemporary, "his limbs lacked the ruddy glow of the players around him."

He was said to be neither "subtle nor scientific," but to be a remarkable maker of the defense splitting-through pass, which left a colleague to bear down on the goalkeeper, alone. Should such passes be wasted, the glare he bestowed on the offender was famous and formidable; in later years it would be matched by the Fulham and England inside left, Johnny Haynes, who captained his country's team in the 1962 World Cup.

When a movement broke down, wrote his Derby teammate Ivan Sharpe, "he would stand stock still, in the centre of the field, strike an attitude by placing his hands on his hips, and fix the offender with a piercing eye." If this were ignored, "he would toss up his head, as if beseeching the recording angel to make a note of this most awful blunder, and stamp back to his position in a manner intended publicly to demonstrate his dis-approval." His bark, or his glare, however, was sub-stantially worse than his bite. Young players tended to throw off their awe quite quickly, and play practical jokes on him.

He had none of the ghostly dribbling powers of his succesor in the England team, David Jack, great goal scorer of the 1920s and early 1930s, whose lovely swerve and delicate touch took him past opponents as though they were made of stone. He seems to have been a curiously modern, functional player; no frills, airs, or graces, just tremendous quickness and efficiency, whether it were to shoot or to pass. The shot was made "from nearer the toe than the instep," where, axiomatically, it should be made, but though—despite Bloomer's reputation for fierce shooting—he obviously lost power as a result, he gained fractionally but invaluably in quickness.

During World War I, while the famous Lancashire coach Jimmy Hogan was interned first in Austria, then in Hungary, Bloomer found himself interned in Germany, where he was a popular figure. "What do you call that, a pass?" he would rumble. "I haven't got an aeroplane!" But these were merely the transient grumbles of a perfectionist.

Hungary, in the 1950s, had Puskás and Kocsis; both went on, in the late 50s and early 1960s, to distinguish themselves in Spain. They shared with Bloomer, and the incomparable Pelé, the ability to do rather more than score goals, though this was their forte; they were also superb users of the ball, makers of passes to other people, able to see in a flash an open space, an opportunity. One remembers three wonderfully deft passes laid off by Pelé in the 1970 World Cup in Mexico, two to the forceful right winger Jairzinho, bringing him the winning goal against England in Guadalajara, the third goal against Italy in the Final, the other for the right back and skipper, Carlos Alberto, fourth and last goal in the Final, Pelé stroking the ball easily aside as Alberto came thundering in to shoot and score. David Webb, a doughty English First Division defender, whose goal won Chelsea the Cup in 1970, summed it up admirably seven years later when he said to me, of Pelé and Beckenbauer, "They do the simple thing as often as they can. They do the difficult thing when it's necessary."

This would almost be a paradigm of Pelé's character: beguiling simplicity, laced by a certain amiable shrewdness. Unlike Bloomer, he was and looked an athlete, though his "fighting" weight was only some 150 pounds; deep chested, thick necked—as was Sandor Kocsis—muscular in thigh and biceps. With Kocsis, Pelé shared a fabled ability in the air, a capacity, at a mere five feet eight in both cases, to rise high above much taller defenders, to achieve not only the spring but the timing of the jump.

Of Ferenc Puskás, I have a favorite memory. He had played in the 1962 World Cup in Chile for Spain, of all people and countries; the Spaniards at this time were shameless about naturalizing anyone and everyone of stature, and the rules of the World Cup were absurdly permissive about such stratagems.

Be that as it may, it was the evening on which Chile, a moderate team wildly well supported, had won a surprising victory in the competition, and the streets of Santiago were full of hysterical celebrants. Unobserved in a doorway, the eternal Budapest urchin, grinning his amusement, munching a handful of monkey nuts, stood Ferenc Puskás. He'd not concealed the fact that he thought little of the standard of the tournament, or of what had happened to football; far too defensive and cautious now for his cast of mind, and style. *His* Hungarian teams, he reminded one, had given goals away; and scored more goals than they conceded, goals in abundance.

He had but one foot, his phenomenal left, but as Danny Blanchflower, captain of Northern Ireland, said of him, "When you have a left foot like that, you don't need a right foot." It was not only capable of scoring fabulous goals of fabulous power—I still remember the sheer strength of his thirty-five-yard shot from the right, which brought him one of his three goals for Real Madrid in the 1962 European Cup Final—but of delightful conjuring. Against England at Wembley, in No-

214

vember 1953, he pulled back a ground pass from Czibor with the sole of his foot, to leave his defender stranded, then, with the same foot and with unbelievable speed, had banged it into goal.

Puskás came from the back streets of Budapest, and for all his unconvincing military rank—the Hungarians made him a major, put most of their best soccer players into the Army to play soccer—an urchin figure he remained. If Bloomer looked unathletic because he was thin, then Puskás looked unathletic because he was fat; thick around the waist and stomach, but heavily muscular in the thighs. It did not stop him getting off the mark so fast that few defenders caught him, once, in his ferret way, he had seized upon a through pass.

Kocsis, he, too, from Budapest, was a rather more delicate player, surprisingly versatile in that his ability in the air was complemented by subtle skill on the ground, an ability to step neatly around tackles. He was the leading scorer in the 1954 World Cup, he left Hungary at the same time as Puskás when, by chance and luck, they found themselves touring abroad with Honved at the time of the 1956 Hungarian Revolution.

Two years later, in Sweden, Pelé went up like a rocket in the World Cup. At the age of seventeen, he scored three in the semi-final against France, two more, two beauties, in the Final against the Swedes themselves. There has never been a more precocious player. At sixteen, he was already a star; a poor boy from the huge state of Minas Gerais, son of a moderate professional footballer, born in the village of Tres Coraçoes, moving as a boy to Bauru, there to be discovered by former World Cup player De Brito and brought to Santos.

On the train from Bauru to São Paulo, en route to Santos, a tremulous 14-year-old, he found himself sitting opposite a pitiful drunk who told him that he, too, had once been a soccer star, but he had broken his leg and look at him now. Beware!

Pelé was so homesick in Santos that he tried to run back home, early one morning, but by chance the club's masseur intercepted him. The rest of the story is well known; sublime talent, even, if one may apply such a word merely to sport, genius; unbroken success for the next twenty years.

A naturally right-footed player operating with the number ten shirt as a notional inside left, there has hardly been a more complete player than Pelé. What could he not do? He had a wonderful right-footed shot; and could use his left as well. He was a superb header of a ball. He had the strength to make and ride tackles, the "vision of play" to bring his colleagues into the game, and to attempt plays, shots, swerves which would have been inconceivable to any other player. He could dribble; and had his own way of using his opponents' legs as a kind of weapon against them; far too many "lucky" bounces returned the ball to his feet for it to be merely an accident. He was immensely acrobatic, could deliver the over the head bicycle kick, body parallel with the ground, feet flailing into the air, with tremendous power. When knocked down, as Phil Woosnam, the NASL Commissioner, once noted, open mouthed, playing against him in Brazil, he was off the ground and up again as though made of india rubber.

Pelé was not a saint, not a Stanley Matthews or a Bobby Charlton, on whose hearts and minds the words "Never Retaliate," one of the great imperatives of British football, seemed engraved. Pelé believed that if a player fouled and intimidated you, the way to stop him was to respond in spades. Once in Chile, he recounted, a player called Cruz had been kicking him hard; till he kicked him back, and that put an end to it.

It did not always work out well for him. In the 1964

216

International Tournament he was brutally marked by Mesiano of Argentina in São Paulo till at last, when he could take no more, he butted Mesiano in the face and broke his nose. Mesiano went off the field, but Pelé was so guilt-ridden and distressed that he did little else in the game. The Argentinians brought on a substitute called Telch, who scored two goals, and won 3-0.

Having played major parts in Brazil's World Cup victories of 1958 and 1970, Pelé retired from international soccer, to the great dismay and despair of Brazilian fans. He was the epitome of what the black had done to revolutionize soccer in Brazil; the black, who had been barred, then actively discouraged, till the 1930s, only to shame those who had opposed him by bringing a new rhythm, style, and detonating force to the game. It is hard to think of any white player who could or ever has matched Pelé's explosive speed of movement, his incredible reflexes. No soccer player has been as famous and as adored. Chinese frontier guards on the Hong Kong border, Communist frontier guards along the Berlin Wall, were alike melted by his presence into simple autograph hunters. When Clive Toye, the English manager, then president, of the New York Cosmos finally persuaded him to return to football, leave Brazil, and come to the States, in 1975, after a long and tantalizing quest, his magnetism was undiminished. Though he might now—as Dr. F. R. Leavis said of the Sitwells—belong chiefly to the history of publicity, rather than that of literature (read soccer), he could still do astonishing things, still enchant, delight, enrapture even those who knew little or nothing of the game. As late as May 1976 he was capable of thundering two of his celebrated, right-footed free kicks past the wall of English defenders in Philadelphia, provoking Ray Clemence to two splendid, plunging saves.

His joy in the game was—is—a very Brazilian thing. I

remember the Brazilians at their training camp at Hindas, outside Gothenburg, in the 1958 World Cup, standing around in a circle, flicking, heading, nudging the ball to one another, never letting it touch the ground, beaming their enjoyment; not doing this because anyone had told them to, but simply because it was a pleasure to them. Pelé retained this marvelous openness, this capacity to gain delight from the game, throughout his unique career.

George Best had some of this as well but perhaps it was less . . . unalloyed. He has said that when he beat a player, it would actually sexually excite him. It might be argued that Best should be placed in the section devoted to wingers, and indeed he began as one, scintillated on the right wing then the left, tied fullbacks up in knots, swerved past them on the outside, danced past them on the inside, made light of kicks, trips, and buffets. Yet the wing was an insufficient domain for him after a few years; he was just as happy to play in the middle, where his electric twists and turns, his courage—another quality Pelé also has had in superabundance—his ability to jump and head, brought him so many goals.

Best is generally acknowledged as the most brilliant forward produced by British football, the most dangerous and the most complete, since the war. All the sadder, them, that his career has been such a switchback of controversy, anticlimax, scandal. Twice he retired, and twice he came back. "If I'd been born ugly," he once said, "you'd never have heard of Pelé." But, in that ugly area, East Belfast, he was not born ugly, he was born unusually good-looking, dark, blue-eyed, cherubic. He was the first soccer star in Britain to be granted, or cursed by, the adulation reserved for film stars or "pop" stars, the first to be as sought after by women as well as admired by men. Stanley Matthews, Tom Finney, and the rest were heroes of the football field; off it, gray and modest figures. Besides, they played in an era when professional footballers were limited to an absurdly low maximum wage which kept them, willy nilly, in close contact with the working class. Even to own a car was unusual.

Best's position was radically different. He had plenty of money, he had national celebrity—at times, notoriety—he came under the kind of pressure that a fundamentally shy, psychologically fragile, young man ultimately could not resist.

He arrived at Old Trafford, Manchester United's headquarters, as a skimpy 15-year-old, in July 1961. Two days later, hopelessly homesick, he went back to Belfast; but United persuaded him to try again. They put him in lodgings with an amiable widow called Mrs. Fullaway, who later recalled, "He was so thin and tiny. He looked more like an apprentice jockey than a footballer." (Twelve years later, when Best was neither thin nor tiny, and was one of the most famous footballers in the world, United, in a desperate attempt to stabilize his life, made him give up the expensive, gadget-filled house he had had built, and put him back with Mrs. Fullaway again.)

"I still hated it," Best has said, of his return to Manchester. "I was homesick, miserable. I felt so bloody ignorant, so terribly puny. God knows what kept me there."

At seventeen he made his debut against West Bromwich Albion in the First Division, and an astonishing career was launched. Since the days of Stanley Matthews and Tom Finney no British player had so delighted the crowds with his magical skills. At a time when football was becoming increasingly dour, in which individualism was discouraged by anxious coaches and managers at every level of the game, in which so few forwards would take the responsibility of trying to beat a man rather than pass to a colleague, in which few in Britain had the skill to do so, Best was a revelation. He could, as the Italians say, "invent the game," conjure goals out of nothing, wriggle his way out of tight corners like Houdini. He had perfect balance, marvelous footwork, terrific speed. He turned like lightning; the speed of his turn alone could leave a defender floundering. He shot hard with either foot, from any angle; he could head the ball. There was no intimidating him.

"This season," I wrote of him in January 1965, when he was still but eighteen, "he has been the terror of the First Division full-backs, a tiny but determined figure with superb control and equilibrium, fine acceleration and the courage both to best bigger men and challenge them in circumstances where he might get hurt. . . . For all Denis Law's brilliance, all Bobby Charlton's moment of genius, Best is vital to United. He was vital to them in the floodlit match they won at Chelsea last September when he outshone everyone else on the pitch, ubiquitous and unstoppable, conjuring the ball away from defenders with magic dexterity."

With fame, alas, came Temptation; Best's scabrous memoirs, written with journalist Michael Parkinson, are reminiscent of Henry Miller; but Miller was not obliged to play professional soccer.

Called in time and again to be reproached by Sir Matt Busby, United's paternalist manager, Best would simply count the animals on Busby's wallpaper: "I used to want the bollocking to last a long time so I could finish my counting." He has admitted that "the only reason I opened a boutique in the first place was because it had a flat above it and it was a great knocking shop."

Bobby Charlton, whose character and style of life, modest and sober, was the very antithesis to his own, he resented. For Best's last three years at Old Trafford, they scarcely spoke. One night, in a Manchester pub, Best threw two dozen eggs at a painting of Charlton that hung on the wall.

Yet Best, who had Pelé's trick of using other players' shins to bounce the ball off, could reach great heights in the most important games. Against the powerful Benfica team in Lisbon, a European Cup tie in March 1966, he ignored Busby's orders to the team to play cautiously. Instead, Best—"I knew I was going to be special that night"—ran the Portuguese defenders ragged scored two fine goals, and United won, 5-1.

The clubs met again in the Final of the European Cup at Wembley. It was 1-1 at half-time and United, who had dominated the earlier stages, looked a weary team. Then Best snapped up a long, high clearance, whirled round a defender who tried to foul him, danced outside the goalkeeper's frantic lunge, and pushed the ball into the net. United won, 4-1, the first English club ever to win the competition.

In the early 1970s, his escapades became impossibly willful. Time and again United "forgave" him, time and again there were new misdemeanors to forgive. In January 1971, when United came to London to play Chelsea, Best missed their train, came down later, in his own time; and spent the week-end in the flat of a young actress, Sinead Cusack, besieged by television and press, as though they were covering an event of global significance. It was hardly Best's fault that the "media" should display such a grotesquely distorted sense of proportion. At the same time, his antics had by now alienated many of those who had most admired him.

Yet he remained, when not involved in scandalous incident, curiously sympathetic and unspoiled, the easy charm, the humor, unimpaired. When he said, for the second time, he would retire, after a disastrous match against Queens Park Rangers in West London at Christmas 1973, when spiteful fans delighted in jeering him, one was filled with a dreadful sense of waste. True, his excesses and absences had left him with a thickened body, had taken the edge off that marvelous quickness, that exhilarating speed. Yet the skills were there, and the hope. He was, after all, still only twenty-seven.

In the summer of 1976 he played in Los Angeles for the Aztecs. In the winter he came back to England and signed on with Fulham, the London club, to play in the Second Division. Thousands poured into Craven Cottage to watch him. He scored a goal in the second minute of his first game, he trained hard, and did delightful things. An understanding Danny Blanchflower, now Northern Ireland's team manager, brought him back into the international side he had so often graced, and he had a fine game in a World Cup eliminator against Holland.

The prodigal son was home; stouter, slower, yet still indisputably a star. One mourned the wasted years, took what comfort one could from the moments of virtuosity. He would never score again the kind of goal which took him, pell mell, across the front of the Sheffield United defense, passing man after man in his cyclonic progress, till at last he turned, shot, and the goalkeeper was beaten. He would never again spin "on a sixpence" to leave a defender standing, as he did for Ireland against England at Wembley, going on to fire his cross shot low into the goal.

Futile to talk about whose "fault" it was, whether more sophisticated handling earlier in his career could have saved Best from himself—what sophistication could you expect from the professional English soccer world?—to speculate on what might have happened to

Best in an earlier, less-pressing era. In a sense, it has been harder to reconcile oneself to the loss of him than if he had died in an air crash, like his unhappy predecessors at Manchester United; been killed in a street accident, like Meroni, of Torino, the Italian star; or simply hurt a knee, broken a leg.

"Do you know what he was really?" asked Pat Crerand, the hardy Scottish international right half who played with Best at Manchester. "I'll tell you, a little Irish kid who had a great gift to play football. If we'd left it at that, there would not have been a problem."

Alas, it was never likely to be left at that.

In June 1978 Best left the Los Angeles Aztecs for the Fort Lauderdale Strikers, after being suspended for constantly missing training. Almost at once, he scored two goals to inspire the Strikers to defeat the New York Cosmos, who at the beginning of the season in New Jersey had threashed the Strikers, 7-0. There was abundant life in George Best yet; though one waited warily for the next crisis.

Meanwhile, on the larger stage of the 1978 World Cup in Argentina, other strikers were gaining fame. Foremost of them was Mario Kempes, Argentina's center forward in the 1974 World Cup, now a goal scorer *par excellence* who began the series playing as a double spearhead with Leopoldo Luque, ended it advancing from a deeper position on the left of midfield, where he found space to make the dazzling, irresistible runs which brought his team three goals in the World Cup Final. Hitting his left-footed shots with tremendous force, beating men with a skill remarkable in one so large, accelerating superbly, Kempes was at once more and less than the center forward he had been. Placed on his own between two wide wingers, as he was against Italy, he foundered. Playing "off" the big, right-footed

Luque, or advancing from behind the front line of three attackers, he looked a player of the highest caliber, immensely dangerous and resourceful.

The man who scored the only goal of the Argentina-Italy game, in Buenos Aires, was the Italian Roberto Bettega, fitting climax to a beautifully adroit performance. Bettega, who began as a left winger where Kempes was at first a center forward, is another who can now be classified only as an all around striker. Tall, elegant, a fine ballplayer, devastating in the air, he is also an original thinker on the game. After he had headed a fine, diving goal for Italy against England in Rome in the World Cup elminator of November 1976, he told me that when playing against a zonal defense, such as England, you could profit from the fractional moments of misunderstanding between the opponents, who weren't quite sure which man was theirs to mark. In Buenos Aires, however, he admitted that on the whole he preferred to play against defenses which marked man-to-man, since you could pull the player assigned to you into whatever area of the field you found him weakest. In a zonal defense, wherever you went, you were simply "passed on" to the next player, who would always be operating in the zone that suited him best.

10
WINGERS

In this era of supposedly Total Football, more than a decade after Sir Alf Ramsey renounced wing forwards and won the 1966 World Cup, the winger may perhaps have an aura of obsolescence. Yet his contribution to the history and the delights of the game is beyond question, while even now, some of the finest, most exciting footballers began as wingers, are clearly most at their ease as wingers, and display the classical talents of the wing forward: Oleg Blokhin of Russia, Rob Rensenbrink of Holland, Kevin Keegan of England, Franco Causio and Roberto Bettega of Italy, Dragan Dzajic of Yugoslavia. It seems to me beyond question that there are certain things a natural winger can do which no other player, not least the overlapping, attacking fullback, can do. Put simply, the born winger has the ability to take the ball up to the opposing fullback on the flank, send him "the wrong way" with a body swerve, flick the ball outside him, take it all the way to the goal line, and from there deliver the most dangerous pass in the game; the center "pulled back" across the defense, to the feet or heads of the advancing forwards.

225

Billy Meredith was the first of the great wingers, and his astonishing career spanned more than a quarter-century. He won his first international cap for Wales in 1895, his last in 1920—fifty in all—and he was forty-nine years old when he played on the right wing for Manchester City against Newcastle United in a semi-final of the F.A. Cup in Birmingham.

Meredith grew up in the North Welsh village of Chirk, where he was discovered and nurtured by the local schoolmaster, a formidable arbiter of talent. Chirk was his first club, after which he played superbly for both the Manchester clubs, City and United. He stood five feet eight and a half inches tall, a gaunt, knobbly figure, renowned for the toothpick he always had in the corner of his mouth, his legs, as a contemporary had it, "rather bony and bowed."

Ivan Sharpe, himself a left winger of renown, thus described his style: "He would sidle down the wing at good speed, at a pace which would not threaten control of the ball. When an opponent barred the way he had a gift, all his own, of somehow wriggling round the obstacle in almost impossible space."

Whenever he could, he would go almost to the goal line, then deliver what Sharpe called "the Meredith hook . . . a neat clip, like the golfer's short approach shot. Not a lofted center; a crisp lob placed . . . in the jaws of the goal." Sharpe said that Meredith "wasn't a roamer, so much as a touch-line expert." For all that, he scored plenty of goals; thirty-one in one Second Division season for Manchester City, a vast haul by any standards. He insisted to the very end of his career that there was always something to learn, and it was said that when he did retire to keep a pub, he could be heard dribbling a football round the beer barrels in the cellar!

Then there was Stanley Matthews, of the astonishing

swerve, as marvelously durable as Meredith, winning his first English cap as a 19-year-old in 1934, playing League football for Stoke City, the club he left in 1946 and rejoined in 1962 after sixteen years with Blackpool, at the age of fifty.

Matthews was born in the Potteries, that once smoke-grimed area of the English Midlands made famous by Arnold Bennett. His town, one of the Five Towns, was Hanley; his father, a boxer called Jack Matthews, was known as the Fighting Barber of Hanley, and made him take deep breaths at the open window every morning. Later, Stanley's own regimen, in which long runs across the beach played a large part, helped him to go on playing when his contemporaries had long since given up.

It was his swerve, his sublime "shuffle," which made him irresistibly brilliant, the swerve which destroyed fullbacks as good as Muenzenberg, the German, in the Berlin Olympic Stadium in 1938, Eliani, the blond Italian in Turin, ten full years later, Nilton Santos, the powerful Brazilian, at Wembley Stadium, on a sunny May afternoon in 1956.

That swerve. There has never quite been anything like it, anything so magically effective, so predictable and yet so impossible to counter. "Don't ask me how I do it," he once said to an inquirer, "it just comes out of me under pressure." Cat and mouse. Receiving the ball, Matthews would bring it slowly up to the tense, waiting defender, a slender, unathletic figure, hair creamed and combed into place, arms slightly akimbo. He would, at the precisely relevant moment, sway slightly to the left. The defender had no doubt heard all about this, had possibly seen Matthews play, may even have played against him before. But he would "buy" the dummy Matthews so insidiously sold him, shift his balance to his right, while Matthews, with a deft flick of the outside of his right foot, went the other way, up the wing. Then catch him if you can!

Few could, for Matthews' other *forte* was his terrific speed off the mark, over the first ten yards or so. By that time, what did it matter? The defender was left stranded, the pass or center had been made. But it would be unwise and unfair to dwell just on Matthews' swerve outside the back; he could manipulate the ball beautifully at speed, pick his way past two or three defenders, conjure the ball deftly away from them, go "inside"—that is, towards rather than away from the goal—as well as "outside," up the flank.

He was not very interested in scoring goals, but when he wanted to, he could. In 1937, at Tottenham, England's unbeaten home record against foreign teams was in considerable danger, at the hands of the Czechs. Jack Crayston, the England right half, was hurt, there were no such things as substitutes then, and in the consequent realignment, Matthews went to inside right. He proceeded to score three goals with his supposedly weaker *left* foot, and England won the game, 5-4.

A footballer as original and unorthodox as Matthews was bound to have his difficulties in the increasingly rigid modern game, and perhaps it was no surprise that he should so often be discarded by England; and so often invited back. True, he could be maddening to play with. He did things in his own time; he was no player of the quick pass, the "one-two" exchange. Forwards could stand in agonized frustration waiting for the ball to come back, while Matthews went through his inspired gyrations on the wing. Yet for those inside rights who really knew how to play with him, and there were several, there could hardly have been a more rewarding partner.

Willy Hall, the little, blond Tottenham Hotspur

player was one. When England played Ireland at Manchester in 1938, they scored seven. Hall scored five, and practically every one of them was created for him by Matthews.

During the war years, when, by an irony, England had one of their most coruscating attacks, doomed to play nothing but unofficial internationals against Wales and Scotland, Matthews found an ideal partner in Raich Carter. This was the more surprising, perhaps, first because Carter, Sunderland-born and bred, and captain of Sunderland as a youngster, was really an inside left, second because his personality on the field was strong to the point of imperious. Yet he and Matthews blended perfectly. He knew just when to give the ball to Matthews, knew that Matthews wanted it, not to run on to, but, as they say in soccer, "to feet," and received many an exquisite pass in return.

Finally, at Blackpool, there was a partner of quite a different genre in Stanley Mortensen, essentially what would be called a "striker," very fast and brave, with an excellent right foot, a dasher through defenses. Both with club and country, he and Matthews had an exceptional understanding.

Matthews never intentionally fouled anybody. When he was tripped or kicked, he never retaliated. He had his own method of setting things right; he would simply proceed to run the offending player ragged, to the joy and amusement of the crowd. It has been said of him, even by one of his former England captains, that he would not, so to speak, roll up his sleeves and fight when the going was hard. I don't think that is either fair or true. I have already given the example of the game against Czechoslovakia. In 1954's World Cup, when England was struggling clumsily against Belgium, it was Matthews who wandered here, there, and everywhere, deserting the wing for the middle, sometimes dribbling past as many as five players at a time, till in the extra half-hour, he pulled a muscle.

Two years later, when he was forty-one, it was Nilton Santos of Brazil who would be his victim, at Wembley; that same Nilton Santos who, in the 1958 Cup Final, would put the ebullient Kurt Hamrin of Sweden quietly into his pocket, who four years after that, at the age of thirty-six, would stroll through the World Cup Final in Chile.

Tall, strongly built, quick, and experienced, there was nothing Santos could do that day against Matthews who, in the dressing room afterwards, talked with some bitterness of how he felt when described by the newspapers as "too old." There were times, he said, "When I could tear the paper across."

Matthews, like Meredith, surely owed his longevity in part to his sheer enthusiasm. Every game was important. I remember, in the last stage of his career at Stoke, being with him in the dressing room before a League game of no special consequence; a mere Second Division match. But for Matthews, it was pressingly real. "I'm not really with you at the moment, Brian," he said, distractedly. Before each game, he confessed, he would have butterflies in his stomach: "You must have butterflies."

For many years, it was reckoned that he would put 10,000 spectators on the gate, whenever he played away from home, particularly in London; for years people flocked to see him, afraid that season might be his last, until it was, indeed, his last.

Between Meredith and Matthews, of course, a revolution had taken place. The offside law had been changed in 1925, Arsenal had developed the "raiding" winger of the 1930s, the winger who would not merely make goals but cut in for goal diagonally to score them, and the philosophy of wing play had greatly changed. Matthews at bottom belonged to the old school. The new men, such as Bastin and Hulme of Arsenal, little Sammy Crooks and "Dally" Duncan of Derby County, the muscular Eric Brook of Manchester City with his fearsome left foot, were goal scorers.

I once saw Bastin, who lived, quiet, calm, shy, and detached in a world of his own, a world in part conditioned by his growing deafness, shake his head at the idea that Brook was as good as he; it was not a matter of immodesty, simply his own deep belief in his own abilities, which were extraordinary.

Arriving in London, at Arsenal, as a shy, 17-year-old inside forward from Devon in 1929, he became a left winger of exceptional gifts, known for his youth as "Boy" Bastin, winning every honor in the game, Cup, League, international caps, before he was twenty. He hadn't the speed of a Joe Hulme, on the opposite wing, nor the ball skills of a Stanley Matthews, yet he remained astoundingly effective, functional, and unflurried, standing well in from the wing, beating men without fuss, always in the right place at the right time, never cooler than in a crisis, when there was a vital game to be saved, or won.

Alan Morton, the Glasgow Rangers and Scotland outside left, was more spectacular. He was a tiny fellow, standing five feet four and a half inches, weighing only 133 pounds; but many of the finest wingers have been small. He could use both feet, though in fact he was a natural right-footer playing on the left wing, just as the extraordinary Tom Finney of England, in later years, was a left-footer playing, for the most part, on the right. Like Matthews', Finney's, and any other great winger's, Morton's balance was exceptional. It helped him to swivel, abruptly and bewilderingly, it helped him perfect what Ivan Sharpe, a lesser outside left but a very acute observer, called "his weaving, dancing-master run."

He began as an outside right, switched to the left, and once said it was a move any winger might profitably make: "The outside-left who is able to dribble and pass with his right foot makes it a cockeyed world for the opposing full-back, who doesn't know which way you are going with the ball. Of course, you will centre as a rule with the left foot."

Morton was a perfectionist, who used to attribute his fine, close control to . . . a cellar door. "There was a hole a little larger than a football in our cellar door. Why, I don't know. Perhaps to let light into the cellar. Anyway, we used to try to shoot or lob or half-volley the ball through the hole. Day after day we did it."

Morton won his first Scottish cap in 1919, his last in 1931. When he retired, he became a director of Glasgow Rangers; in those days a most unusual distinction for a professional footballer. He was also wont to play with a "twopenny" ball, a little rubber ball which he would kick against the garden wall and trap before it bounced back over the footpath. It helped him, as he realized in later years, "to develop a quick touch and speed off the mark. You have to be nippy to gather a small ball before it bounces off the footpath." How diligently he worked on his art, and before he even knew he would become a professional!

While he was still playing for the celebrated Glasgow amateur club, Queens Park, he practiced every Tuesday and Thursday, first dribbling a ball all the way around the field. "Then I would prance some steps, as in shadow-boxing. Visitors to the grounds have said, 'What is that crazy stuff?' They may have wondered whether the little chap was quite right in his head. The idea was to build-up weaving and wobbling while running with the ball. Balance is necessary to change direction at speed. Mind and feet in due time synchronize. Weaving and swaying then come automatically."

Morton's style was quite different from Matthews'. "He could take a short step with one foot," Ivan Sharpe wrote, "and then suddenly switch the other way, carrying the ball along with him. Thus, if near the touch-line on the left-wing, he might take a short step to the left as if to move along the touch-line and then, directly his opponent moved that way, Morton could switch to the right and carry away the ball *inside* the defender."

Like Matthews, he was very quick off the mark and practiced this in terms of short steps, in the manner of a sprinter making a start. "At my weight, I needed acceleration to escape charges." And in his day, the British shoulder charge was very much alive and alarming. As late as 1934, Vittorio Pozzo, team manager of Italy, was speculating on whether Continental players would ever be able to stand up to its ferocity.

Morton went on playing till 1933, and it is not surprising that he should call his "most memorable match" that of the Wembley Wizards, the nickname given to the Scottish team which thrashed England 5-1 in April 1928, at Wembley. A little Scottish forward line in which the largest man was the right winger Alec Jackson, scorer of three of the five goals, at five feet seven, took the English defense apart.

"Stanley Matthews, of course, is a genius," said Morton, in the early 1950s, "but I should have admired him more if he had been quicker to centre the ball." He was also an admirer of Tom Finney, "a splendid example of the player who can use both feet expertly and confidently."

Indeed he could. Known as the Preston Plumber, since he came from that Lancashire footballing town, and was indeed trained as a plumber, Finney joined

Preston North End as a boy inside left, was switched to the right wing, and was already making a name for himself when, in the last war, he was posted to North Africa with the renowned Eighth Army. Among those who saw and admired him there was Alec Jackson, who was also serving in that campaign.

When Finney returned in 1946, there was no keeping him off the England team; even if it meant excluding Matthews. The comparison between them has been made from that day to this; there will always be those who prefer Finney to Matthews, always those who would have Matthews rather than Finney. I would agree that Finney was, as has so often been said, the complete footballer. Small, wiry, beautifully balanced, as clean and sportsmanlike a player as Matthews himself, he had Matthews' ability of getting an opponent on the "wrong" foot, off balance, then coasting past him up the touchline, to deliver a killing center from the goal line.

Finney could play on the left as well as the right, could score goals as well as create them, could play his part in midfield, if necessary, as well as up the front. When in the England vs. Scotland game at Wembley in April 1951, Wilf Mannion, a famous England inside forward, cracked a cheekbone, reducing the team to ten men, Finney took his place and was sensationally good, an inside forward to perfection, working and running and dribbling and creating. Towards the end of his splendid career, in the later 1950s, he became with Preston a deep lying center forward, hovering just behind the strikers, using his sublime balance and control to hold the ball, beat men, work openings.

After the 1946–47 season—the first "official" one after the war—in which Finney had largely kept Matthews off the England team, the English selectors finally made, in Lisbon, what today might be known as an historic compromise. Exploiting the fact that Finney was a natural left-footer, they played him on the left, Matthews on the right, against Portugal; and the English forwards scored ten goals, without reply!

The succession of Brazilian right wingers, Julinho, Garrincha, Jairzinho, was rather different; there was a pantherine element about them, a quality of detonation. If they were graceful, it was a pantherine grace, where Matthews and Finney, for all their speed off the mark, had also something deliberative about them.

Julinho, with his mournful, American Indian, moustached face, his long upper body, his astounding speed, his immaculate close control, his fulminating right-footed shot, was a revelation of the 1950 World Cup, in Switzerland; Garrincha, a revelation of 1958, in Sweden.

That Garrincha was a simple soul there was never any doubt. The psychologist whom the Brazilians had imported from São Paulo to soothe their wayward players, a sweatered, amiable, unshaven, bespectacled man, had Garrincha ineluctably tagged as an "instinctive"; his method of typology was to get the players to draw a man. Those who, like Garrincha, drew matchstick men, were instinctives. They made, the psychologist told me one sunny morning in the Ullevi Stadium, Gothenburg, good wing partnerships with more sophisticated players.

Garrincha, whose nickname was the name of a small bird, came from the village of Pau Grande, where he fathered eight daughters. He was born crippled, and although an operation allowed him to walk, his right leg was always a little crooked and distorted. Some felt, in Adlerian fashion, that it was for this very reason that he was able to produce his astonishing feints and spurts.

Though Brazil brought him to Sweden, he was not initially on the team; his reputation for inconsistency was too well established. Eventually a deputation of players went to the coach, Vicente Feola, and persuaded him to pick Garrincha against Russia in the third game, at Gothenburg. As the team stood listening to the national anthems before the game, Nilton Santos, a colleague of Garrincha at the Rio club, Boxtafogo, said, "Don't let us down!" but all Garrincha could say was, pointing at the linesman, "Look at that chap! He's just like Charlie Chaplin!" Which said, he went out to demolish the Russian left back.

Garrincha, you might almost say, was Matthews to the power of ten. He had, as he showed when setting up two goals in the Final, the same amazing swerve, the same burst of speed, but carried out with an altogether different rhythm, an almost savage suddenness.

That he was a child as well as a force of nature, there can be no doubt. Not for him the introversion of Stanley Matthews, the solidly pursued engineering career of Alan Morton, the sober dedication of Tom Finney. A singer called Elsa Soares followed Brazil to the 1962 World Cup in Chile; Garrincha left his wife and all his daughters to marry her. When he smashed his knee in a motor accident, the chips were inevitably down. His career was cut short, he played a bit in France, he played in charity games at home, but the long, sad years of anticlimax stretched ahead.

Meanwhile what player, even Pelé, had done more for Brazil? For Pelé dropped out of the 1962 World Cup after a couple of games. It was the marvelous running, swerving, shooting, and, yes, heading of Garrincha that kept Brazil in contention. Spain, England, and Chile could do nothing with him. He had by then developed a finishing power with both feet and with his head which few other wingers could have dreamed of; certainly not Matthews, who scarcely headed the ball at all. He was muscular and combative. He could jump enormous heights and score goals, either foot, from a prodigious distance. The odd thing was that, having torn Chile to pieces in the semi-final—then been sent off the field for retaliation and cut on the head by a missile as he left it—he did little in the Final itself.

I remember the last minutes of that game in Santiago. Czechoslovakia, having taken the lead, had given away three goals. The game was lost and won. Out on the right, Garrincha got the ball, dancing and swaying over it, bringing it up to the massive, bald Czech center half, Jan Popluhar. And Popluhar put his hands on his hips, resigned and exasperated; stood there regarding him as much as to say, like some New York Lower East Side mother, "What do you want of my life?"

As for Jairzinho, who, like Garrincha, played in three World Cups, he was a tank, a glorious runner, strong enough to run through tackles, not to mention run around them, as willing to play center forward—his position with Botafogo—as on the wing.

Dzajic, Blokhin, Rensenbrink are left-sided players, as was Italy's Gigi Riva before he became an all-purpose striker. This was really a matter of Darwinian evolution. In Italian football the tight man-to-man marking, the inferiority in numbers of attackers to defenders, has long been so great that for reasons of sheer survival, Italian strikers have had to become incredibly resourceful; physically strong, very fast, very brave, clever in control. There were no frills about Riva; he was as fast and as direct as any W formation winger, he had a great turn of speed, a fine left-footed shot, and was good in the air.

Dragan Dzajic has been a more subtle player. A Red Star, Belgrade, player since boyhood, he did not leave them till 1975, when, finally given permission to leave Yugoslavia and seek his fortune abroad, he surprisingly decided to join a small club in the French League, Bastia, of Corsica, where the attendances were minuscule, where success had never smiled, but where the shy and modest Dzajic was quite happy.

He has certainly been an authentic star ever since, as a 21-year-old, his effervescent wing play, his dazzling goals, deserved to give Yugoslavia the Nations Cup in 1968. But some dreadful, deeply suspicious, refereeing in the Final in Rome cheated Yugoslavia of their due. The match was drawn 1-1 after extra time, and in the replay Italy won 2-0, calling up Riva to drive home one of their goals.

Dzajic had scored the only goal of the semi-final, in Florence, against England, drifting into the center, controlling a high ball magisterially when it floated over Bobby Moore's head, and volleying it home. He also scored for Yugoslavia in the first Final against the Italians. Like Cliff Bastin, he was always a left winger who would move into the right place at the right time.

On the ball, he was an artist, wonderully supple, able to work the ball this way and that, whipping it either inside or outside the defender, then leaving him beaten hopelessly for speed. Balance, yet again, was the essence; Alan Morton would have admired Dzajic. We did not see the best of him in the finals of the 1974 World Cup, in West Germany, when he was said to be at odds with the team coach Miljan Miljanic over tactics he considered, not without reason, too defensive. Curiously, he has had, for all his mild and friendly temperament, a surprising amount of trouble with Yugoslav team coaches. Miljanic's successor, Mladinic, seemed bent, mysteriously, on leaving him out as often as possible, though he had finally to restore him to the team which played such exciting football in the finals of the European Nations Cup of 1976.

Again, a winners' medal escaped Dzajic, but his galvanic opportunism brought him a goal in the semi-final against West Germany, in Belgrade, pouncing on a German mistake; another in the Third Place match, in Zagreb.

Oleg Blokhin, European Footballer of the Year in 1975, a blond Ukrainian from Kiev with high cheekbones, a mother who was an 80-meter hurdles champion, was the most spectacular Russian forward since the days of the great Moscow Dynamo team which toured Europe in 1945. A thoroughly modern player obliged to be much more than just a winger, to cover far more ground, he is, nevertheless, a winger by origin and a winger at heart, with the classical gifts of speed, control, and, for an outside left, the necessary fine left foot. Blokhin began his career in the Russian national team of 1972 as a left winger, and when Dynamo Kiev blossomed in the late 1970s to dominate Russian football and, for a while, provide the whole of the Russian international team, he was their star.

Blokhin, like Riva, could be something of a one man forward line, prepared to take on several defenders at a time with the end in view of a shot at goal, rather than a pass. It was significant that Dynamo Kiev should acquire from Zaria Voroshilovgrad, champions of the Soviet Union in 1972, another international left winger and left footer in Onishenko. Clearly it was not their intention to play either of them merely on the left wing, or they would have cancelled each other out, and indeed they showed themselves capable of striking from almost any angle or position.

Tremendous speed has been one of Blokhin's chief assets, a quality shared by another, rather more orthodox, left winger, Francisco "Paco" Gento, the dark, stocky little winger who played in all six of their European Cup-winning teams. Blokhin, who can run the hundred meters in 10.7 seconds and is one of the quickest soccer players in the world, still believes that he could be faster, and that his heading could be improved. Perhaps it could; but there are few clubs which would not willingly pay an immense sum of money to acquire Blokhin just as he is.

One of the ironies of the 1978 World Cup competition, in Argentina, was that West Germany, who came to the finals with a team famous for its use of two orthodox wingers, should abandon the tactic at once, while Argentina, who began with only one recognized winger, should eventually win the Cup with two; themselves chosen from among three.

Early in the season 1977–78, West Germany appeared to have a splendidly effective attack in the shape of Rudi Abramczik and Karl-Heinz Rummenigge, on the wings, flanking the resourceful and acrobatic Klaus Fischer, in the middle. By the time June 1978 and the World Cup came around, however, the virtue seemed to have gone out of the formation, and even when the three men did play together, late in the competition, Rummenigge was used more as a midfielder than a true winger.

Argentina, however, was obliged to reassess their tactics after their second game, when an injury deprived them for a time of their powerful striker, Leopoldo Luque. Their coach, Cesar Luis Menotti, decided to use Daniel Bertoni wide on the right, Oscar Ortiz wide on the left, first with Mario Kempes, later with Luque himself, in the middle, bringing René Houseman on from time to time as a substitute winger. The tactics were successful, giving Argentina the "width" which only true wingers can give.

Rob Rensenbrink, the Dutch international outside left, finished just behind Franz Beckenbauer of West Germany in the voting for European Footballer of the Year. Had he been fully fit in the World Cup Final of

240

1974 in Munich, it may well be that Beckenbauer would never have received the trophy. But Rensenbrink, whose pace, incision, and great strategic intelligence had done so much to take the Dutch to the Final, pulled a muscle, and ultimately had to be substituted, having shown little of his prowess.

In 1978, Rensenbrink was not injured, but he had another somewhat disappointing World Cup. How easily he could have been the hero of the Final, a shot in the first half being splendidly saved with his legs by Ubaldo Fillol, the Argentinian goalkeeper, another, in the ninetieth minute, failing by the width of the post it struck to give Holland victory!

In contemporary fashion, Rensenbrink, a Dutchman who has played most of his senior career for Belgian clubs, such as Bruges and Anderlecht, can strike from the right as well as from the left, but it is from the left that he does most damage, a player of great facility and poise, with the traditional winger's capacity to *beat* people.

And there, I think, we have it; or at least a salient part of it. A natural winger will take defenders on and get past them, whether he does it with a Matthews swerve and flick or with a Gento turn of speed, whether he has Alan Morton's delicate footwork, or Jairzinho's pace and power. When Ramsey won the World Cup for England without wingers, there was a feeling of dissatisfaction, even displeasure, in England itself. Ramsey defended his tactics on the grounds that he had tried several wingers, right into the tournament itself, and they had failed; but in fact he had successfully espoused similar tactics with Ipswich Town, in League club football. Total Football or no, the game would be much the poorer without wingers; and who can imagine its history without Meredith and Matthews, Morton and Bastin, Julinho, Garrincha, and Jairzinho?

11
CENTER FORWARDS

Some would have it that there ain't no such animal today as a center forward; there are merely strikers. They would be wrong. There will always be center forwards, and they will always be heroes. They will come, as they have invariably come, in all shapes and sizes. Johan Cruyff of Holland is wiry, tall, and slim. Franco Graziani of Italy is tall and robust, Gerd Müller, the most phenomenal goal scorer of all time, the center forward who can, so it seems, conjure goals out of the air, is quite short, with massive thighs. Hughie Gallacher of Scotland was short, if sturdy. Dixie Dean and Tommy Lawton, both of whom played for Everton and England, were tall and very muscular. Uwe Seeler, Müller's predecessor, and still more a German hero, was of modest height, but square and strong. And G. O. Smith, the great English center forward of the early years of this century, was described by an illustrious contemporary, C. B. Fry, as "of medium height, slight and almost frail in build."

Fry, himself a protean figure, athlete and Oxford scholar, soccer international, cricketer, long jumper, fine Rugby player, went on to describe Smith as "a quick mover but not a sprinter. He was uncannily prehensile of foot and almost delicately neat. What made him was his skill in elusive movements, his quickness in seeing how best to bestow his passes, his accuracy and his remarkable penetrative dribbling. He swung a marvellously heavy foot in shooting—always along the turf and terrifically swift."

Smith was that now remote and obsolescent figure, an English gentleman. Like Charles I, he nothing common did nor mean, were he playing for the Old Carthusians, the former pupils of Charterhouse, where he learned the game and played four years in the first eleven, the illustrious Corinthians, or the England international team, for whom he appeared twenty-one times between 1893 and 1901, and would have done many more had it not been for an early retirement.

The reasons for this were in some sense characteristic. Coming down from Oxford University, where he successfully played cricket as well as soccer, Smith, like so many "Oxbridge" athletes, became a prep school master. Ludgrove School "prepared" its pupils largely for Eton; its headmaster, Arthur Dunn, had been an English international center forward himself, in the 1880s. In 1902 he died of a heart attack at the early age of forty-one. G. O. Smith became joint headmaster with another famous Corinthian, W. J. Oakley, and remained at the school, then at Cockfosters, in Hertfordshire, for the next thirty years. He had, alas, no more time for football.

"Mr. Smith," Jack Robinson, an illustrious England goalkeeper from Southampton, once said to him, "I'd sooner keep goal against his Satanic Majesty than against you."

Looking at photographs of Smith, one is astonished that this small, pale, slender, narrow-shouldered figure should so triumphantly have survived against the defenders of his day, players for whom the heavy shoulder charge was *de rigueur;* but then Tinsley Lindley, his predecessor on great Corinthian teams at center forward, was not much bigger. It is further evidence that soccer is a game in which physique comes always in second place to skill.

Though the controversy has long since faded away, there was debate, right through to the 1940s, over whether Smith was the greatest center forward ever to play for England, greater than Lawton and Dean. My own view is that, whatever his excellence, his immaculate technique, his opportunism, he was an incomplete center forward to the extent that he so seldom headed the ball. Soccer, he felt—with the Scots in their classic period—was a game to be played on the ground, and though the best soccer always *is* played on the ground, one cannot denigrate the sheer excitement, the fine spectacle, of the headed goal. It was often said of Tommy Lawton that when he went up in the air, there was a point at the very top of his jump where he seemed to pause and *hover.* An optical illusion, we were told, but more recent scientific work on the subject has suggested that a Lawton, like a Nijinsky, may have had some special power.

After Smith, the great English amateur center forward was Vivian Woodward. Fittingly, Woodward was inspired by G. O. Smith, whom he used to watch at Kennington Oval, the South East London cricket ground which for many years was the scene of Cup finals and internationals, and near to which Woodward himself was born. Like Smith he showed, in the words of his great admirer and sometime colleague Ivan Sharpe, "that brain and a gentlemanly bearing can beat brawn and brutish methods." By Woodward's time, English international teams were made up almost wholly of professionals, and his achievement in winning twenty-one full international caps, plus another three on tour in South Africa, was extraordinary. Like Smith, he was slight in the shoulders, but unlike Smith he did not have a compensatory strength of shot. He was the star of the United Kingdom team which won the Olympic soccer tournament in Stockholm in 1912, he could fill any of the three inside forward positions, he played regularly in League football for the two celebrated London clubs, Tottenham Hotspur and Chelsea.

Unlike G. O. Smith, he *was* a good header of a ball, and his splendid leaps, his brisk deflections, brought him many a goal.

For Ivan Sharpe, Hughie Gallacher was "the deadliest center forward" in his experience of the game, as G. O. Smith had been, before his time. Short and compact, a magnificent ball player, splendidly quick to shoot with either foot, Gallacher scored no fewer than 386 League goals in Scotland and England.

Among his feats were five goals for Scotland against Ireland in 1929, five for the Scottish League against the Irish League in 1925, each time away from home, in Belfast. He was too small to make much impact when the ball was in the air, though he judged high balls well, and had the courage to go for them against much bigger men. He might have sympathized with the views of G. O. Smith, who wrote, in 1942, "Backs and half-backs have to use their heads at times, but, in my opinion, if forwards have to there is something wrong with the side."

Gallacher came from the Scottish mining village of Bellshill, where he was brought up with another legendary little Scottish forward, Alex James. Undisciplined, inflammable, a drinker, he wandered from club to club, never staying anywhere for very long; Airdrieonians in Scotland, Newcastle United, Chelsea, Derby County,

Grimsby Town. He had a fierce temper which opposing defenders callously exploited; when they kicked him, they knew there was every possibility he would flare up. He led the attack of the Wembley Wizards when they thrashed England 5-1 in 1928; not one forward but for Jackson, the right winger, stood over five feet six.

It was said that the experience of his friend, Scottish center forward Hughie Ferguson, scorer of the strange goal that won the Cup Final for Cardiff in 1927, turned Gallacher sour. Gallacher felt that rough usage by defenders and spectators knocked the heart out of Ferguson, who went back to Scotland, lost form, was barracked by the crowd, and eventually committed suicide by hanging himself in the dressing room.

Gallacher himself committed suicide more miserably still, died on the railway line at Gateshead in the North East of England, still only in his fifties, the day before he was due to appear in court for ill-treating his son. It was a pitiful end to the pitiful life of one of the best of all center forwards.

Dixie Dean, Gallacher's contemporary, was made in a quite different mould: strongly built, a superb header of a ball. Born near Liverpool in Birkenhead, his real name was Bill and he hated to be called Dixie. In season 1927–28, when the third back game was still settling down, he scored no fewer than sixty goals for Everton in the Championship; three of whose forty-two matches he missed. Significantly, his last three goals, to make up the magic sixty, were scored in the very last game of the season against . . . Arsenal, the team which had invented and, it was supposed, perfected, the third back game. It was a deep disappointment to Charlie Buchan, Arsenal's famous captain, inventor of the third back game, whose last appearance in football this was. In later years, however, he would pay this tribute to Dean:

Dean, tall, dark-haired and magnificently built, was then at the height of his powers. His headwork was beautiful, so well-timed that it seemed effortless. He headed two goals that day, one from well outside the goal-area with just a nod of the head. Everton planned their game around Dean. A long, high ball up the middle to Dean's head, a clever deflection to the feet of an inside-forward and Everton's attack was in full cry for goal.

The center forward, as you will have gathered, is the *fer de lance* of soccer, the player who takes his chance, and his chances, in the imminent, deadly breach. When, in season 1976–77, a volley of splendidly taken goals established Andy Gray, of Aston Villa and Scotland, as a center forward with all the natural gifts and courage, his coach, Ron Saunders, said of him, "Instead of joining the queue waiting for chances at the far post [*i.e., the goal post farther from where the center is made*] Gray attacks the six-yard box, making his own chances. We know that if we put enough balls into that area he will be on the end of most of them." The lean and fair-haired Gray was thus essentially a center forward, not merely that generic creature, a so-called "striker," supposed in some way to combine the qualities of winger, center forward, and attacking center forward.

Dean's successor at Everton, when no successor seemed possible, was Tommy Lawton. Lawton came from Burnley as a 17-year-old, already coveted by half the First Division clubs in England, but he was born in that other Lancashire town of Bolton, famous for producing center forwards.

Albert Shepherd, esteemed by Charlie Buchan as the best of all center forwards before 1914, had played for Bolton Wanderers. Such was the savage power of his shot that it is said that George, Aston Villa's international goalkeeper, danced up and down on his line, beating his knees with his hands as Shepherd advanced, and crying, "He's coming again! He's coming again!"

Later, Bolton would have Nat Lofthouse as their center forward, star of a famous English victory against Austria in Vienna in 1952, and of Wanderers' win in the Cup Final in 1958. But Lawton, like the much slighter but considerably gifted Paul Mariner, who joined Ipswich Town for the equivalent of £200,000 in 1976, was a Bolton man who eluded Bolton Wanderers.

Instead, Lawton went to Burnley, dissatisfied with the offers Bolton made him to work part-time either as a clerk or as a butcher's boy. At Turf Moor, Burnley, where they gave him a job working in the office, he was under the stringent tutelage of the former Manchester United halfback, Ray Bennion, who would switch him across the buttocks with a stick if he didn't jump high enough to head the ball in training, and would make him dribble around and around the field, stopping to hit all the "B's" in the advertisement, "Burnley's Beer Is Best." Either because of or despite such draconian methods, Lawton was good enough to play Second Division football at sixteen, score goals, and at seventeen join Everton at a record fee for so young a player.

He would have been a bargain at almost any fee, for there could scarcely have been a more complete center forward. His physical strength was exceptional, he was, as we have seen, a magnificent header of the ball, capable of jumping great heights, he was quick, he was a powerful shot, and he could, as they used to say and demand of center forwards, "hold his line together," giving the ball as well as receiving. He was England's center forward at the age of nineteen, and who knows what records he might have set up had the war years not intervened, years in which official League and international football were scrapped, when he was at the peak of his powers. Thus there was never any hope that he would match Dean's extraordinary record of 379 goals in the Football League, but some of those he did score were extraordinary.

None was more dramatic than the late goal he headed to give England a 2-1 win against Scotland in April 1939 at Hampden Park, their first in Glasgow for a dozen years. Stanley Matthews, out on the right wing, took the ball up to George Cummings, a strong and rugged left back, went round him as though he didn't exist, and centered high. Lawton wrote, in his "ghosted" autobiography, that as the ball came over he told himself, "Use your loaf, son, it's your only chance!" (Loaf of bread—Cockney rhyming slang for "head.") At all events, up he went in what came to be celebrated, journalistically, as the Lawton Leap, soaring high above the Scottish defenders, to head the ball firmly into the top corner of the goal. 2-1.

Europe in the 1930s produced three especially fine center forwards: Mathias Sindelar of Austria, Giuseppe Meazza and Silvio Piola of Italy; though George Sarosi of Hungary, who could also turn a trick as an attacking center half, was close behind them.

Sindelar was a G. O. Smith figure, tall and so very thin that he was nicknamed in Vienna *Der Papierener,* The Man of Paper. Of this wispy, blond figure, Willy Meisl, by then a sports journalist in Central Europe, wrote:

> He was truly symbolical of Austrian football at its peak period: no brawn but any amount of brain. Technique bordering on virtuosity, precision work and an inexhaustible repertoire of tricks and ideas. He had a boyish delight in soccer exploits, above all in unexpected twists and moves which were quickly understood and shared by his partners brought up on the same "wave-length," but were baffling to an opposition mentally a fraction of

a second slower. Sindelar, though a soccer genius, was never an egotist. [He] commanded a rasping shot, but . . . preferred to walk, or rather to dance the ball not only towards the goal, but almost literally into the net. It did not always come off, but with such artists you have to take the rough with the smooth.

Sindelar died a wretched and mysterious death, yet one more famous center forward who was a suicide, expiring in a gas-filled room in Vienna. He was partly Jewish, and it was said he had been betrayed to the Gestapo by his fellow Austrian international Mock, an ardent Nazi.

Meazza and Piola could scarcely have had a more different approach to center forward play, but they complemented one another admirably when they played for the Italian World Cup winning team of 1938. Piola, big and forceful, in the middle, Meazza, quick, slight, and elusive, at inside right, beside him. Of Meazza, his Italian team manager, Vittorio Pozzo, wrote, "He was a born attacker. He 'saw' the play, understood the situation distributed the ball judiciously, made the whole attacking section function. He wasn't as a young man, nor even as a veteran, robust. His concept of the game was all skill . . . he was one of the most skilful Italian forwards who ever existed."

Meazza scored 355 goals in his career, 33 of them in his 53 games for the Italian international team. He was not only immensely quick and incisive on the ground, but surprisingly good with his head. The burly Piola eventually overtook his total of goals; he was three years younger than Meazza, but played till he was nearly forty. In his thirty international games, he scored no fewer than 34 goals; a record which would be surpassed in Europe only by the unique Gerd Müller.

When Meazza made his debut for Italy in Rome in February 1930 against Switzerland, a party of Neapolitans traveled up specially to jeer him, much to the fury of his mother, who was watching from the stand. The cause of their wrath was that Pozzo had preferred Meazza to their own idol Sallustro, the Naples center forward, who was actually an Argentinian.

Of the many splendid goals Meazza scored for Italy, Pozzo thought one of the best was the one he scored on a muddy February day of 1931 in Milan, against Austria; the first time Italy had ever managed to beat them. Receiving the ball from the Argentinian left winger, Raimondo Orsi, Meazza drew the famous Viennese keeper, Hiden, out of goal, left him sprawling with a feint, and pushed the ball into the net.

Piola's "finest hour" was the World Cup competition of 1938 when no defense could stop him, but his most bizarre goal was surely the one he punched for Italy against England in Milan in 1939. Five years earlier, at the Arsenal Stadium, in London, Meazza had scored two graceful goals for Italy against England, just about the only graceful things in a brutish Italian performance, after they had been reduced to ten men early in the game. A kick on the foot broke the toe of Luisito Monti, Italy's ruthless Argentinian center half, he was taken to hospital in great pain, a handkerchief stuffed in his mouth at his own request, and the other Italian players decided it had been done on purpose. England won what England knows as the Battle of Highbury 3-2.

The war over, Italy drew fine center forwards from all over Europe, seduced by the money rather than the climate. Gunnar Nordahl, a massive Swede from Norkopping, known as The Fireman for the career he originally followed, arrived from Norkopping, in 1948, and stayed to score an avalanche of goals for Milan, concluding his sojourn in Rome. Heavy thighed yet adroit, efficient in control, strong in the air, a thundering right-footed shot, Nordahl had led the attack of the fine Swedish team which won the Olympic soccer tournament of 1948, in London. Nor, despite his size, was he slow when there was a through pass to be chased. On his right, in the Milan attack, he had the shrewd Gunnar Gren, on his left the tall, skillful, infinitely versatile Nils Liedholm, who stayed in Italy to become a successful manager; three Swedes, making up the so-called Grenoli Trio.

In 1957, John Charles arrived in Turin from Leeds, to become the most popular center forward Juventus, the crack club of Italy, has ever had, a Welshman from Swansea who had begun his career as a center half, played there for Wales at seventeen, then been converted at Leeds United into a still more successful center forward.

Charles had a massive physique, a thundering turn of speed, immense ability in the air, and no small capacity on the ground. In Turin he was nicknamed King John, and for five years his fame surpassed even that of his inside forwards, the *jeune premier*, fair-headed captain, Giampiero Boniperti, and the fiery little Argentinian, Omar Sivori.

There was a bleak, ironic side to Charles's heroic days in Turin; his wife ran away with an Italian lover and, it was alleged, took much of his money—*their* money?—with her. He was a simple, decent, honest man, who played the game hard and always with straightforward courage. Once, when he had been fouled more often than he could bear during a game, he turned to Boniperti and pleaded with him, "*You* do something to them, Boni; *I* can't."

Now and again, Gunnar Nordahl would drop back and play in a "deep lying" position, but the prince of the so-called deep lying center forwards was Hungary's Nandor Hidégkuti. In the great Hungarian team of the early 1950s, his role was to fall back into midfield, leaving the formidable Puskás and Kocsis up front, but he was always capable of moving up into the attack and scoring splendid goals.

Never had he played better than he did against England at Wembley in 1953, when Hungary took away their unbeaten home record against foreign "invaders." He scored three fine goals, the first of them in ninety seconds when, with a cunning feint, he drew Harry Johnston, England's center half, out of the defensive "wall," and scored with a fulminating right-footed shot. His second came from an equally powerful shot, right foot again after England had briefly drawn level; the third, and Hungary's sixth, volleying in a lob from Puskás. Hidégkuti was thirty-one years old at the time, but his energy was fathomless; and energy, as he once told an interviewer, was essential for the kind of game he played, and preferred. As he also explained, it was feasible only when a team had a couple of inside forwards capable of scoring goals. He himself liked to hover in the rear and be a playmaker; besides, he admitted, his heading had never been very good.

What those who tried to imitate Hidégkuti's play, such as the future Leeds and England manager, Don Revie, neglected was that it entailed not only leading one's troops from the rear, like Gilbert and Sullivan's Duke of Plaza Toro, but also coming up to support them. Revie was a distinguished general, as he showed with a memorable performance for Manchester City against Birmingham City in the Cup Final of 1956 at Wembley but he hadn't Hidégkuti's balance, acceleration, stamina, and shot.

Alfredo Di Stefano had; and a great deal more besides. Whether or not he was the greatest center forward of all time must be a matter of opinion; he was surely the most complete. An Argentinian from Buenos

Aires, he built up his astonishing stamina as a long-distance runner; though a distinguished coach, Dave Sexton, who did so well with London's Chelsea and Queens Park Rangers, once told me he felt stamina was as much a gift as ball control. Be that as it may, Di Stefano, long before anybody played Total Football, was Total Football incarnate; one moment, it seemed, averting a goal with a slide tackle in his own penalty area, the next racing through the opposing defense for a shot at goal. He could execute a defense splitting through pass to perfection, and when Ferenc Puskás arrived in 1959 to join him in the Real Madrid attack, he exploited the tubby little Hungarian's shot, speed, and opportunism to perfection. They scored seven goals between them in Hampden Park, Glasgow, against Eintracht Frankfurt in the European Cup Final of 1960; when the hypercritical Glasgow fans stayed behind to give Real an ovation.

Two years later, in Amsterdam, when Real lost the Cup 5-3 to Benfica, and Puskás got another three goals, I still recall the sublime precision and judgment of the through ball with which Di Stefano sent Puskás galloping half the length of the field to score.

Di Stefano was tall, fair-haired, deep-chested, the son of an immigrant from the Isle of Capri who himself had been a professional footballer. He began with River Plate, left, with a drove of other Argentinian stars, to make money in Colombia when that country dropped temporarily out of FIFA in 1948 and paid high wages, and returned to Argentina as a coach only at the end of his playing career.

In 1953, at the age of twenty-seven, he came to Spain. Real Madrid wanted him; so did Barcelona. The Spanish Federation issued a judgment of Solomon: they should share him. Real Madrid had him first; and that was that. At the end of that season, they bought out

Barcelona's interest, and Di Stefano stayed to inspire their remarkable monopoly of the European Cup, five victories in the first five years of the competition.

Imperious, intransigent, but the essential motor and mentor of his team, Di Stefano would brook no rivals. Didì arrived from Brazil, star and strategist of the 1958 World Cup, and cooled his heels on the sidelines, hardly getting a game. Little Raymond Kopa came from France, a deep-lying center forward of exquisite balance and control, whose Reims team had very nearly beaten Real in the first European Cup Final of all, in 1956. He was banished to the right wing, and came into his own only when, in the summer of 1958, he was released to play for France and inspired them to take third place in the World Cup. It is said that when Ferenc Puskás arrived, a refugee from Hungary, he mollified the great man by presenting him with an easy chance to score in the last League game of the Spanish season, when he and Di Stefano were level on goals as the competition's chief scorers.

An equally mighty ego, that of the successful coach, Helenio Herrera, clashed with Di Stefano's in the 1962 World Cup, when he traveled, naturalized now, with the Spanish team to Chile, Di Stefano didn't play a game. Officially, he was injured. There were those who felt he had no great desire to play.

What remains beyond doubt is that without him, Real would never have established their monopoly of the European Cup. They had many fine players, some unexceptional ones, but what made the wheels turn round was the brilliant ubiquity, the endless stamina and versatility, of Di Stefano. Perhaps he was not so good with his head as the Charleses, Lawtons, and Deans; but he *could* score goals with it when it was necessary, and there was scarcely another aspect of the game in which he was not outstanding.

The moral effect Di Stefano had on Real Madrid, Uwe Seeler, though a much less talented player, had on West Germany. Short, squat and powerful, infinitely brave, he came into the international team as an 18-year-old, just after it had won the 1954 World Cup, and went on playing till after the World Cup of 1970. "If the ball was on the other side of that wall," an Irish international forward once said to me, "Seeler would get it." He was fast, he was intelligent, he moved out of the middle well when the occasion suggested it, he jumped remarkable heights and headed some remarkable goals; none more so than the one against England in León in the 1970 World Cup quarter-final.

England was 2-1 in the lead, the end of the game was approaching, and there seemed no danger at all when a high ball dropped into the English penalty area. Somehow, however, Seeler managed to leap, his back to the goal, twist, and head the ball over the English goalkeeper, Bonetti, in an extraordinary parabola, into the net. Germany went on to win.

That was the tournament in which Helmut Schoen, the West German team coach, had to square the circle or, to be more precise, reconcile the claims of Seeler with that of the Young Pretender, the still more remarkable center forward, Gerd Müller. It was not easy. Seeler had become the most magnetic, popular player in West Germany. In the 1966 World Cup, when England had beaten West Germany in the Final, the war cry of the German fans had been, "Uwe, Uwe, Uwe!" Schoen, taking a leaf out of the book of Vittorio Pozzo when he was Italian team manager, put Müller and Seeler into the same room; and into the same forward line, with Müller in the middle, Seeler as inside right. It worked extremely well, for the two blended nicely, and the goal they worked out together against Italy in the semi-final with a sweet exchange of headers was a triumph of unselfishness.

Twenty-four years old at the time, Müller, though he scored the amazing total of 68 goals in his 62 games for West Germany, at a time when defenses had never been more heavily manned or better organized, never won the hearts of the German public as did Seeler. "Germans like a fighter," Udo Lattek, his manager at Bayern Munich for some years, explained to me during the 1974 World Cup, "and Müller is not a fighter." This was not a criticism; merely a statement of fact. The criticism that *has* been made of Müller is, in schoolboy parlance, that he is a "goal hanger," merely loitering about the goal area with intent to score. Sheer nonsense. In the first place Müller can, when it is necessary, play just as great a part in the team effort as anybody else. In January 1977, shortly before he had to go into hospital for an operation on his spine, he played in extreme pain against Duisburg, against medical advice, and ran himself into the ground in his team's cause.

Leading scorer in the 1970 World Cup, scorer of the winning goal in the 1974 World Cup Final, he is well used to being undervalued. Playing for his local, Bavarian, club at Noerdlingen he impressed none of the great clubs much. Zlatko Cjaicowski, the Bayern manager, Czechoslovakia's World Cup captain in the 1950s, thought so little of him that he had to be persuaded to sign him by the Bayern president, Herr Neudecker. Müller proceeded to show that there *are* times when directors know more than their managers.

Thick-thighed, with a very low center of gravity, extraordinary pivotal ability, superb anticipation, the coolest of cool heads, Müller proceeded to score a fusillade of goals. Let me recall a few of them. Against England, in León, he scored the winner with a ferocious left-footed volley, at point-blank range. Two years later, in Antwerp, a European Nations Cup semi-final, he somehow managed to get under a cross into the goal area, and urge it, rather than head it, over the Belgian goalkeeper, into the net. In May 1974 in the replayed European Cup Final against Atlético Madrid, he saw the Madrid goalkeeper off his line, and with the most delicately judged lob, floated the ball tantalizingly over his head, and home. I do not think there has ever been anyone quite like him.

Johan Cryuff, it is true, does more; though never as much as Alfredo Di Stefano, the player whom he most admired. Born into a poor family in Amsterdam, Cryuff's mother used to clean the floors of Ajax, Amsterdam, the club he would join, inspire, and transform into the best team in Europe, the finest since Real Madrid.

Cruyff meant as much to Ajax, who won the European Cup three years in a row, as did Di Stefano to Real. Had he stayed in Amsterdam, rather than go to Barcelona, no doubt they would have equaled Madrid's record of five successive wins. Sheer, galvanic speed has been the essence of Cryuff's game; speed of thought as much as speed of movement. He has said that in fact he is not particularly fast; that he is simply quicker off the mark than his opponents. Be that as it may, he has a remarkable aptitude for being first to the ball, an electric turn, a whiplash shot with either foot. If he hasn't the physical strength of a Di Stefano, his eye for making or taking an opening is as marvelously alert. He acquired the hallmark of a great player by showing he could be great in the World Cup Final; even if, after his early, scintillating run through the German defense had brought a penalty, he was seldom outstanding in the rest of the game.

That one man can, indeed, make, or at least transform, a team, contrary to the soccer adage, Cruyff would prove when he joined Barcelona in 1973. They were near the bottom of the League when he began to play. By the end of the season, they had won it comfortably.

When he signed for his third season with them in 1976, Cruyff was promised 48 million pesetas, some $800,000; more than all the other players on the roster were earning among them. There is no doubt that he is interested in money, yet one can also find a beguiling openness in him, and for one with so little schooling, he is a remarkable linguist, fluent in English, German, French, Spanish, and Italian.

The salient thing about the greatest center forwards— G. O. Smith, Gallacher, Lawton, Di Stefano, Müller, Cruyff—is that they are unique, yet all generically, indisputably, center forwards. The position obstinately, sturdily, survives.

Evidence of this, and of the fact that center forwards need not be large, was clearly demonstrated in the 1978 World Cup by Paolo Rossi and Andres Toroscik, the first a 22-year-old Italian, the second a 23-year-old Hungarian, the first dark, the second blond.

Rossi, who came with little expectation of playing, in fact had a much happier and effective World Cup than Toroscik, so highly quoted before the start. Toroscik, beautifully balanced, an exquisitely nimble player on the ground—as indeed is Rossi—was so severely provoked by the tactics of the Argentine defenders in Buenos Aires that in the last minutes he kicked one of his tormentors to the ground, was sent off, and thus suspended from the next game. Nevertheless, his persecution was itself a negative tribute to the way he flitted past defenders whose only means of stopping him was desperately to foul him. Toroscik does not head the ball much, but his skill, positional sense, and elusiveness in the penalty area embody the Hungarian tradition at its best.

Paolo Rossi, a Tuscan, came to Argentina with a $5,000,000 price on his head; the amount at which he'd just been valued in an absurd auction in which his club, Lanerossi Vicenza, bid $2,500,000 for the half share in him which the much wealthier Juventus club of Turin still held. Rossi had had an outstanding season in the Italian Sèrie A, the First Division. His form in practice games led to his being put into the Italian World Cup team, for which he performed with consistent dash, courage, skill, and speed. As the watching England team coach, Ron Greenwood, remarked, he was faster at the end of his runs than at the beginning. He could move out to either wing and sprint with success, he was lethally quick around the goal, he showed his strength of character—despite his boyish demeanor—when he insisted on playing against Argentina, though Enzo Bearzot, his coach, wanted to rest him. In the event, he set up the only goal of the game, for Roberto Bettega.

12
TOURNAMENTS AND TEAMS

The *Football Association Challenge Cup,* as it should properly be called. The F.A. Cup is the great progenitor of all competition; indeed, it may be said, of soccer itself. The allure of it made, with fantastic speed, a national sport of soccer in Great Britain in the 1880s, fired the enthusiasm of the Scots, who would revolutionize tactics, brought about the birth of professionalism. The F.A. Cup is the natural father of the World Cup, the European Cup, and all those other, lesser, cups we know today, whether they be the Copa de los Libertadores of South America, or the Intercontinental Cup, that grandiose abortion. The F.A. Cup has maintained an astonishing vitality. It is still the most attractive and most passionately followed competition in England, still famous for its feats of "giant killing." It still builds up to a spectacular crescendo when the Final is played at Wembley Stadium each May, watched by 100,000 fortunate enough to get a ticket, but by millions more on television, not only in England but throughout the world.

It was on July 20, 1871, that C. W. Alcock, secretary of

the eight-year-old Football Association, proposed at a meeting in London "that it is desirable that a Challenge Cup should be established in connection with the Association, for which all clubs belonging to the Association should be invited to compete." Note this last proviso: *all* clubs. There is the glory and the glamor of it. Where in most other countries the national cup is a limited affair, confined to teams in the Football League, in England the humblest, most obscure little amateur club is entitled to take part, entering at the stage of the Preliminary Round in September, near the very start of the season. Four rounds of the qualifying competition will then be played, until the Competition Proper begins in late November.

To this a number of the lesser Football League clubs will have exemption, but it is only with the Third Round proper, traditionally played in early January, that the competition gets right off the ground, only then that the major First and Second Division clubs of the Football League enter the lists. At this stage, there will be sixty-four clubs remaining in the tournament. After the Fourth, Fifth, and Sixth rounds there will be only four, contesting the semi-finals, which are both played in neutral stadiums. These take place now in April, though when the season was shorter they were played in March, with the Cup Final itself in April.

Alcock, an Old Harrovian, was inspired by Harrow's Cock House competition; the "houses" into which the school was divided competed at Harrow Rules football on a knockout basis. With the exception of 1945–46, the first post-war season, when the Cup was revived after seven years, this has remained the pattern.

Then, somewhat obscurely, even perversely, it was decided to play the matches not on the basis of "sudden death"—the result of a single game being decisive—but on that of home and away ties, the winning club being that which scored more goals in the two games. It is this method which, for better or for worse, has been adopted for the three major European cups, of which the UEFA Cup—the European Union Cup, first known as the Fairs Cup—retains the practice even for the Final. There will be more to say of the consequences of this, elsewhere; for the moment let it be observed that what it tends to cut out of a tournament is that very element of surprise, the prodigies of David against Goliath, which makes the F.A. Cup so exhilarating. David, playing on his own ground, can always hope to defeat Goliath but if, having defeated him, he must play a return game on Philistine territory, then his hopes are greatly diminished.

Nowadays, when a first game is drawn, it must be replayed on the ground of the away club. If there is a second draw, then extra time of a quarter-of-an-hour each way is played. If the game still results in a draw, then a second replay is scheduled, again with extra time if necessary, on a neutral ground. So it must go on, always on a neutral ground, until a result be reached. In the Third Round of 1953, it took Stoke City and Bury five games before Stoke at last had the better of the argument.

There were no replays in the early versions of the F.A. Cup; one does not find them until the fourth version of the F.A. Cup, in 1874–75. Initially, the F.A. itself had discretion as to which club should go through in the event of a draw, just as it could give clubs exemption when they had long distances to travel. Moreover, till the 1873–74 tournament, it was a Challenge Cup in the traditional manner of the Davis Cup for tennis; the holders were exempted until the final, challenge, round.

Fifteen clubs competed for the first F.A. Cup, among them Queens Park of Glasgow, who were given exemption till the semi-final. They were among those clubs who subscribed for the initial F.A. Cup itself, of whose £20 cost they generously provided a guinea (one pound, one shilling), which was fractionally more than one-sixth of their annual income. They came to London to contest the semi-final against the powerful Wanderers, made up of players from the public schools, surprised everybody with their modern conception of football, which eschewed individualism for the passing game, drew 0-0, went back to Scotland, and hadn't the money to come down for the return game. They withdrew.

Byes, exemptions, and manipulations did not last very long. Soon it was customary to "draw" the pairings for each round. Today, the draw is a national event, numbered balls representing the clubs concerned being dropped into a bag, and pulled out in pairs by officials of the Football Association. The first club out of the bag has the advantage of playing at home. Thus there is a double element of chance and, if you wish, mystery; a team does not know whom it will play, nor whether it will play at home or away.

Originally, it was decreed that captains of competing teams should toss a coin for choice of venue, while all matches after the Second Round were to be played in South East London at the cricket ground, Kennington Oval; or as the Committee decreed. The location of the Final, however, was at the discretion of the club holding the trophy.

Between 1872 and 1892 the Final took place regularly at The Oval, with the one exception of 1873, when the Wanderers, as holders, decided they wanted it to be played at Lillie Bridge in South West London, a ground which no longer exists, though some thirty years later the Chelsea Football Club would use nearby Stamford Bridge for their home field; as they do to this day. The kick-off at Lillie Bridge was at eleven in the morning,

264

for the quaint and indicative reason that the players and their friends wished to watch the Oxford and Cambridge Boat Race, on the Thames. For all that, the Final began a half-hour late.

The first Final was watched by the surprising number of nearly 2000 spectators; a sporting newspaper of the day opined that there would have been still more, had an admission charge of one shilling not been levied.

A decade later, the advent of the professional clubs from the North sent the numbers up. There were 7000 to watch the Old Etonians beat Blackburn Olympic 1-0 in 1882; 12,500 two years later when Blackburn Rovers, for the second consecutive year, kept the Cup in England by beating Queens Park. Thereafter, the Cup became an all-English affair.

The 20,000 mark was passed in 1889 when mighty Preston North End beat the Wolves 3-0, in front of 22,000; there were 25,000 on the occasion of the last Final at The Oval in 1892, between the two Midland clubs, Aston Villa and West Bromwich Albion. The following season the Final at last moved to Fallowfield, Manchester, where a staggering 45,000 watched Wolves beat Everton. Next it was the Everton ground itself, at Liverpool, which had 37,000 fans for the Notts County vs. Bolton Wanderers game. Then the Final moved to the huge expanses of the Crystal Palace, in South East London, where it stayed till 1915.

Crowds, there, increased almost by geometrical progression. There were 42,560 at the first Final; 65,000 in 1897, when Villa beat Everton; and 110,000 when Sheffield United played North London's Tottenham Hotspur in 1901. Even this extraordinary record was beaten twelve years later, when 120,081 spectators watched a famous Final between Aston Villa and Sunderland.

That was the game in which Clem Stephenson, Villa's famous inside left, one of the finest of all constructive inside forwards, though he was only capped once by England, turned to the no less distinguished Charlie Buchan of Sunderland and said, "We're going to beat you by a goal to nothing. I dreamed it last night. Also that Tom Barber's going to score the winning goal." Sure enough, with about a half-hour to go, Charlie Wallace took a poor goal-kick for Sunderland, Barber, Villa's right half, dashed forward, headed it, and the ball went into the net for the only goal of the game. Of such strange incidents is the lore of the F.A. Cup composed.

A far stranger goal, which might almost be called The Goal That Never Was, had been scored (if that is the word) in the 1901 Final. Tottenham Hotspur, the Spurs, had reached it, through they were only a member of the Southern League, a competition which lay outside the Football League, with its two divisions. In 1920 the League would co-opt the Southern League as a Third Division. Meanwhile, for a team from so lowly a competiton to confound the mighty, as Spurs had done, scoring four goals alike against Preston and West Bromwich, was phenomenal. So the 110,000 poured into the Palace, some of them perched in the trees, Spurs twice shot past the massive Sheffield United goalkeeper "Fatty" Foulke, and had made it 2-1 when, within a minute, United scored their strange equalizer.

Lipsham dashed down Sheffield's left wing, and shot; Clawley, the Spurs keeper, well off his goal line, stopped the ball, but did not catch it cleanly. It went behind the line, and the linesman signaled for a corner kick. The referee indicated he did not agree, so Clawley took the ball and placed it for what seemed the only logical alternative, a goal kick. The referee did not agree with this, either. He awarded a goal, maintaining that when Clawley fumbled the ball, it had crossed the Tottenham goal line between the posts! He refused to consult his linesman. He was much too far up the field possibly to have seen what occurred. Clawley, in fact, had been yards out of his goal. But the goal stood, the game was drawn, and justice was done only when the Final was replayed on the ground of Bolton Wanderers.

In 1923, after a couple of years on Chelsea's ground at Stamford Bridge, the Cup Final came to Wembley Stadium, where it has stayed ever since. The North London suburb had been the scene of an Imperial Exhibition. Crystal Palace was considered, now, too primitive for modern needs, and in 1921 the Football Association made an agreement for twenty-one years with the proprietors of the Exhibition. A quarter of a million tons of clay were removed and the vast stadium, ample if aesthetically negligible, went up. It had none of the grace of the structures being designed at this time by Pietro Nervi, its granite towers were a monstrosity, it would wear on into the twentieth century as an increasing anachronism, but there are undoubted accretions of history there, and soccer has had few more dramatic days than the playing of the first Wembley Cup Final in April 1923.

The F.A. left the organization of the Final to the proprietors of Wembley, the Empire Exhibition, themselves. These authorities decided that the stadium could hold 127,000 which, at 1.45 p.m., it did, the gates accordingly being closed. But walls were scaled, barriers beaten down, and shortly before the game was due to start there were some 200,000 fans inside the stadium, hundreds of them on the field of play itself. The calm diligence of a mounted policeman on a white horse, an almost legendary figure in the history of the Cup, did much to see that the field was cleared, though the crowd still stood around the touchline, one player allegedly joked afterwards that the best pass he received came from a spectator, while a West Ham defender, George Kay, was enmeshed in the crowd when Bolton, the winners, scored their second goal. "If our supporters had known the result of the game was going to stand," said an official of West Ham United, the beaten, East London, club, "I am afraid they would have protested by swarming over the pitch." So Bolton Wanderers won the first Wembley Cup Final, 2-0.

The *European Cup*, sometimes known as the Champions' Cup, born in 1955, was conceived by a famous French sporting journalist and former player, Gabriel Hanot. The idea was that the League champions of each European country should compete each season for a Cup on a knock-out basis with the variant, as we have seen, that the ties should be decided on a home-and-away, aggregate of goals, basis. The anomaly, of course, was that a knockout tournament should decide the Championship of Europe, all of whose participants had qualified for it by winning their *League*. Cups may have the allure and the excitement; it is generally agreed, throughout the world of soccer, that League championships, lasting over a protracted period in which luck, hypothetically at least, should even out, are a fairer test of quality. The same objection may be raised with even greater validity to the World Cup which succeeded the Olympic soccer tournament— another to be conducted from the first on a knockout pattern—as the most important in football.

A European *League*, however, has always presented too many difficulties, above all that of reconciling its massive demands with those of a country's domestic competition. Take Manchester United out of the Football League, Rangers and Celtic out of the Scottish League, Juventus out of the Italian League, Saint Etienne out of the French League, and what have you left? At best, a seriously diminished competition.

The English Football League, renowned as a deeply insular and reactionary body, in fact "advised" Chelsea, English League champions at the time (ironically, the only time), not to take part in the first European Cup tournament: and Chelsea cravenly bowed to their behest.

Manchester United, the following year, simply told the Football League to go to the devil, and competed, reaching the semi-final. Under the progressive, internationally minded leadership of their Scottish coach Matt Busby, they were not inclined to put up with the League's authoritarianism. But the League would take an especially mean and churlish revenge. In 1958, when United lost more than half their team in the appalling Munich air crash, on their way back from playing a European Cup tie in Belgrade, the European Union, organizers of the European Cup, invited them to take part in the 1958–59 tournament as a gesture of sympathy. The Football League forbade it! Their grounds were devious in the extreme; for they maintained that since United were not the English champions, the rules of the European Cup did not permit them to participate! Shameless sophistry. The fact that the European Union had decided to waive their own rules was happily ignored by the Football League.

Manchester United appealed to the Football Association, the overall ruling body, whose writ runs not only at the level of international competition but among *all* clubs, inside and outside the 92-team strong Football League. The F.A. upheld United's appeal; whereupon the League flew into a fury, insisted on a joint F.A.–F.L. committee to appeal the appeal, and got its own, sour way. Manchester United was forbidden to compete.

For its first five seasons, the European Cup was synonymous with Real Madrid, and Real Madrid was synonymous with Alfredo Di Stefano, the great Argentinian center forward. Real was a club which did things on a scale undreamed of in Britain; and in most other European countries. They enlarged their stadium at Chamartin into a huge bowl, capable of taking 125,000 spectators, and named it after Santiago Bernabeu, their paternalist president. They spent huge sums of money buying the best players from all over the world, though several of these, including such heroes of the 1958 World Cup as Didì of Brazil and Agne Simonsson of Sweden, did little or nothing when they reached Madrid.

They say in football that one man doesn't make a team, but Di Stefano ridiculed the apothegm. Without him, Real would never have got off the ground. With his stamina, his skill, his versatility, his inspiration, his tremendous finishing power, he was the heart, soul, and lungs of the team. By 1960, when Real had the last of their five victories with a coruscating 7-3 win against West Germany's Eintracht in the Final in Glasgow, Di Stefano had Hungary's Ferenc Puskás on his left, the sturdy, tireless Del Sol, bought from Betis, Seville, at inside right. By and large, however, it is strange to see how few other players of major status played in those Real Madrid teams, when one looks back to consider them. They never did find a satisfactory outside right, though they tried the famous Raymond Kopa of France, and Canario from Brazil. For the first three tournaments, Di Stefano's first lieutenant was another Argentinian, the tall, clever inside left Hector Rial, with whom he combined so smoothly. Two of the five successful Finals were against Reims, and the first, played in Paris in June 1956, was a very close-run thing. Inspired by the splendid play of Kopa as a deep lying center forward, Reims actually went into a two-goal lead in the opening ten minutes, through Leblond and

Templin. Di Stefano and Rial had squared that by half-time, but Hidalgo restored the French team's advantage, and it was only a remarkable goal by the Spanish center half Marquitos, setting off on a long, lone raid to score, which put Real on terms again. Eleven minutes from full-time, Rial got the winner.

Francisco "Paco" Gento played outside left in all five games, a squat, dark, little winger of tremendous pace, whom Di Stefano knew exactly how to bring into the game. Their understanding was at times almost telepathic. The following season, Gento scored Real's second goal when they beat Fiorentina—which boasted the illustrious Brazilian right winger, Julinho—2-0 in rather a dull Final in Madrid. On the way, they had knocked out the rising young Manchester United team in the semi-final. "We have learned quite a lot," said Roger Byrne, the England and Manchester United left back and captain, fated to die in the Munich air crash. "I think these two games against Real have shown every ingenious device to stop a team playing football."

This, alas, was the other side of Real's coin; just as it would be the other side of Internazionale's, the Milan club. The Real defenders could be quite ruthless; none more so than the big, fair-haired Uruguayan stopper José Santamaria, who joined them in time to participate in their 1958 success. This was another near-run game. Milan, in Brussels, was every bit as good and lively as Real, strong in the possession of two splendid inside forwards in Liedholm of Sweden and Ernesto Grillo, the Argentinian. Real escaped when Tito Cucchiaroni, Milan's outside left and another Argentinian, hit the bar in the closing minutes. After 107 minutes, Gento scored to keep the Cup for Real.

Tactically, Real was not innovative; the concept of the deep lying, roving center forward, though brought to perfection by Di Stefano, was not new; it had been developed by Nandor Hidégkuti of Hungary. Nor, despite that famous goal by Marquitos, were they a team which habitually launched defenders into attack. Technical excellence, quickness of eye, mastery of the ball, great finishing power were their chief weapons. They were also extremely adept at keeping possession of the ball with a maze of short passes, then suddenly changing rhythm to burst into penetrative attack; much as the Brazilians do, at their best.

They were succeeded by another splendid team from the Iberian peninsula, Benfica of Lisbon, under the canny managership of Hungarian Bela Guttmann. Benfica won the Cup at Berne in March 1961, defeating Barcelona, Real's conquerors, in the Final. (It is a rule of the European Cup that the League champions of a country whose team holds the Cup can compete, as well as the holders.) The following year, at Amsterdam, in one of the most dazzling and dramatic football games ever seen, Benfica thrashed Real 5-3 in a fusillade of astounding goals, most of them smashed home from well outside the penalty box. Three of them went to Puskás, two to the mighty right foot of the young Eusebio, from Mozambique. At the end, in a generous, if histrionic, gesture, Puskás took off his shirt and gave it to Eusebio.

Eusebio, lissome, tall, an immensely graceful mover, a superb controller of the ball at speed, had the round and soulful face of some gentle, threatened animal. Often comparisons would be made between him and Pelé, but they were gratuitous. Neither in style, build, nor temperament were they alike, though each had a devastating right foot. Eusebio was essentially a marvelous runner, over long distances—in soccer terms—a faculty never better shown than when he scored four goals for Portugal in the World Cup finals of 1966, a tournament in which he finished leading scorer. Pelé, by contrast, moved very quickly over short distances, was a much better header of the ball, quite fearless, where Eusebio, at times, could be intimidated. Eusebio would score another goal the following year in the Final against Milan, at Wembley Stadium, but Coluna, the left-half, another African with a left foot almost as good as Eusebio's right, was kicked out of the game and off the field. Milan, with two well-taken goals engineered by the subtle Gianni Rivera for the rampant Brazilian José Altafini, brought the Cup to Italy.

Coluna was at inside left in Benfica's first two Finals, a poised, muscular, moustached figure who dominated the midfield; strong, skilled, and a fine distributor. Germano, who played center half in the first two Finals, and again in 1965, was one of the best in the world; tall and bald, heavily moustached, immensely athletic and resilient. "He *bounces* with energy," said the England team coach, Walter Winterbottom, admiringly. Alas, Germano was not only a late starter, he was also subject to injury, so that the gloss was taken off a distinguished, sadly short career.

Benfica had a tall, calm goalkeeper in Costa Pereira, excellent wingers in José Augusto, who became a midfield man, and the exuberant Antonio Simoes, later, like Eusebio, to play in America. Eusebio, indeed, gained a late and unexpected honor when, in 1976 at the Seattle Kingdome, he materially helped the unfancied Toronto Metros to beat the Minnesota Kicks 3-0, scoring the first goal himself with a typically potent free kick.

They were, these Benfica players, a versatile lot. If Augusto was transmuted from a winger into a midfield player, good enough to figure prominently in the 1966 World Cup, then Coluna, scorer of a spectacular left-footed goal against Barcelona in Berne, moved easily back to left half, while Cavem—who scored a beauty in

Amsterdam—had moved by then to right half from the left wing.

In 1964 and 1965 the Cup went to Helenio Herrera's Internazionale, of Milan. Inter was superbly prepared and exceedingly efficient. They played *catenaccio*, with a sweeper at the back, yet could certainly not be said to be merely a defensive team, for in front of the sweeper, or *libero*, Armando Picchi, there were no more than three players who tight-marked their man; and of these the huge fullback, Giacinto Facchetti, was forever moving up in quest of goals.

What detracted from their victories was the suspicion, later to be given chapter and verse, that they suborned referees. The semi-finals of the 1964 and 1965 competitions provided particular evidence. In 1964, having drawn 2-2 in the away leg with the West Germans, Borussia Dortmund, Inter played them at San Siro, Milan. Their Spanish inside forward Luis Suárez kicked a Borussia halfback so severely that he had to leave the field, and the Germans, down to ten men, lost, 2-0; for Suárez was not sent off. The following summer, Tesanic, the Yugoslav referee, was discovered by a Yugoslav tourist with his linesmen, on holiday at an Italian seaside resort; paid for, he confessed, by Inter.

A year later it was Liverpool's turn to be shabbily treated at San Siro. They had won the first leg of the semi-final—at Anfield, only three days after winning the English Cup Final. Before the game began, the irrepressible Bill Shankly, Liverpool's Scottish coach, was told sadly by an Italian journalist, "You have no chance. They'll never let you win."

Soon, he would see what this meant. The Spanish referee allowed two extraordinary goals. One was scored by Inter's Peiro, a long-legged, talented Spaniard, when he hooked the ball virtually out of the goalkeeper Tommy Lawrence's hands, as he was bouncing it preparatory to clearing. The other, which outraged Shankly still more, came when the referee gave an indirect free kick, one from which no goal can be scored with a direct shot. Mario Corso, the Inter left winger, shot straight past Lawrence into the net; and the referee gave a goal.

In the 1964 Final in Vienna, Inter beat Real 3-1, exploiting weaknesses in the Spanish defense. In 1965, on their own San Siro field, they were lucky to win 1-0, in a deluge of rain, against Benfica, who lost their goalkeeper, Costa Pereira, injured, and had to put Germano in goal. The following year, Real regained the Cup by beating Partizan of Belgrade in the Final; but even the emergence of such admirable players as Pirri, at right half, and the stocky Amancio, on the right wing, could not make up for the going of Di Stefano.

In 1967 and 1968, Britain at last took the trophy, first through Glasgow Celtic, then through Manchester United, who at long last achieved the "Grail" for which Matt Busby had been so long in quest. Celtic's win was a particularly popular one, for in the Final their exuberant football finally overwhelmed a stale and negative Internazionale team. Their little, red-headed outside right, Jimmy Johnstone, with his superb swerve and footwork, his great speed, his ability to take the ball close up to an opponent before whisking it away from him, was certainly among the best wingers in the world at that time. Jock Stein, who had actually moved out of League football in Scotland to play minor League football in Wales, before returning to Celtic to help, initially, with their reserves, had proved an outstanding coach.

His team, it should be said, had little about it of the classical Scottish style, moving rather at immense pace, with an overlapping fullback in Tommy Gemmell who scored a goal that day which Facchetti might have envied. Inter defended; Celtic's whole ethos was one of attack. So, indeed, was Manchester United's when they deservedly beat Benfica at Wembley, the following year, after losing their grip on a game they seemed to have well won.

In 1969 Milan brought the Cup back to Italy, easily defeating Ajax Amsterdam in Madrid; three of the goals going to the talented left winger, Pierino Prati. Ajax, however, would come into their own two years later, to win the Cup three times in a row and emerge as the finest club team in Europe since Real Madrid. In the meantime, their compatriots, Feyenoord of Rotterdam, impressively beat Celtic in the 1970 Final at San Siro, Milan, playing a fast, economical, modern game which exposed Celtic's tactical deficiencies.

Ajax and Bayern Munich now brilliantly exploited the methods of Total Football, with its attacking sweeper, its perpetual interchanging of roles, its emphasis on extreme physical fitness; though not, as in Alf Ramsey's England teams, in the mere cause of "work rate," in an attempt to make up for lack of talent with sheer hard grind.

If Cruyff, the tall, boyish looking, vibrant center forward was the motivating force of the Ajax team, then Franz Beckenbauer, inventor of the attacking sweeper, was the linchpin of Bayern's. Ajax beat the Greek team, Panathinaikos of Athens, coached by Ferenc Puskás, in a dull Final at Wembley in 1971, then two Italian teams, Internazionale and Juventus, in the ensuing Finals. Juventus' progress to the 1973 Final in Belgrade was blemished by an attempt to bribe the Portuguese referee, Francisco Lobo, of the semi-final against England's Derby County.

Dezso Solti, an expatriate Hungarian, domiciled in Italy, visited Lobo in Lisbon and offered him $500 and

276

a car to favor Juventus at Derby. Lobo, a telephone engineer and a profoundly honest man, tape recorded the conversation, reported Solti—who had previously worked, officially, for Internazionale, on their managerial staff—to his Federation, and they, in turn, reported it to UEFA, the European Union. UEFA's disciplinary sub-committee staged an extraordinarily haphazard inquiry a few months later in Zurich, mysteriously exonerated Juventus, but suggested that Solti be made *persona non grata* in European football.

UEFA's Executive Committee, meeting in Glasgow, turned down that suggestion, which was implemented only in December 1974 after an investigation conducted by Keith Botsford and myself for the London *Sunday Times* had, as Macbeth would put it, blown the horrid deed in every eye. Juventus swore Solti had nothing to do with them, which reminded one a little of the Duke of Wellington's riposte to a man who inquired of him, "Mr. Smith, I believe?" "Sir, if you believe that, you will believe anything."

Strange creatures crawled from under stones. It emerged that in 1972, on their way to the Final against Ajax, Inter had played in the quarter-finals against Standard Liège, in Belgium, where two of their players had been cautioned for fouls by the Hungarian referee Mr. Emsberger. Of these, one was the Brazilian outside right Jair, the other the halfback Bedin, who had been cautioned before. Two cautions meant automatic suspension. To Mr. Emsberger, as he left the field, came another Hungarian referee, Istvan Szolt, a theater director in Budapest, famous in his time, though now retired from refereeing. He told Emsberger—whom Botsford and I visited at the mining town of Tatabanya, outside Budapest, in December 1974—that he would fill in his official report for him; he knew that Emsberger had a plane to catch. Emsberger gratefully agreed. But when the report arrived at UEFA headquarters in Berne, the booking of Bedin was not recorded. Szolt explained that he must have been talking to some journalists at the time Bedin was booked. UEFA noticed the disparity, suspended Bedin, suspended Emsberger. Szolt himself visited me in London in 1975, grew curiously silent when I outlined to him what Emsberger alleged had occurred, and muttered merely that if Emsberger had said so, then it must be right.

The refereeing of the 1975 European Final in Paris, when Bayern Munich beat Leeds United 2-0, was little more satisfying. Leeds was refused a manifest penalty, when Allan Clarke was tripped by Franz Beckenbauer, and what seemed a good goal when Peter Lorimer shot home; though Billy Bremner was standing in an offside position, even if he was not interfering with the play. The European Union awarded M. Kitabdjian, the French referee, only two marks out of twenty and deplored his performance. The French press was equally severe in its judgment.

Solti, a very popular man in Hungarian football circles till his banning, had clearly infringed the Eleventh Commandment, Thou Shalt Not Be Found Out. On his return to Budapest in 1975, he was thrown into prison for several days, threatened with proceedings for alleged contraband and favoring of prostitution, and told that the real object of the exercise was to make him aware he was no longer *persona grata* in his native country, either. Solti retired into a sad obscurity in Milan. By contrast Italo Allodi, who had been Secretary of Internazionale, then General Manager of Juventus at the time of the Lobo affair, attained high office with the Italian Soccer Federation (FIGC).

Solti deserved little sympathy, but he was merely a tool, used by more powerfully connected people who had "run" him both in Milan and Turin, and had themselves skillfully avoided impeachment, though not suspicion. To know is one thing, to prove, quite another, and the European Union had neither the will nor the means to dig very deep.

Bayern Munich, though they too succeeded in winning the European Cup three years in a row, did not do so with the facility of Ajax, let alone the splendor of Real. Of the Leeds United Final I have written already. Against Atlético Madrid, in Brussels in 1974, they were actually a goal down till the closing seconds, when a Marquitos-like burst, if one may so call it, from their center half Georg Schwarzenbeck, a mighty drive, gave them the equalizer. In the return game, Madrid had shot their bolt, and Bayern had won with a fusillade of glorious goals, two each for Müller and Uli Hoeness, who twice showed to perfection how to beat a goalkeeper when through on one's own. The second goal was taken with extraordinary *sang froid*, Hoeness first exploiting the fact that he had been left with one defender to beat, and beating him, then dodging coolly round the keeper, to shoot into the empty net.

In 1976, at Hampden Park, Glasgow, where Real had enraptured the crowd in 1960, Bayern merely labored against a splendid Saint Etienne team. The Frenchmen, playing a wonderfully modern game, twice hit the bar in the first half, but the burly Roth drove in the only goal of the game after Beckenbauer, masterly throughout, rolled a free kick to him. Bayern had played cautiously, reminding one of Inter in the 1960s, but with the same facility for devastating breaks; Roth, Hoeness, and the dark Kappelmann showing an impressive ability and readiness to run alone with the ball over long distances.

The two other European competitions for clubs are inevitably overshadowed by the European Cup which is, after all, the Cup for Champions.

The *UEFA Cup* had a strange beginning. It was conceived in 1955 as the Inter-Cities Fairs Cup, with the rather curious and arbitrary qualification that competing clubs must come from a city which staged an industrial fair. Louis Malle, the distinguished French film director, once remarked to me that it might as well be confined to cities which had bordellos!

Gradually and inevitably, the rules were relaxed, though they have remained arbitrary, some countries being allowed more entrants than others—there are now sixty-four, where formerly there were but thirty-two—and these being chosen on a widely varying basis. Thus in England the Football League has tried to make its own knockout Cup more attractive by giving the winners an automatic place in the Fairs Cup. They were left with egg on their face when, on the first occasion they meant to do so, Queens Park Rangers, then a Third Division club, won their trophy, and were denied admittance by the Cup Committee on the ground that they didn't play in the First Division!

The first version of the tournament dragged on, believe it or not, for three full years, till Barcelona beat London—then fielding a representative, rather than a club, team, in the two-legged Final. In 1971, the European Union elbowed the Inter-Cities Fairs Cup Committee aside, and took the competition over, rechristening it the UEFA Cup. It remains attractive; but arbitrary.

The *European Cup Winners' Cup* was born in 1960. Again, it is flawed. The Cup competition is taken very seriously, needless to say, in England; also in Scotland, France, West Germany, and Spain. Elsewhere, it induces little passion. Sir Stanley Rous, for years the president of FIFA, used to say when he was secretary of the English F.A. that he hoped (quite why is obscure) that the tournament would promote interest in national cup competitions. It hasn't, though it has produced some distinguished Finals; and one notorious one. That was in Salonika in 1973 when Milan beat Leeds United 1-0 in a game refereed with such outrageous bias by the Greek Michas that he was suspended by UEFA, who never embarked on an investigation. Don't make waves.

One of the great problems raised by all three competitions is that of time. In 1967–68, the habit of "playing-off" on a neutral ground when the teams finished level on aggregate was abandoned. Now, in such cases, the team scoring the greater number of goals *away* from home would qualify, on the basis of away goals counting double. There's arbitrary for you! A still greater element of chance and ridicule was brought into the European Cup competition in 1971, when it was decided that in the event of teams finishing level, after extra time in the second leg, on goals, the decision would be made on penalty kicks, each team taking a series of five; then, in case of equality, five more. What connection this had with the true nature of a game or, indeed, *two* games, defied analysis. This fatuity, however, has now been wished not only on the very Final of the European Cup, since 1976, but on the World Cup Final too. May it never, in either competition, come to pass! Time, time, time; which means money, money, money, is at the bottom of it all.

The *European Nations Cup*. Otherwise known as the *European Championship*. Where the European Cup long preceded its South American equivalent, the South American Championship came many years before the European Nations Cup, begun by UEFA rather as a self-aggrandizing exercise, in 1958. Then, it was a rather half-baked affair. None of the British countries entered, and when Spain was drawn against Russia in the quarter-finals, they refused to play them on political grounds. The semi-finals and Final, not to speak of that egregious non-event the Third Place Match, which still clutters up the Nations and the World Cup, were played in France, Russia beating Yugoslavia in the Final.

It has been customary for these last two rounds to be played on the grounds of one of the four countries surviving till the semi-finals. In the case of the World Cup, the host country is designated in advance and has exemption to the Finals, as has the holder of the trophy. In the first and second Nations Cups, the tournament was run on a straight knockout basis, teams meeting at home and away, as they did in the European cups for clubs, up to the semi-finals. Since the 1966–68 tournament, however, it has been customary for them to compete in eight qualifying groups, the winners being drawn against each other in the quarter-finals, which are played on a home and away basis.

Spain, playing at home, won the 1964 tournament. Italy, most contentiously, that of 1968, in Rome, when there was reason to believe the Yugoslavs were cheated out of victory in the Final by bizarre refereeing; when Ferrini charged Pavlovic in the back in the Italian penalty area, there could have been no one but the referee, unless he were an impassioned Italian supporter, who did not think it a penalty. I certainly did; and I was there.

Not till 1972, when a brilliant West German team, playing Total Football, won the Final in Brussels against lumbering, outclassed Russia, did the Nations Cup seem something more than a mere superfluity. The 1976 finals were better still, reaching a memorably high standard, as Yugoslavia, West Germany, Czechoslovakia, and Holland (torn by dissension) played each other in

Zagreb and Belgrade. Seldom has one seen so much gloriously enterprising and gifted football, effort matched and crowned by virtuosity. In the Final, Holzenbein headed an equalizer for West Germany from a corner kick in the very last second. The fiasco of penalty kicks followed, and the Czechs, a splendidly organized and talented team, won; but it must be said in defense of UEFA that the teams themselves agreed that there would be no replay, so exhausted were they by the efforts and the climatic conditions of the tournament.

The *Copa de los Libertadores,* or *South American Cup.* This began purely—if that be the word—and simply for the purpose of throwing up a challenger to the holders of the European Cup, to compete for the alleged world title. It has been almost from the first a horrid affair. For years FIFA, the world body, would have nothing to do with it, and it has been kept alive by the greed of the European clubs, the desperate economic need of the South American clubs, who clung to it almost pitifully at a time when the Europeans were treating it with disdain.

Things were not quite so bad until the Argentinians, in the later 1960s, became embroiled. It should be made clear that there are traditionally, in Argentinian football, two strains, one of sheer artistry, of virtuosity bordering on exhibitionism, on effortless control of the ball, amazing pyrotechnics, the other of violence, sheer thuggery. Sometimes these qualities can be found in one and the same player. There is no doubt that from Orsi, fifty years ago, through Di Stefano and Sivori in the 1950s, to Houseman, Brindisi, and Ayala in the 1970s, Argentina has provided some of the most gifted and exciting players in the history of the game. But something turned very sour in Argentinian football after the 1958 World Cup, in which their team was humiliated 6-1 by the Czechs in Sweden and, to rub salt in the wound, the Brazilians—traditionally considered their South American inferiors by the Argentinians— walked off with the trophy; as they did again in 1962.

The Argentinians overcompensated. They became harder, more functional, more destructive than the most parsimonious European teams. They produced, in such clubs as Racing, Independiente, and the dreaded Estudiantes de la Plata, teams to be feared throughout the world; not for their prowess but for their physical threat.

Not till the fourth version of the Libertadores Cup, in 1964, were they successful. In 1960 and 1961 it was won by the famous Uruguayan team, Peñarol, of Montevideo. In 1963, Peñarol was beaten in the Final by Pelé's magnificent Santos team, in which Pelé combined so sweetly, worked such fabulous one-two exchanges, with the black center forward, Coutinho. On the left wing was Pepe, with his incredible free kicks; he could score with a deadly swerving shot from thirty yards. In midfield was the tall, jog trotting Mengalvio, and the famous attacking right half Zito. In goal was the faultlessly calm Gilmar, picked up for a song, and enjoying a protracted Indian summer. Santos won the Cup again in 1964, their victims in the two-legged Final being Boca Juniors, of Buenos Aires.

The competition was run on the basis of qualifying groups till the semi-finals, when it became a two legged, knockout, affair. The Brazilians were disenchanted by the fact that the representation was increased to two clubs per country. They resented having to play matches against obscure little teams in "lesser" footballing countries. In 1965, 1969, and 1970 they entered no teams. When they did return to the competition, the frequently intimidatory methods of the Argentinian teams made it a dangerous and dubious

284

prospect. As often as not, the two-legged Final went to a third, play-off, game, in neutral territory, bad blood building up along the way.

The *Intercontinental Cup*, or world championship for clubs, began in July 1960; not inauspiciously.

Real Madrid twice played Peñarol, drawing in Montevideo, winning the return in Madrid 5-0, with two goals from Puskás, one from Di Stefano. Six years later a splendid Peñarol team, strong in the possession of Ecuador's black Spencer, Peru's black Joya, in attack, had ample revenge, winning 2-0 both at home and away. Concetto Lo Bello, an admirably honest Italian referee, scorned all half-time blandishments in the return game.

By a rule as bizarre as it was recklessly ill-judged, the team drawn *away* in the first leg of the two-legged championship had the privilege of playing a decider on its own territory, if each game were drawn; or if each team won one game, no matter by what margin. Goal average, that's to say, didn't count. This caused no great grief on the first occasion it was implemented, in 1961. Benfica, beating Peñarol 1-0 in Lisbon, lost the return in Montevideo 5-0, which by all logic should have been the end of it. Instead a third game was played, to which Benfica flew out the then 19-year-old Eusebio, who scored a splendid goal but couldn't prevent Peñarol winning 2-1.

In 1962, Benfica had the misfortune to run up against Santos at their apogee, one of the greatest club sides ever seen. They lost 3-2 in Brazil, they lost by a shattering 5-2 at home, an irresistible Pelé scoring three of the goals, having got two in the Rio game. 1963 saw Santos lose 4-2 in Milan, with Pelé, then win the next two games in Rio, which grew thoroughly nasty, thanks chiefly to the Brazilians, in Rio.

But this was nothing to what lay in store; for Milan, again, among others. True, it was only some thoroughly doubtful refereeing in the play-off in Madrid which enabled Internazionale to prevail against Independiente of Buenos Aires; that same Spanish referee was in charge who had taken the notorious game against Liverpool. It is doubtful if any referee could have done much about what happened in the bloodcurdling series between Racing Club of Buenos Aires and Glasgow Celtic, two years later.

The first game, at Hampden Park, Glasgow, saw Celtic win laboriously, 1-0, and Jimmy Johnstone get hacked down or body-checked almost every time he had the ball. In Buenos Aires, the return game had not even begun when a missile from the terraces struck Ronnie Simpson, the unfortunate Celtic goalkeeper, on the head, and knocked him out. To their credit, Celtic agreed to play with their reserve goalkeeper, Fallon. They lost 2-1, and were subjected to perpetual provocation, incessant fouling, by the Argentinians. It was a foregone conclusion that the third game, in Montevideo, would be a cauldron. Glaswegian Scots, too, have their *machismo*, and they had had enough of being kicked, pinched, struck, taunted, and incited by the *portenos*. Johnstone was one of the worst sufferers, spat at so often in Montevideo that at half-time he had to come into the dressing room and wash the spittle out of his hair.

It was all too much for the Glaswegians. Big John Hughes, known as "Yogi Bear," a forward whose robust play harked back to Sunny Jim Quinn, but who was generally as lacking in malice ("All the men Jim Quinn killed," said a contemporary, "are living yet"), had a rush of blood to the head and kicked the Racing goalkeeper. He was sent off. Tommy Gemmell sneaked around the back of a posse of players, arguing with the referee, kicked one of the Argentinians, and ran away; an incident pitilessly recorded by the television cameras. Racing, I suppose you could say, had the better of it. They had two players sent off to Celtic's four, and they won the game (game?) 4-2.

The following year, it was Manchester United's turn to suffer. They had to play Estudiantes in the first leg at the Boca Stadium in Buenos Aires; a game I was unfortunate enough to attend. After twenty minutes even George Best decided to stop playing, knowing he was in physical danger every time he went near the ball. Nobby Stiles was headed in the face and cut above the eye by Bilardo, a medical doctor with an evident penchant for providing his own patients. Bobby Charlton had three stitches in his shin after being kicked by Pachamé. Estudiantes won 1-0, and drew a bruisingly ill-tempered return in Manchester. The thing about the Argentinians, one British critic pointed out, was that they could behave like thugs *and* play football. It came less naturally to the British, who had to choose when provoked between one or the other.

The Italians, generally considered well capable of looking after themselves, were the next sufferers. Milan had the temerity to beat Estudiantes 3-0. In Buenos Aires, Nestor Combin, Milan's Argentina-born center forward, had his nose broken by the blow of an elbow from Aguirre; Prati, while sitting on the ground having treatment, was kicked in the back by Poletti, the Estudiantes goalkeeper. General Ongania, then President of Argentina, had both Estudiantes players and Manera imprisoned, then suspended.

From that point, as you will appreciate, European teams were none too keen to play the Argentinians, though Feyenoord had the courage—rashness?—to do so in 1970 and beat them; Van den Deale, the Feyenoord goal scorer in the return, having his glasses broken for his trouble.

You would have thought that UEFA, the European Union, would have sympathized with any of their clubs which wanted to avoid risking life and limb against South American teams. Not a bit of it. When Ajax found one excuse or another for not playing Nacional Montevideo in 1971, UEFA threatened to fine them; then compounded their own crassness by delegating Panathinaikos, the runners-up, to compete. The Greeks lost their right back with a broken leg in the first game in Athens, a 1-1 draw. They were beaten in Montevideo. Only the fact that all three of the Nacional's goals were scored by the elegant Argentinian center forward Luis Artime, *El Hermoso*, the handsome one, conferred a little distinction on the games.

That UEFA should have devalued what there was to be devalued about the grandiosely named Intercontinental Championship was lamentable but predictable, in view of their strange, illogical attachment to it. Things became more ludicrous still in November 1973. Ajax—who had unwisely changed its mind about entering the fray, their players lured by the sums of money involved (there never was a great team more thoroughly motivated by money than Ajax)—was still licking their wounds after coming up against Independiente in 1972. It would be Independiente again in 1973, and Ajax decided that discretion would be the better part of . . . profit. Consequently, they stood down, the UEFA once again yielded to the desperate pleas of the impoverished South Americans, entering the runners-up of the 1973 European Cup, Juventus.

The Turin club, however, having no wish to be kicked to pieces on the River Plate, insisted there be but one game. This was played not in Turin but in Rome. The Juventus team approached it as though it were a training game, and Independiente won 1-0.

A certain dignity and authenticity were restored to the competition in 1977 when a Brazilian club, Cruzeiros of Belo Horizonte, endured the thousand natural shocks of playing an Argentinian team in the South American Cup Final, and qualified to meet Bayern Munich. The Germans played superbly, winning in Munich, drawing 0-0 but, by general consent, deserving to win, in Brazil.

The *South American Championship* for nations goes back to 1917.

In the early years of the century, Argentina and Uruguay competed for a trophy presented by Sir Thomas Lipton, the tea millionaire, known as the Lipton Cup. The South American Championship had over forty years of vigorous life, being played usually, but not always, in alternate, odd-numbered, years. By the early 1960s, however, it had run out of steam, overshadowed by the World Cup, undermined by the Copa de Los Libertadores. The custom was to play it, on a knockout basis, in a given city; the first—just like the World Cup—took place in Uruguay, in Montevideo.

Argentina dominated it, winning it nine times between 1917 and 1959, thrice in a row between 1927 and 1929—after which there was an eight-year gap—1955 and 1959. Their victory in 1957 in Lima, Peru, was a particularly distinguished one, achieved with the so-called Trio de la Muerte, trio of death; three dazzling young inside forwards in Humberto Maschio, Valentino Angelillo, and Omar Sivori; all of whom were promptly snapped up by Italian clubs and thus denied to the Argentinian World Cup team of 1958. It was in Lima, too, four years earlier that a combative Paraguayan team surprised everyone by taking the Championship, beating Brazil in the Final.

Attempts to revive the Championship in the 1960s and 1970s proved largely abortive; the virtue, alas, had gone out of it.

The *Olympic Soccer Tournament* was born in 1908 in London, won by the United Kingdom, but sternly contested by a fine Danish team. The French entered two sides, each of which was well beaten, in a knockout tournament. In 1912 the United Kingdom, a team consisting on each occasion of English amateurs with experience of professional football, beat Denmark in the Final in Stockholm. Italy and Austria entered the lists. There was a consolation tournament, in which J. Fucks of Germany established a record by scoring ten out of twelve goals against Czarist Russia. His brother later became a distinguished psychoanalyst in London, and it was strange to be asked in a suburban garden in Hampstead, London, whether one had heard of J. Fuchs.

After the Great War, "shamateurism" became the custom, as it has been ever since. Most countries entered their full international team during the 1920s, though not Britain. 1920's was a torrid tournament. Belgium won the title in Antwerp, the Czech team walking off en masse in the Final when they were losing 2–0. 1924 and 1928 saw the domination of a superb Uruguayan team, which beat Switzerland in Paris, Argentina, in the second of two riveting Finals, in 1928 in Amsterdam. Los Angeles, in 1932, had no soccer. In 1936, in Berlin, an Italian team consisting of alleged students—almost all of whom were League club professionals—labored to an uneasy victory.

After World War II, Sweden's admirable team beat

290

Yugoslavia in the Final at Wembley; again, these were scarcely amateurs. So strong was Sweden that the illustrious Nils Liedholm, inside forward, could find a place only on the left wing. Then it was the turn of the Communist "shamateurs" to enter and to dominate the tournament. The brilliant Hungarians cut their teeth on it in 1952—Puskás, Kocsis, and all, winning in Helsinki—the Russians made heavy weather of winning it in Melbourne in 1956; Yugoslavia beat a fine young Danish team in Rome.

That—1960—was the tournament in which Italy, the hosts, performed a superb feat of sophistry. They must, they knew, appear to field a team of amateurs. Ah, but what was an amateur, pray? Well, in Italian soccer law, no player could technically turn professional until he was over twenty-one. What was he, then, if under twenty-one? Why, obviously an amateur! So it was that the Italian team consisted wholly of gifted professionals . . . under the age of twenty-one. When they tried it again in 1964, even *they* grew ashamed, and pulled out just before the final rounds in Tokyo.

There the Hungarians fielded what amounted to a B team to win—with considerable style; the Final against a similar Czech team was of high quality. In Mexico, in 1968, they won again, with a team of the same composition; B rather than A. This was a tournament enlivened by the defeat of the young Mexican professionals by the French amateurs, and the taking of third place by a remarkable Japanese team with a splendid center forward in the powerfully built Kamamoto.

The Polish victors of 1972, in Munich, were a full-strength international team of great quality. 1976, in Montreal, saw crowds of extraordinary size for a North American venue, a victory for East Germany (and Iron Curtain shamateurism) over Poland. The tournament was played on a basis of eight qualifying "pools" providing eight quarter-finalists, to compete thereafter on a knockout basis, and the Final, whatever one may think of the *mores* of its contestants, was an excellent one, won by a fine team.

Enough, however, was enough, and FIFA, under their new President Joao Havelange, debated the feasibility of making the tournament one confined to players under twenty-one. Its inequalities, its hypocrisies, had simply become too much.

The late Avery Brundage was never much of a man for jokes, but he did produce one when Sir Stanley Rous, then president of FIFA, defended the soccer tournament on the grounds that the vast majority of soccer players in the world were amateurs. "I know," said Brundage, wryly, "but none of them seems to play in the Olympics."

APPENDIX

1930
Montevideo

Uruguay 4
Ballesteros, Nasazzi,
Mascheroni, Andrade,
Fernández, Gestido, Dorado,
Scarone, Castro, Cea, Iriarte

Argentina 2
Botasso, Della Toree,
Paternoster, J. Evaristo,
Monti, Suarez, Peucelle,
Varallo, Stabile, Ferreira,
M. Evaristo

1934
Rome

Italy 2
Combi, Monzeglio,
Allemandi, Ferraris, Monti,
Bertolini, Guaita, Meazza,
Schiavio, Ferrari, Orsi

Czechoslovakia 1
Planicka, Zenisek, Ctyroky,
Kostalek, Cambal, Krčil,
Junek, Svoboda, Sobotka,
Nejedly, Puc

1938
Paris

Italy 4
Olivieri, Foni, Rava,
Serantoni, Andreolo, Locatelli,
Biavati, Meazza, Piola, Ferrari,
Colaussi

Hungary 2
Szabó, Polgár, Bíró, Szalay,
Szucs, Lazar, Sas, Vincze,
Sarosi, Szengellér, Titkos

1950
Rio de Janeiro

Uruguay 2
Maspoli, Gonzáles, Tejera,
Gambetta, Varela, Andrade,
Ghiggia, Pérez, Miguez,
Schiaffino, Moran

Brazil 1
Barbosa, Augusto, Juvenal,
Bauer, Danilo, Bigode, Friaca,
Zizinho, Ademir, Jair, Chico

1954
Berne

West Germany 3
Turek, Posipal, Kohlmeyer,
Eckel, Liebrich, Mai, Rahn,
Morlock, O. Walter, F. Walter,
Schaefer

Hungary 2
Grosics, Buzansky, Lantos,
Bozsik, Lorant, Zakariás,
Czibor, Kocsis, Hidégkuti,
Puskás, J. Toth

293

1958 Stockholm	**Brazil 5** Gilmar, D. Santos, Bellini, Orlando, N. Santos, Zito, Didì, Garrincha, Vavà, Pelé, Zagalo	**Sweden 2** Svensson, Bergmark, Axbom, Boerjesson, Gustavsson, Parling, Hamrin, Gren, Simonsson, Liedholm, Sköglund
1962 Santiago (Chile)	**Brazil 3** Gilmar, D. Santos, Mauro, Zozimo, N. Santos, Zito, Didì, Garrincha, Vavà, Amarildo, Zagalo	**Czechoslovakia 1** Schroiff, Tichý, Pluskal, Popluhar, Novák, Masopust, Kvasniak, Pospíchal, Scherer, Kadraba, Jelinek
1966 London	**England 4** Banks, Cohen, J. Charlton, Moore, Wilson, Stiles, R. Charlton, Peters, Ball, Hurst, Hunt	**West Germany 2** Tilkowski, Hottges, Schulz, Weber, Schnellinger, Beckenbauer, Overath, Haller, Held, Seeler, Emmerich
1970 Mexico City	**Brazil 4** Felix, Carlos Alberto, Brito, W. Piazza, Everaldo, Clodoaldo, Gerson, Jairzinho, Tostão, Pelé, Rivelino	**Italy 1** Albertosi, Burgnich, Cera, Rosato, Facchetti, Bertini, Mazzola, De Sisti, Domenghini, Boninsegna, Riva Substitutes: Juliano and Rivera
1974 Munich	**West Germany 2** Maier, Vogts, Schwarzenbeck, Beckenbauer, Breitner, Bonhof, Hoeness, Overath, Grabowski, Müller, Hölzenbein	**Netherlands (Holland) 1** Jongbloed, Suurbier, Rijsbergen, Haan, Krol, Jansen, Van Hanegem, Neeskens, Rep, Cruyff, Rensenbrink Substitutes: De Jong and R. Van De Kerkhof
1978 Buenos Aires	**Argentina 3** Fillol, Olguin, Galvan Passarella, Tarantini, Ardiles, Gallego, Kempes, Ortiz, Luque, Bertoni Substitutes: Larrosa and Houseman	**Netherlands (Holland) 1** Jongbloed, Krol, Poirvloet, Brandts, Jansen, Haan, Neeskens, W. Van De Kerkhof, Rep, Rensenbrink, R. Van De Kerkhof Substitutes: Suurbier and Nanninga

THE EUROPEAN CUP

1956	Paris	Real Madrid 4, Stade de Reims 3
1957	Madrid	Real Madrid 2, Fiorentina 0
1958	Brussels	Real Madrid 3, AC Milan 2
1959	Stuttgart	Real Madrid 2, Stade de Reims 0
1960	Glasgow	Real Madrid 7, Eintracht Frankfurt 3
1961	Berne	Benfica 3, Barcelona 2
1962	Amsterdam	Benfica 5, Real Madrid 3
1963	London	AC Milan 2, Benfica 1
1964	Vienna	Internazionale Milan 3, Real Madrid 1
1965	Milan	Internazionale Milan 1, Benfica 0
1966	Brussels	Real Madrid 2, Partizan (Belgrade) 1
1967	Lisbon	Celtic (Glasgow) 2, Internazionale Milan 1
1968	London	Manchester U 4, Benfica 1
1969	Madrid	AC Milan 4, Ajax (Amsterdam) 1
1970	Milan	Feyenoord (Rotterdam) 2, Celtic 1
1971	London	Ajax 2, Panathinaikos 0
1972	Rotterdam	Ajax 2, Internazionale Milan 0
1973	Belgrade	Ajax 1, Juventus 0
1974	Brussels	Bayern Munich 4, Atlético Madrid 0 (after 1-1 tie)
1975	Paris	Bayern Munich 2, Leeds U 0
1976	Glasgow	Bayern Munich 1, St.-Etienne 0
1977	Rome	Liverpool 3, Borussia Mönchengladbach (West Germany) 1
1978	London	Liverpool 1, Bruges 0

THE UEFA CUP

(Originally the Fairs Cup, for teams from European cities that held industrial fairs, it became the UEFA Cup in 1972, run by the European Union, which chooses the 64 contestants.)

1955–58	London 2, Barcelona 2
	Barcelona 6, London 0
1958–60	Birmingham C 0, Barcelona 0
	Barcelona 4, Birmingham C 1
1961	AS Roma 2, Birmingham C 0
	Birmingham C 2, AS Roma 2
1962	Barcelona 1, Valencia 1
	Valencia 6, Barcelona 2
1963	Dynamo Zagreb 2, Valencia 1
	Valencia 2, Dynamo Zagreb 0
1964	Real Zaragoza 2, Valencia 1 (one game)
1965	Ferencváros 1, Juventus 0 (one game)
1966	Barcelona 1, Real Zaragoza 0
	Real Zaragoza 4, Barcelona 2 (Barcelona won on away goals.)

THE UEFA CUP (continued)

1967	Dynamo Zagreb 2, Leeds U 0
	Leeds U 0, Dynamo Zagreb 0
1968	Ferencváros 0, Leeds U 0
	Leeds U 1, Ferencváros 0
1969	Newcastle U 3, Újpest Dosza (Hungary) 0
	Újpest Dosza 2, Newcastle U 3
1970	Anderlecht 3, Arsenal 1
	Arsenal 3, Anderlecht 0
1971	Juventus 2, Leeds U 2
	Leeds U 1, Juventus 1 (Leeds U won on away goals.)
1972	Wolverhampton W 1, Tottenham H 2
	Tottenham H 1, Wolverhampton W 1
1973	Liverpool 3, Borussia Münchengladbach 0
	Borussia Münchengladbach 2, Liverpool 0
1974	Tottenham H 2, Feyenoord 2
	Feyenoord 2, Tottenham H 0
1975	Borussia Münchengladbach 2, Twente Enschede (Holland) 0
	Twente Enschede 1, Borussia Münchengladbach 5
1976	Liverpool 3, Bruges 2
	Bruges 1, Liverpool 1
1977	Juventus 1, Atlético Bilbao 0
	Atlético Bilbao 2, Juventus 1 (Juventus won on away goals.)
1978	Bastia 0, PSV (Eindhoven) 0
	PSV 3, Bastia 0

THE EUROPEAN CUP WINNERS' CUP

1961		Glasgow Rangers 0, Fiorentina 2; Fiorentina 2, Glasgow Rangers 1
1962	Stuttgart	Atlético Madrid 3, Fiorentina 0 (after 1-1 tie)
1963	Rotterdam	Tottenham H 5, Atlético Madrid 1
1964	Brussels	Sporting Lisbon 1, MTK Budapest 0 (after 3-3 tie)
1965	London	West Ham U 2, Munich 1860 0
1966	Glasgow	Borussia Dortmund 2, Liverpool 1
1967	Nuremberg	Bayern Munich 1, Glasgow Rangers 0
1968	Rotterdam	AC Milan 2, Hamburg 0
1969	Basel	Slovan Bratislava 3, Barcelona 2
1970	Vienna	Manchester C 2, Gornik (Poland) 1
1971	Athens	Chelsea 2, Real Madrid 1 (after 1-1 tie)
1972	Barcelona	Glasgow Rangers 3, Dynamo (Moscow) 2
1973	Salonika	AC Milan 1, Leeds U 0
1974	Rotterdam	FC Magdeburg (East Germany) 2, AC Milan 0
1975	Basel	Dynamo Kiev 3, Ferencváros (Hungary) 0
1976	Brussels	Anderlecht (Belgium) 4, West Ham U 2
1977	Amsterdam	Hamburg SV 2, Anderlecht 0
1978	Paris	Anderlecht 4, FK Austria 0

THE EUROPEAN NATIONS CUP
(or European Championship)

1960	Paris	U.S.S.R. 2, Yugoslavia 1
1964	Madrid	Spain 2, U.S.S.R. 1
1968	Rome	Italy 2, Yugoslavia 0 (after 1-1 tie)
1972	Brussels	West Germany 3, U.S.S.R. 0
1976	Belgrade	Czechoslovakia 2, West Germany 2 (Czechoslovakia won on penalties in overtime.)

SOUTH AMERICAN CHAMPIONSHIP
(Campeonato Sudamericano de Fútbol)

1917	Uruguay	1926	Uruguay	1953	Paraguay
1919	Brazil	1927	Argentina	1955	Argentina
1920	Uruguay	1937	Argentina	1957	Argentina
1921	Argentina	1939	Peru	1959	Argentina
1922	Brazil	1942	Uruguay	1963	Bolivia
1923	Uruguay	1947	Argentina	1967	Uruguay
1924	Uruguay	1949	Brazil	1975	Peru
1925	Argentina				

COPA DE LOS LIBERTADORES
(South American Cup)

1960	Peñarol (Uruguay)	1970	Estudiantes
1961	Peñarol	1971	Nacional (Uruguay)
1962	Santos (Brazil)	1972	Independiente
1963	Santos	1973	Independiente
1964	Independiente (Argentina)	1974	Independiente
1965	Independiente	1975	Independiente
1966	Peñarol	1976	Cruzeiro (Brazil)
1967	Racing Club (Argentina)	1977	Boca Juniors (Argentina)
1968	Estudiantes (Argentina)	1978	Boca Juniors
1969	Estudiantes		

OLYMPIC SOCCER TOURNAMENT

1908	London	United Kingdom 2, Denmark 0
1912	Stockholm	United Kingdom 4, Denmark 2
1920	Antwerp	Belgium 2, Czechoslovakia 0
1924	Paris	Uruguay 3, Switzerland 0
1928	Amsterdam	Uruguay 2, Argentina 1
1932		No competition
1936	Berlin	Italy 2, Austria 1

OLYMPIC SOCCER TOURNAMENT (continued)

1948	London	Sweden 3, Yugoslavia 1
1952	Helsinki	Hungary 2, Yugoslavia 0
1956	Melbourne	Russia 1, Yugoslavia 0
1960	Rome	Yugoslavia 3, Denmark 1
1964	Tokyo	Hungary 2, Czechoslovakia 1
1968	Mexico City	Hungary 4, Bulgaria 1
1972	Munich	Poland 2, Hungary 1
1976	Montreal	East Germany 3, Poland 1

NORTH AMERICAN SOCCER LEAGUE CHAMPIONS

1967 Oakland Clippers 4, Baltimore Bays 1
   (aggregate score of two games as National Professional Soccer
   League)
1968 Atlanta Chiefs 3, San Diego Toros 0
   (aggregate score of two games)
1969 Kansas City Spurs 110 (points), Atlanta Chiefs 109 (points)
   (point totals for the season—there were no league play-off games)
1970 Rochester Lancers 4, Washington Darts 3
   (aggregate score of two games)
1971 Dallas Tornado 7, Atlanta Chiefs 4
   (aggregate score of three games)
1972 New York Cosmos 2, St. Louis Stars 1
1973 Philadelphia Atoms 3, Dallas Tornado 0
1974 Los Angeles Aztecs 4, Miami Toros 3
1975 Tampa Bay Rowdies 2, Portland Timbers 0
1976 Toronto Metros-Croatia 3, Minnesota Kicks 0
1977 New York Cosmos 2, Seattle Sounders 1
1978 New York Cosmos 3, Tampa Bay Rowdies 1

INTERCONTINENTAL CUP

1960 Real Madrid
1961 Peñarol (Uruguay)
1962 Santos (Brazil)
1963 Santos
1964 Internazionale Milan
1965 Internazionale Milan
1966 Peñarol
1967 Racing Club (Argentina)
1968 Estudiantes (Argentina)
1969 Milan

1970 Feyenoord
1971 Nacional (Uruguay)
1972 Ajax
1973 Independiente (Argentina)
1974 postponed until 1975
1975 Atlético Madrid
1976 Bayern Munich
1977 postponed until 1978
1978 Boca Juniors (Argentina)

FA CUP FINALS 1872–1978

1872	Wanderers 1	Royal Engineers 0
1873	Wanderers 2	Oxford University 0
1874	Oxford University 2	Royal Engineers 0
1875	Royal Engineers 2	Old Etonians 0 (after 1-1 tie)
1876	Wanderers 3	Old Etonians 0 (after 0-0 tie)
1877	Wanderers 2	Oxford University 0
1878	Wanderers 3	Royal Engineers 1
1879	Old Etonians 1	Clapham R 0
1880	Clapham R 1	Oxford University 0
1881	Old Carthusians 3	Old Etonians 0
1882	Old Etonians 1	Blackburn R 0
1883	Blackburn Olympic 2	Old Etonians 1
1884	Blackburn R 2	Queen's Park, Glasgow 1
1885	Blackburn R 2	Queen's Park, Glasgow 0
1886	Blackburn R 2	WBA 0 (after 0-0 tie)
1887	Aston Villa 2	WBA 0
1888	WBA 2	Preston NE 1
1889	Preston NE 3	Wolverhampton W 0
1890	Blackburn R 6	Sheffield W 1
1891	Blackburn R 3	Notts Co 1
1892	WBA 3	Aston Villa 0
1893	Wolverhampton W 1	Everton 0
1894	Notts Co 4	Bolton W 1
1895	Aston Villa 1	WBA 0
1896	Sheffield W 2	Wolverhampton W 1
1897	Aston Villa 3	Everton 2
1898	Nottingham F 3	Derby Co 1
1899	Sheffield U 4	Derby Co 1
1900	Bury 4	Southampton 0
1901	Tottenham H 3	Sheffield U 1 (after 2-2 tie)
1902	Sheffield U 2	Southampton 1 (after 1-1 tie)
1903	Bury 6	Derby Co 0
1904	Manchester C 1	Bolton W 0
1905	Aston Villa 2	Newcastle U 0
1906	Everton 1	Newcastle U 0
1907	Sheffield W 2	Everton 1
1908	Wolverhampton W 3	Newcastle U 1
1909	Manchester U 1	Bristol C 0
1910	Newcastle U 2	Barnsley 0 (after 1-1 tie)
1911	Bradford C 1	Newcastle U 0 (after 0-0 tie)
1912	Barnsley 1	WBA 0 (after 0-0 tie)
1913	Aston Villa 1	Sunderland 0
1914	Burnley 1	Liverpool 0
1915	Sheffield U 3	Chelsea 0
1920	Aston Villa 1	Huddersfield 0

299

1921	Tottenham H 1	Wolverhampton W 0
1922	Huddersfield 1	Preston NE 0
1923	Bolton W 2	West Ham U 0
1924	Newcastle U 2	Aston Villa 0
1925	Sheffield U 1	Cardiff C 0
1926	Bolton W 1	Manchester C 0
1927	Cardiff C 1	Arsenal 0
1928	Blackburn R 3	Huddersfield T 1
1929	Bolton W 2	Portsmouth 0
1930	Arsenal 2	Huddersfield T 0
1931	WBA 2	Birmingham C 1
1932	Newcastle U 2	Arsenal 1
1933	Everton 3	Manchester C 0
1934	Manchester C 2	Portsmouth 1
1935	Sheffield W 4	WBA 2
1936	Arsenal 1	Sheffield U 0
1937	Sunderland 3	Preston NE 1
1938	Preston NE 1	Huddersfield T 0
1939	Portsmouth 4	Wolverhampton W 1
1946	Derby Co 4	Charlton Ath 1
1947	Charlton Ath 1	Burnley 0
1948	Manchester U 4	Blackpool 2
1949	Wolverhampton W 3	Leicester C 1
1950	Arsenal 2	Liverpool 0
1951	Newcastle U 2	Blackpool 0
1952	Newcastle U 1	Arsenal 0
1953	Blackpool 4	Bolton W 3
1954	WBA 3	Preston NE 2
1955	Newcastle U 3	Manchester C 1
1956	Manchester C 3	Birmingham C 1
1957	Aston Villa 2	Manchester U 1
1958	Bolton W 2	Manchester U 0
1959	Nottingham F 2	Luton T 1
1960	Wolverhampton W 3	Blackburn R 0
1961	Tottenham H 2	Leicester C 0
1962	Tottenham H 3	Burnley 1
1963	Manchester U 3	Leicester C 1
1964	West Ham U 3	Preston NE 2
1965	Liverpool 2	Leeds U 1
1966	Everton 3	Sheffield W 2
1967	Tottenham H 2	Chelsea 1
1968	WBA 1	Everton 0
1969	Manchester C 1	Leicester C 0
1970	Chelsea 2	Leeds U 1 (after 2-2 tie)
1971	Arsenal 2	Liverpool 1

1972	Leeds U 1	Arsenal 0
1973	Sunderland 1	Leeds U 0
1974	Liverpool 3	Newcastle U 0
1975	West Ham U 2	Fulham 0
1976	Southampton 1	Manchester U 0
1977	Manchester U 2	Liverpool 1
1978	Ipswich T 1	Arsenal 0